MARY PICKFORD

Sincerely
Mary P

HARTSOOK
PHOTO
S.F.-L.A.

MARY PICKFORD

QUEEN OF THE MOVIES

Edited by Christel Schmidt

 LIBRARY OF CONGRESS  UNIVERSITY PRESS OF KENTUCKY

Copyright © 2012 by The Library of Congress

The University Press of Kentucky

Scholarly publisher for the Commonwealth,
serving Bellarmine University, Berea College, Centre
College of Kentucky, Eastern Kentucky University,
The Filson Historical Society, Georgetown College,
Kentucky Historical Society, Kentucky State University,
Morehead State University, Murray State University,
Northern Kentucky University, Transylvania University,
University of Kentucky, University of Louisville,
and Western Kentucky University.

Editorial and Sales Offices: The University Press of Kentucky
663 South Limestone Street, Lexington, Kentucky 40508-4008
www.kentuckypress.com

16   15   14   13   12   5   4   3   2   1

Library of Congress Cataloging-in-Publication Data

Mary Pickford: queen of the movies / edited by Christel
Schmidt.
    p.   cm.
    Includes bibliographical references and index.
    ISBN 978-0-8131-3647-9 (hardcover: alk. paper) — ISBN 978-0-
8131-3667-7 (pdf) — ISBN 978-0-8131-4055-1 (epub) 1. Pickford,
Mary, 1892–1979. 2. Motion picture actors and actresses—
United States—Biography. 3. Motion picture producers and
directors—United States—Biography. I. Schmidt, Christel.
    PN2287.P5M38 2012
    791.4302'8092—dc23
    [B]
                                    2012019015

⊚ This book is printed on acid-free paper meeting
the requirements of the American National Standard
for Permanence in Paper for Printed Library Materials.

Printed in China.

Member of the Association of American University Presses

Composed in Kennerley Old Style (originally created
by Frederic Goudy for Mitchell Kennerley's 1911 edition
of *The Open Door* by H. G. Wells and digitized in 2001
by Berthold LLC).

Designed by Robert L. Wiser, Silver Spring, Maryland.

Frontispiece: Photo by Hartsook, circa 1919.

Pickford with her niece Gwynne on the set of
Rebecca of Sunnybrook Farm *(1917).*

*To Robert Cushman (1946–2009) for his passionate commitment to
Mary Pickford throughout his thirty-seven-year career at the Academy of
Motion Picture Arts and Sciences. His love for the actress began when he
was a teenager and lasted a lifetime. Robert's curatorial accomplishments
on her behalf live on through the institution's Mary Pickford Collection.*

*To Gwynne Pickford Ornstein (1916–1984), who had a deep love for her
aunt Mary and an endless interest in her career.*

CONTENTS

EDITOR'S PREFACE

Christel Schmidt

It has been 100 years since Mary Pickford was first dubbed the Queen of the Movies. At the time, the phrase simply noted her popularity in the huge field of actors who appeared in short films shown at nickelodeons. Though it was a gratifying compliment, the title had inherently ignoble associations. After all, most people considered the movies to be a low form of entertainment. Pickford winced at the label, but it was remarkably prophetic of her future triumphs.

As the movies expanded to feature length, Pickford's skyrocketing fame created box-office gold; meanwhile, her widely heralded acting prowess advanced the medium's quest for respectability. In 1915 Pickford formed her own corporation and began hardball negotiations with her studio, Famous Players. This led to a landmark film contract the following year, in which Pickford received her own production unit, a strong creative voice in the making of her movies, and a salary rivaled only by that of Charlie Chaplin. Just two years later, she left Famous Players for First National in a deal that gave her complete creative control and more money. Then, with the ink barely dry on her contract, she became involved in plans to form a new company, United Artists, which she cofounded with Chaplin, actor Douglas Fairbanks, and director D. W. Griffith in 1919.

Throughout the 1910s, the fervor of Pickford's massive fan base never wavered. In fact, the craze amplified, especially when the Queen of the Movies—a title that now defined her position as both an industry leader and a superstar—married Fairbanks. As Hollywood's most popular leading man, Fairbanks was a king in his own right, and he shared Pickford's passion for filmmaking. The pair became the first celebrity supercouple; their movies spread American culture and values around the world and made them the nation's unofficial ambassadors. During their international travels, they were coveted guests of royalty, presidents, and prime ministers. At home, they ruled Hollywood from Pickfair, their Beverly Hills mansion, which became a social center for the cultural elite.

By the mid-1920s, newer and younger stars were challenging Pickford's box-office supremacy. Several, including Clara Bow, Colleen Moore, and Gloria Swanson, temporarily won the mantle of movie queen, but Pickford remained an enduring favorite. Then suddenly the industry underwent a radical change: silent film was out and the talkies were in. Within a few years, most of the era's great stars had toppled from their lofty positions, and Pickford's acting career and marriage floundered. During the Depression, she sought refuge in new ventures—forming a cosmetics company, performing on radio, and writing books. These projects met with varying success, but none captured her soul as the movies had. And though she continued to work with United Artists and occasionally produced films for other people, nothing matched the thrill of creating her own. A decade of professional disappointment was matched by profound personal losses; her mother, Charlotte, died in 1928, followed by her younger siblings, Jack and Lottie, in 1933 and 1936, respectively. Fairbanks died in 1939. These painful events exacerbated a growing struggle with alcohol that plagued her until the end of her life.

Meanwhile, Pickford's on- and offscreen achievements were fading from memory. Silent film, an art form she had helped pioneer and later dominated, was considered archaic. Fearing ridicule, Pickford did not allow her work to be exhibited in the rare revival screenings of silent films. Unfortunately, this lack of access prevented generations of moviegoers from discovering her work and allowed a distorted view of her movies to take hold. For decades, her twenty-four-year screen career—with an output of more than 200 shorts and features— was believed to be a series of saccharine performances in retrograde plots too unsophisticated for contemporary audiences. Several film historians, including James Card, Lary May, and Alexander Walker, valiantly tried—but ultimately failed—to correct this impression. As Pickford expert Robert Cushman once told me, "it was like whistling in the wind."

Fortunately, Pickford's reputation has changed remarkably in the past fifteen years. This reversal was due in large part to the publication of two superb books: Eileen Whitfield's biography *Pickford: The Woman Who Made Hollywood*, and Kevin Brownlow's *Mary Pickford Rediscovered*. But despite an *American Experience* documentary, an international film tour, a research project that located some of her missing films, and the release of several of her movies on DVD in the intervening years, only a few film critics and scholars (most notably Jeanine Basinger, Richard Corliss, and Gaylyn Studlar) have since written in depth on the actress.

Pickford, circa 1933. © Estate of George Hurrell.

The recent centenary of Pickford's first movie appearance prompted this celebration of one of early cinema's key figures. Here, Pickford scholars (past and present) delve into her onscreen persona, her impact on modern celebrity culture, and her transformation from popular actress to national icon. Her frequent turns in nonwhite roles and as teenagers are explored, as is the glorification of the Pickford curls and her companionate marriage to Fairbanks. Other pieces examine her role as a Hollywood philanthropist and her interest in the fledgling archival film movement and the preservation of her film legacy.

Pickford's life and career are illuminated by the presentation of more than 235 images and illustrations. Most are from the personal collections of films and photographs she donated to the Library of Congress and the Academy of Motion Picture Arts and Sciences, respectively. Her collection of costumes and other memorabilia, housed at the Natural History Museum of Los Angeles County, is also showcased. Together, these magnificent images and revealing essays offer a fascinating portrait of a brilliant woman whose influence on the film industry remains unmatched. ❧

Christel Schmidt

INTRODUCTION

Molly Haskell

S O QUICKLY DID CINEMA move from the stagy theatrics of one-reelers to the fluid intimacy of silent cinema and then to the completely different registers of sound that Mary Pickford, who had been in the forefront of the first revolution, came to seem old-fashioned in the second. It wasn't just a matter of acting style and voices, but the zeitgeist as well. The Victorian ideal of child-like innocence and can-do spirit that Pickford brought to luminous perfection crashed on the shoals of a more cynical age. The brittle disillusion that followed the First World War, the end of Progressive Era idealism, and audiences' hunger for more sexually daring stories and stars—all these combined with the coming of sound to render Little Mary's brand of optimism passé. Against this harsher background, Pickford's image crystallized and hardened into a stereotype of a Pollyanna with golden ringlets and simpering charms. It has been left to devotees of silent cinema to rescue her reputation and convince moviegoers, who today consider even black and white archaic, to take another look at the exquisite gems from the silent past over which this lady reigned—with spirit, gumption, beauty, and (perhaps most of all) tenacity.

She was the first great star and, as historian Robert Cushman states without exaggeration, "the most popular, powerful, prominent and influential woman in the history of cinema."[1] Yet no one so vital to the development of motion pictures in the first half of the twentieth century fell so far from fashion in the latter half. Even in the fervent cinephilia of the 1970s, when film buffs excitedly disinterred early movies as if they were time capsules from the past, the poison-pen letters of Erich Von Stroheim were more welcome than the valentines from America's Sweetheart. Charlie Chaplin, director D. W. Griffith, and Buster Keaton made their claims on modern audiences who were much too sophisticated, much too liberated to look upon "the girl with the golden curls" as anything but a quaint curiosity.

Precisely for this reason—fearing that she would be laughed at—Mary Pickford withdrew her films from distribution. At the time, she was living out her days at her Beverly Hills home, Pickfair, in her own, rather more benign version of *Sunset Boulevard*. We critics colluded in turning Pickford into a joke by circulating the story that she was the arch-prude who had ended Mae West's career by complaining to newspaper magnate William Randolph Hearst about the bawdy lyrics of her songs.

This introduction is drawn from a book review published in the New York Times, *June 6, 1999.*

The Ladies' World *(April 1915).*

Anyone who has seen more than one of the major Pickford films knows that she was a great deal more than a cuddly little girl in pinafores. In appearance alone, she ranges from the winsomely beautiful to the almost unrecognizably, even grotesquely, plain. Then there are her amazingly varied incarnations: she is child, adolescent, and mother (in one 1921 film, *Little Lord Fauntleroy,* she plays both mother *and* son and, in an astonishingly sophisticated sleight-of-camera scene, kisses herself); she is tomboy and coquette, the queen of Herzegovina and a cockney laundress, a coddled rich girl and a misshapen slavey (in extraordinary dual roles in 1918's *Stella Maris*); she is obstreperous, belligerent, sweet, fierce, and ingenious; a spitfire and a street fighter; a lady, singer, dancer, and daughter. She plays Spanish, French, Scottish, and even Asian in a version of *Madame Butterfly* (1915). If these impersonations were not uniformly successful, they testify to the way her vast ambition dovetailed with the rich pantomimic possibilities of silent cinema, before sound narrowed its vocabulary, exacting authenticity of diction and accent.

The scope of Pickford's popularity in the 1910s and 1920s is difficult to imagine now. Discovered by audiences when actors were unbilled and unidentified, she emerged from the pack at Biograph to become the first real star and the begetter of what would emerge as the star system. By 1914, just a year after signing with Adolph Zukor, she had experienced an almost frighteningly meteoric rise, becoming beloved above all others in every country where movies where shown. Vibrant, sincere, disarmingly funny, and, above all, good, she had an appeal that was spiritual rather than erotic and was all the more powerful because of it. "The whole world wanted to put its arms around her," Cushman notes, "and in a way it did."[2] Americans had fallen deeply in love with "our Mary" in a strange mixture of idealization and identification, of worship and familiarity, that would connect moviegoers and stars, mutating into America's twentieth-century religion.

Yet there was nothing awesome or grand in her vision of herself or in her approach to her roles, which was that of a miniaturist. She was a naturalistic actor by instinct, feeling her way into character, at a time when broad gestures and melodramatic expressions were common currency. Director George Cukor used to say that Pickford invented screen acting and was the first method actress. She and her friend Lillian Gish acted in Griffith's early films, and (as film historian Kevin Brownlow has argued) Griffith developed the close-up to capture their extraordinary faces and the subtlety of their expressions. But whereas Gish, astonishing actress that she was, evolved very much as Griffith's creation, Pickford went her own way, choosing the heroines she would play, becoming the architect of her own persona. Rarely a shrinking violet or a beautiful victim, she was more active and physical, a resourceful fighter who was likely to strike back if provoked, clobbering abusers and standing up to bullies.

No less important to her phenomenal success was her grasp of both the art and the business of moviemaking. Born poor, but willful and determined, she acted on stage from the age of seven and shortly afterward became the family's breadwinner. At fourteen, depressed by the shabbiness of her life in third-rate stock companies and seedy boardinghouses, she conducted a successful campaign to get into a David Belasco Broadway show. From there, she made her way into movies. She took cinema seriously almost from the beginning. Pickford was the first female star to form her own corporation (in 1915), and to the roles of star and producer she added that of distributor when, in 1919, she formed United Artists with Chaplin, Griffith, and actor Douglas Fairbanks. She was a perfectionist, enlisting top directors, cinematographers, art directors, and screenwriters. The childhood she had missed out on as a precocious trouper she re-created and enjoyed in her films, and she devoted enormous thought and care to reproducing the gestures and movements of a child, even devising special lighting and makeup that would smooth her adult features into the rounder face of a little girl. However harsh the life and the obstacles portrayed—and her films often surprise modern audiences with their grimness—Pickford saw childhood as a blessed state. Now, as a powerhouse star, she could create and preserve what she never had—the lost paradise of childhood innocence.

But times were changing, and seams began to show. There was something incongruous in that image of innocence and Pickford's ferocious shrewdness as a businesswoman. Being a dynamo herself, in ways that make today's feminist superwomen look like dilettantes, it was inevitable that she would clash with "star" directors such as Maurice Tourneur and Ernst Lubitsch. Still, the films they did together are among the most remarkable of her career.

Like so many show business superachievers, Pickford's fear of failure lurked beneath her success. She once described the hellhole of her early stage career. She was acting in the dilapidated old Thalia in the Bowery, where "everything inside and out spoke of decaying grandeur: cracked marble, dulled gilt, [and] creaking seats."[3] Of all the hardships, the only one she couldn't accept was "the fact that the dreariness and fatigue which we felt seemed to be reflected in the audience. Night after night I watched their bored apathetic faces, their entire lack of response, and I felt I could have borne the discomfort of it all if our performance had brought some satisfaction to them."[4] The need to please is, of course, both the genius and the curse of the star, and Pickford's celebrity became a kind of gilded cage from which she dared not break out; she could not roam too far afield in her choice of parts, for fear of losing her fans.

Douglas Fairbanks, Charlie Chaplin, D. W. Griffith, and Pickford announce the formation of United Artists in 1919.

MARY PICKFORD
in
"Tess of the Storm Country"

Lobby card for Tess of the Storm Country *(1922).*

Some viewers, unable to get past the Victorian plot conventions, will always resist Pickford, but I find her films a revelation. Those values that once seemed archaic—the intense family feeling, the sanctity of home and hearth, the championing of female virtue (always accompanied by spirited competence)—now look refreshing. Moreover, her films deal imaginatively and feelingly with real issues such as adoption, child abuse, and poverty. If the plots veer to Dickensian extremes, they are extremes that Pickford knew: wealth and destitution, fame and anonymity. Happiness is rarely won without unbearable cruelty. The trials of Unity Blake, the much-abused cockney orphan in *Stella Maris,* are heartbreaking, and the glow of happiness that surrounds the lovers at the movie's end is clouded by Unity's ultimate sacrifice. Even the dogs—in the canine subplot—behave more nobly than the people do in today's movies.

There are other chords that seem alien to contemporary moviegoers, chords of spiritual rapture in *Sparrows* (1927) and in *Tess of the Storm Country* (1914 and 1922), when Tess, the pariah, carries a dying baby to the baptismal font and performs the rite herself. Yet such ecstatic moments make one understand the wrenching regret felt by viewers of silent movies with the coming of sound.

Mary Pickford was in the middle of it all, presiding over so much of what was exciting and groundbreaking, both technically and emotionally, in the silent cinema. ❧

THE
NATURAL

Transitions in Mary Pickford's
Acting from the Footlights
to Her Greatest Role in Film

Eileen Whitfield

Pickford and Harold Lockwood
in a scene from Tess of the Storm
Country *(1914).*

There was something about watching Mary Pickford that moved silent-era moviegoers in a way no other actor has ever achieved. And to find out why, one has only to watch her smashing work in *Tess of the Storm Country* (1914), the first surviving feature to fully convey what one fan, in *Photoplay,* called her "weird magnetic grip."[1]

The grip still holds, from the moment Pickford (as Tessibel Skinner, a ravishing, unkempt young woman in rags) awakes from a nap beside a fishing shack. Disentangling herself from a heap of ropes and leaves, she shakes Tess to life with the force of a shock wave. And yet, on paper, the role is unplayable, a schizophrenic mess of clashing traits.

Tess is rustic and ignorant of the world. Still, she knows enough to contact a lawyer when the squatters in her fishing village face eviction. She tosses her hair like Rita Hayworth and sashays across the screen, hands on hips. Even so, if a man responds, she kicks him violently out the door. In the face of the law, she becomes a hooligan, leading a riot and hurling sticks. A devoted Christian, Tess owns a Bible because she stole it. She sets a snarling dog on a man she hates and cheers when it almost takes his hand off. Later, she weeps when a bunny is killed. A foster mother, she is tender but unsentimental as she cares for a dying child. When she baptizes the child herself to make sure he goes to heaven, she's a model of that other Mary's saintly devotion.

Still, Pickford fuses these contradictions. In fact, her Tess is so commanding, so elemental, that she seems to have leaped, fully formed, from the celluloid itself. It's a startling achievement. *Tess of the Storm Country* was released in 1914, when the art of silent acting—especially at feature length—was still evolving. Add to this the fact that, even for its day, the film was rushed and badly made. But somehow Pickford created a character who is pure, transcendent cinema. How did she do it—and so early?

Silent film acting is a hybrid of styles. In 1909, when Pickford auditioned for film director D. W. Griffith, she knew only one of them. First known as *Delsarte* (for semiotician Francois Delsarte's nineteenth-century theory), the style was all the rage in North America for decades. Unfortunately, it also devolved from a search for emotional truth into a code of declarative gestures to magnify passion, excitement, and thrills. These histrionics were common when Pickford, age seven, made her Toronto stage debut.[2] Players brandished fists at God or dramatically pointed enemies from the room; women received bad news by placing a hand to the brow. In moments of complete defeat, they threw themselves prostrate to the ground.

Pickford's business card from her early years working with Broadway impresario David Belasco.

The fact that this system seems dated today does not mean it was a bad one. The language of acting always changes, defined by an unspoken pact between audience and players about the kind of stage behavior they are willing to believe. In addition, melodrama (then the Western world's favorite genre) demanded flamboyance from performers, who appeared as forthright heroes, nefarious villains, plaintive children, and virtuous mothers in nick-of-time, roller-coaster plots. Pickford, who followed a year in Toronto with six years touring in such plays, worked with creatively jaded actors who (pushing histrionics to the edge) tore each character to tatters. She began to fear that her own work was ragged, too.

To solve this problem, she sought and won a small role on Broadway in *The Warrens of Virginia* (1907). The play, a Civil War romance, was produced and directed by David Belasco, a glittering figure on the Great White Way and an icon of showmanship and taste. Under his direction, Pickford (playing a child in the Warren family) learned a subtler approach than the rip-roaring antics of the road. Unfortunately, she never explained Belasco's specific views on acting or how he taught them. Luckily, Belasco's greatest star, Mrs. Leslie Carter, recalled that the maestro stressed a measured pace. In addition, he preached that histrionics should "subordinate themselves to the requirements of the action ... the meaning sometimes lies latent, and can be brought to light by a gesture, a walk across the stage, a look."[3]

Pickford cherished her position in Belasco's ranks—a prestigious connection that became her shield when, at the end of her *Warrens* contract and with money short at home, the seventeen-year-old risked her pride by doing something most actors considered no better than looking for work in a freak show. Donning her best clothes, she visited Biograph's New York brownstone. There, on April 19, 1909, she asked film's foremost director, D. W. Griffith, for a job.

Biograph made short films, six to twelve minutes long, shown in converted storefronts known as nickelodeons. The low ticket price attracted viewers who couldn't afford Broadway's upscale attractions. But even though she had her hand out (Biograph paid five dollars a day), Pickford kept her nose in the air, calling movies "a comedown" compared to the "prouder heritage" of the stage.[4] Just as strongly, Griffith believed he was shaping a new era's cultural vanguard. Pickford's first day with him was traumatic.

First, he auditioned her, smearing her features with bright white greasepaint (without it, the studio's blinding lights filled even a young face with deep, dark lines). Then she faced the camera: an alien, boxlike machine with the lens poking through it like a swollen eye. Also jarring, when the action started, the camera burst into a rat-tat-tat as it filmed and punched out sprocket holes. Pickford, deep in culture shock, felt like the floor was "going up and down in waves."[5] For the first time, she lost her creative bearings.

But she got them back. Just two days later, she played the romantic heroine in Biograph's *The Violin Maker of Cremona* (1909). As Giannina, whose hand in marriage is the prize in a violin-making contest, Pickford clung to what she knew—Belasco's modified histrionics. At one moment, she holds her arms out toward her beloved, takes a few steps, then stops as though tugged by an unseen leash. To show frustration, her fists are clenched. The result resembles a porcelain figure twirling on a music box—elegantly rendered, posed with care, but lacking any sense of a real, live girl.

Pickford was probably happy with her work. But in terms of film, her strength lies less in her gestures than in what happens between them. Waiting for the contest results, she clings to her father in a state of dread. She uses no semaphores for her feelings. In these moments, she is simply being. Of course, body gestures have a place in performing; indeed, the silents needed such signals to clarify action. But they coexisted with a radical change that film brought to acting. The camera moved viewers closer to the actor's face than at any time in history. Watching, audiences sensed what Griffith called "the light within"—the actor's resonance and presence, as well as the state of his or her thoughts and feelings.[6] Stillness from the performer was key in these new, almost shockingly intimate moments.

Later, an actor in the Biograph troupe recalled that Pickford's gift for film acting was innate: "we all saw it as well as Griffith."[7] That said, her breakthrough did not occur in a single film, then flower in a straight line. Nickelodeon films were made in a matter of days, with roles assigned at a moment's notice. Accordingly, Pickford's insights waxed and waned as she plunged into "the novelty, the adventure, from day to day, into unknown areas of pantomime and photography."[8] She plunged into a new range of characters, too.

Onstage, Pickford had always played children. But because film lighting aged performers, her repertoire grew to include adolescents, young women, and wives. She also discovered that early film gave her far more creative power over her roles than she ever had on stage. In a play, the script is the character's blueprint. One-reel films, in contrast, used scenarios—brief, sketchy plots with generic roles (mother, daughter, temptress, maid). Performers chose how to turn these stereotypes into *people,* improvising while the film rolled and the director shouted suggestions from the sidelines. This rapid-fire, on-the-spot way of playing meant that an actress usually turned to her quickest, most natural impulse in a scene. Along the way, she replaced the playwright as the role's prime authority, building the character straight from her inner self.

Pickford was exhilarated: "Everything's fun when you're young," she remembered, "and we were pioneers in a brand new medium of art."[9] Anxious to test her mettle, she played a stream of leading and minor roles, tapping into strengths that soon informed her screen persona. The first of these surfaced in just six weeks while shooting *The Renunciation* (1909), in which her beau, an "effeminate, namby-pamby dude," is played by Biograph's Billy Quirk.[10] Namby-pamby dudes were his stock in trade, as well as a finicky, fussy technique. Griffith liked the contrast with Pickford's down-to-earth approach and cast them as sweethearts in a comedy series. The result was revelation.

Pickford (as Giannina) and Owen Moore in The Violin Maker of Cremona *(1909).*

Kitty (Pickford) chooses a fastidious dandy (Billy Quirk) over rugged miners Joe (James Kirkwood) and Sam (Harry Solter) in The Renunciation *(1909). Quirk, a frequent Pickford costar in Biograph comedies, had a gestural and frenetic performance style.*

A few times, Pickford tried to match Quirk's elaborate style. In *His Wife's Visitor* (1909), for instance, she plays a young wife whose husband neglects her. In a moment alone, she thinks through her problems: her better half spends too much time at the club, and she wants him at home. Then she suddenly sees how to teach him a lesson. Unfortunately, the sequence involves so many gestures that Pickford seems more like a party guest playing charades than a newlywed considering a marital crisis.

Much more often, film comedy put her in urgent touch with her feelings, releasing her fiery, assertive self in a way that stage roles had never allowed. As she coaxes, needles, and manipulates Quirk, Pickford's comic reactions flow so fast that she bypasses coded gestures in favor of simply getting on with things. And extreme rage helped her reach the heights. Offscreen, her anger erupted suddenly. At Biograph, *Photoplay* reported, she would enter the studio "and sit unobtrusively on one side until called. Occasionally her very real sense of humor would prompt her to speech. Once in a great while the resounding temper that lurks unsuspected under her serenity would smash forth in an abrupt, natural, flashing explosion."[11] It also smashed forth in a confrontation with Griffith when, while rehearsing *To Save Her Soul* (1909), he actually shook her, calling her "a piece of wood." In return, Pickford shocked herself by sinking her teeth into his hand, "the first and last time I have ever bitten anyone."[12]

As an ingénue, Pickford's pique may start with a shrug, a pout, and a toss of her hair—but all the while, she is simmering inside. In 1910's *When We Were in Our 'Teens,* her beau refuses to admire a canvas she has been painting; she promptly tries to crash it around his ears. In *The Smoker* (1910), she plays a wife who hates the smell of tobacco and believes her husband has dropped the habit. When she hears that he has rented a private room, she assumes he is having an affair (in fact, he is using the space to smoke) and runs down the road, fists flying at nothing. When she finds him, she vents her rage by shaking the blinds and manhandling a chair.

An angry Pickford catches smokers Billy Quirk (right) and Frank Opperman (left) in The Smoker *(1910).*

In this mode, Pickford's tour de force is *Wilful Peggy* (1910), in which she plays a sexy, hotheaded Irish colleen who responds like a wildcat to matters of courtship. When a man tries to steal a kiss, she furiously beats him to the ground. (He exits running.) When a lord tries to woo her with the gift of a bouquet, she snatches it from him and stamps it flat. Later, when he returns to propose, her mother pushes her from behind, forcing her to walk in his direction. Defiantly, Peggy digs in her heels with each step and wrinkles her nose as though she smells a skunk. After she finally consents to marry, she breaks into sobs as her mother holds her. Meanwhile, her feet are seen stomping below her long skirts in a tantrum.

An emotional explosion has unstoppable life; it bursts from a sliver of feeling into a flood that rises, builds, and courses until it spends itself. Similarly, Pickford's onscreen anger sweeps histrionics aside as it surges, crests, and dissipates. The result feels so true that, as Leonard Bernstein said of great music, it is "fresh but inevitable."[13] Indeed, when Pickford lets loose, her passion transcends the embroideries of acting in different styles and eras. She is simply an actress in enthralling flight.

Comic rage made Pickford a star in nickelodeons (in 1910, only one year after she entered film, *Moving Picture World* christened her the "queen of comediennes").[14] And a short fuse was crucial to her rowdy Tess. For instance, when Tess grows impatient with suitors, Pickford (channeling Peggy) sends them out the door with a kick to the rear end, booting the last man's hat out after him. In a much grimmer scene, she turns her fury on three men who are burning the squatters' nets. One has a gun, and he points it at her. Tess doesn't care; she's as mad as an attack dog and faces him directly with a warrior's wrath. At that moment, she's a supernova, and her cowed opponent never fires a bullet.

The spirited Peggy (Pickford dressed in men's clothes) threatens an unwanted suitor in Wilful Peggy *(1910), a popular Biograph comedy.*

But in some ways, Tess was a challenge for her. Beyond its heroics and comic charm, the role is filled with melodrama (sad lamentations, appeals to fate). Pickford, who quickly learned to trust her comic instincts, was far less consistent in her approach when rendering heartbreak for the camera. For some, histrionics were the best solution. Silent star Lillian Gish, in particular, used them to escalate drama to tragic heights, but the style fit her fragile, neurotic image.[15] Pickford's warm and capable presence was far less suited to high-flown signals. When she used them onscreen, the results were mixed.

Her least successful attempt occurs in *An Arcadian Maid* (1910), in which she plays Priscilla, a slavey (or household drudge). Near the film's end, the bewildered girl goes searching for the roué who has left her. At first, she runs a distance with her arms out, and the effect is poignant. But the gesture plays less well when Priscilla, learning that her lover has left by train, dashes aimlessly about with her arms held straight up over her head. Still holding the posture, she runs through a field—and nearly crashes into the man himself. Known to be a crook, he has been thrown off the train and is critically wounded. When he dies, Priscilla visibly declaims him "Dead!"—then shudders, clutches her head, and writhes. This is not only frantic; it feels untrue, as though even Pickford doesn't really believe it. The sequence is a sudden lapse in a portrait that, according to scholar Tom Gunning, is filled with "revolutionary moments in the development of screen acting."[16]

Pricilla is an odd duck, first seen doggedly trudging down a dirt road, head bent low beneath a heavy hat. When the hat comes off, she's revealed as a plain girl with dark, thick brows and a grin like a grimace. Hired as a laundress, she responds to everyone with curtsies—quick, constant efforts to please that might as well be cringes. Indeed, she is happiest while scrubbing, nodding to herself in approval, socially inept but relaxed in the realm of small, practical tasks. She doesn't know that she's gauche and slow-witted. Instead, she manages life as she knows it, marching to a tune only she can hear.

Apparently, Pickford was touched by Priscilla; she played six more slaveys throughout her career.[17] Perhaps she welcomed the chance to act "plain," a choice that reassures the player that the public loves her for more than her beauty. Perhaps her poverty as a child gave her a sympathetic link to the destitute. For whatever reason, the actress often seems to inhabit (rather than act) Priscilla—suffused, soul to skin, with her earnest but primitive grasp of life.

In the same way, Pickford inhabits Tess, with whom she seems to mesh completely. Probably the character's can-do energy chimed with Pickford's confident offscreen self. Yet, as she does with Priscilla, the actress breaks into histrionics—but this time, she shapes the code to her talents. The solution is simple: cut the tension. When Tess accepts bad news, she simply dangles her arms at her sides, head down. In another scene, she kneels, dejected, and crumples to the floor. These are moments of surrender, and Tess's intensity is depleted. Pickford no longer treats histrionics as though the technique is holy ground. Instead, it is a tool in her acting kit. When she places the back of her hand to her brow, the movement joins the flow of the performance, as everyday as tucking back a lock of hair.

Pickford as the unattractive household drudge Priscilla in An Arcadian Maid *(1910).*

She also knows when to take her time, profiting from a series of Biograph films in 1912 in which Griffith gave her generous footage to calibrate emotion.[18] In *Tess,* the heroine watches as her father, on trial for murder, is sentenced by a judge to be hanged. Just as she does in *An Arcadian Maid,* Pickford mouths the word "dead." But her follow-up choices are radically different. She shows Tess slowly sinking into shock, then walking toward the judge in disbelief. Tess reasons with him, explaining sweetly that God has told her that her father will be freed. Emotions shimmer across her face, allowing the "light within" full resonance. The judge watches, mesmerized, as Tess then takes her father's hand and tries to lead him from the chamber. Only when an official stops her does Tess finally see that the cause is lost.

It's a spellbinding scene. After all, Tess is almost never submissive. She's a master and commander who defends the helpless and battles landlords, courts, and the church. In fact, through *Tess of the Storm Country,* Pickford's image was distilled and deeply planted in the public mind, although the words to describe it proved elusive. An eloquent fan told a film magazine that Tess was "ragged ... dirty yet beautiful, full of naughty vagaries yet capable of great sacrifices—she is the uncivilized woman."[19] Julian Johnson evoked Pickford's "luminous tenderness in a steel band of gutter ferocity" in a *Photoplay* piece that sang her praises.[20] But even these tributes fail to mention an unexpected aspect of Tess's nature: she can, at any moment, behave like a child.

"I didn't have a childhood," said Pickford. "Not any."[21] From the age of five, her alcoholic father's death and her widowed mother's plight obsessed her. As the new, self-appointed head of the family, she helped raised her siblings and became her mother's confidante. Even onstage she could not, vicariously, feel like a child, because melo-drama's young roles were stiff and unbelievable. And, as a juvenile on tour, she seldom met anyone in her age group. Still, she never forgot how her brother, sister, and other children looked and moved while they amused themselves.

Poster for The School Teacher and the Waif *(1912).*

In early films, most actors who were physically small appeared sporadically as children and young teens, and Pickford (who was five feet tall) did her share of such parts as a matter of course. They were usually brief, generic roles. But in 1912, when she starred in *The School Teacher and the Waif,* she brought her character to life so vividly that it seemed like a dam had burst inside. Indeed, as Nora (the Waif), she plays a survivor who, in some ways, reflects Pickford's younger self. Nora has grown up in an isolated shack with her alcoholic father. Like Pickford traveling alone on tour, she is self-sufficient but lonely, with few (if any) young companions. Ordered to attend school by "the commissioners," Nora knows nothing of playground dynamics. Taunted by schoolmates, she tries to engage them by throwing a rock. The gambit fails when the rock is thrown back and the group deserts her. Shaken, Nora retreats to a birch grove, where she hides her head in the crook of her arm, cries in fear of her own emotions, then violently shakes two slender trees. When panic returns, she frantically flings an arm on her face, shudders with sobs, then falls against a sapling as though into the arms of a human being. None of this is histrionics. Instead, it is harrowingly real, and raw.

Few adults remember childhood clearly; much of the experience is lost or blurred. Through Nora, Pickford realized that her childhood had been "walled up inside of me ... I needed to express it."[22] And express it she did, with an acuity few artists achieve. She engages with Nora's world directly, miraculously reengaging with a juvenile's pain, confusion, and joy. And she never "plays cute" just because the girl's feelings are bundled in a small, young frame. Instead, she simply plays her without the distortions caused by the filter of adulthood.

Throughout her features, Pickford continued to play a subset of roles that ranged in age from eleven to early adolescence. Almost all of them express the duality of girls who are young enough to play with dolls but old enough to look at boys, care for their parents and other children, and may even carry guns.[23] In fact, their exact age is often blurred. This tangled development starts with Nora, who enters *The School Teacher and the Waif* in outraged pursuit of two boys who are trying to steal the family goat. Her movements (hair flying, arms flung every which way) are those of a ten-year-old. At the same time, her face and physique are those of a gorgeous adolescent. The paradox continues: In one scene, she wears a poor girl's version of the topknot bow common among little ones of that era. In another, she almost elopes with a con man, mistaking his appraising stare for love. In line with these contradictions, Pickford's Nora often wanders along in skips and jumps, then falls into a purposeful, grown-up stride with a more adult friskiness to her walk.

The beautiful, unruly, and immature Nora (Pickford)
attracts the attention of the teacher (Edwin August) in
The School Teacher and the Waif *(1912).*

Pickford's genius for playing children comes from the recognition that they don't live in a vacuum; sometimes they feel mature emotions or emulate what they see grown-ups doing. By the same token, from time to time, her grown-up characters behave like children—such as when Peggy (whose age might be anywhere between late teens and early twenties) throws a heel-kicking tantrum. Similar in age, Tess still prays to "Goddy" and insists that her father give her piggyback rides. She also takes unabashed pride in her skill at killing bugs and, during a shampoo, uses the lather to paint a curly mustache on her face. Such moments are delightful. Rather than infantilizing Tess, they add yet another capricious layer to a temperament marked by violence, maturity, humor, and virtue. This is layered, nuanced work, delivered with a full dose of star charisma.

The heart of today's psychological acting is transfiguration, a process in which the player's own feelings are shifted, reinvented, and adapted to create an imagined being. Such notions were far from common in the theater of 1909. But when Pickford chose to stay in film, improvisation at Biograph allowed her to transfer and adapt her own being to the screen. The results reverberated with viewers because they were genuine to the actress. By the time Pickford appeared in features, her fans were already bonded to the fireball she had played in early films. In Tess, they found its apotheosis. Pickford was affected the same way; she declared Tess to be her favorite role and spent most of her career playing permutations of the same fighting underdog. How could she help it? Aside from the box-office gold it promised, Pickford's Tess was a second self, created from the personal materials we now take for granted in American acting. Traditionally, historians turn to Pickford to find the first great movie star. One has only to watch her spontaneous Tess to see the soul of modern acting in the first great performance of feature film. ঌ

Pickford gives a powerful and nuanced performance in Tess of the Storm Country *(1914).*

ODY BACK?

MARY PICKFORD IN
"TESS OF THE STORM COUNTRY"
PRODUCED BY THE
FAMOUS PLAYERS FILM CO.

CHILDHOOD REVISITED

An Evaluation of Mary Pickford's Youngest Characters

Eileen Whitfield

*It is childhood and its environment which teaches
us things that are poignantly influential on our later lives.*

Mary Pickford, Visual Education, July 1924

*Pickford was twenty-four when she portrayed
a ten-year-old in* The Poor Little Rich Girl
*(1917). Her remarkable re-creation of childhood
was praised by critics and fans alike.*

No ASPECT of Mary Pickford's career is as misunderstood as her work playing children. These characters, featured in a fraction of her movies, are beautifully rendered and deserve their popular and critical success. But after the close of the silent era, distortions and half-truths about their nature had a toxic effect on Pickford's image. Writers repeatedly claimed that Pickford usually or always played children on the screen. Others incorrectly wrote that the films in which she played adults were box-office failures. Critics who apparently had not seen the movies described the portrayals as false and coy. Indeed, her "anachronistic little girl roles" were deemed a "bizarre preoccupation."[1]

In fact, such work by actors was common. As Pickford grew up in the 1890s, both adults and juveniles played prepubescent roles. In 1904 Maude Adams gave one of Broadway's landmark performances as the title character in James M. Barrie's *Peter Pan*. The actress was thirty-three years old, while Peter still had all his baby teeth.[2] Broadway regulars such as Ruth Chatterton (*Daddy-Long-Legs*) and Patricia Collinge (*Pollyanna*) played both waifs and ingénues, while Pickford, Norma Talmadge, Lillian Gish, and others appeared in one-reel films as children, adolescents, and newlyweds. In January 1913, when Pickford took a respite from film and opened on Broadway as a blind girl in *A Good Little Devil,* she was twenty years old, a married woman, and an old hand at suggesting that her character was younger than her actual age.

A *Good Little Devil* is a fairy tale, adapted from a story by George Sand. Its first and only Broadway production was lavishly designed, with winged sprites hanging in the air, a picturesque apple tree, and a magic well. Pickford added to the enchantment and was praised for giving "real childish spirit" to a character so "demure and tender" that the play's "wild [[animal]] friends of the forest . . . come to her garden because they trust her."[3] To the staff of *Theatre* magazine, her ethereal streak and unadorned manner recalled Adams's star performance in *Peter Pan.* Nodding to Pickford's fame in one-reelers while claiming her as Broadway's own, they dubbed her "The Maude Adams of the 'Movies.'"[4]

When Pickford returned to film later that year, one-reelers had given way to features. But the custom of casting both grown-ups and juveniles as children continued. The actress starred in a few roles in which she appears briefly as a child and becomes an adolescent. In 1917 she played a child for the entire length of *The Poor Little Rich Girl,* a film that brings her gift for playing preteens to remarkable life. As one critic observed, "There is never a false move or expression" to spoil the illusion that Gwendolyn (Pickford's character) is ten years old.[5] It helped, of course, that the star was only five feet tall and looked even smaller when surrounded by oversized furniture, props, and actors who were chosen for their height. She could also mirror children's body language, writing later in *Vanity Fair* that a child moves "freely, its arms [[swing]] carelessly, its shoulders droop very slightly . . . the knee joints are loose, and the toes point inward."[6]

Pickford frequently appeared with tall actors such as Winifred Greenwood, pictured here in an off-camera shot from M'liss *(1918), to make her look even smaller onscreen.*

Eileen Whitfield

Actor Ernest Truex sits with Pickford under an apple tree in the 1913 stage production of A Good Little Devil.

But these would have been mere technical tricks had Pickford not instinctively related to the inner life of a child. Most of us remember only glints of childhood, and the fragments we retain are either overintense or blurred. Pickford had a gift for connecting freshly to the way a child assimilates the world. In addition, Gwen—who is virtually a prisoner in her mansion, due to the chance that she might be kidnapped—often has hypersensitive reactions. Accordingly, Pickford's face is bathed with Gwen's desolation, neurotic fears, and occasional rage and self-assertion.

Adapted from the 1912 book by Eleanor Gates and the subsequent Broadway play, the movie was a smash and encouraged Pickford to turn more young-adult novels into features. The films *Rebecca of Sunnybrook Farm* (1917), *A Little Princess* (1917), *Daddy-Long-Legs* (1919), *Pollyanna* (1920), and *Little Lord Fauntleroy* (1921) place her characters at about age twelve, and some reach their late teens by the end.[7] Critics noted that Pickford's versions of the books were far more robust than their lachrymose Broadway adaptations. Indeed, the Pickford persona in these films is a good-natured, take-charge type; she is "practical, high-spirited, independent and, above all, an imaginative creature determined to confront and cope with the adult world's miseries and inequities."[8] In addition, the actress had an uncanny insight into the quicksilver mood swings of a child. Using these mercurial transitions, Pickford (especially when paired with director Marshall Neilan) created scenes that ring intimately true.

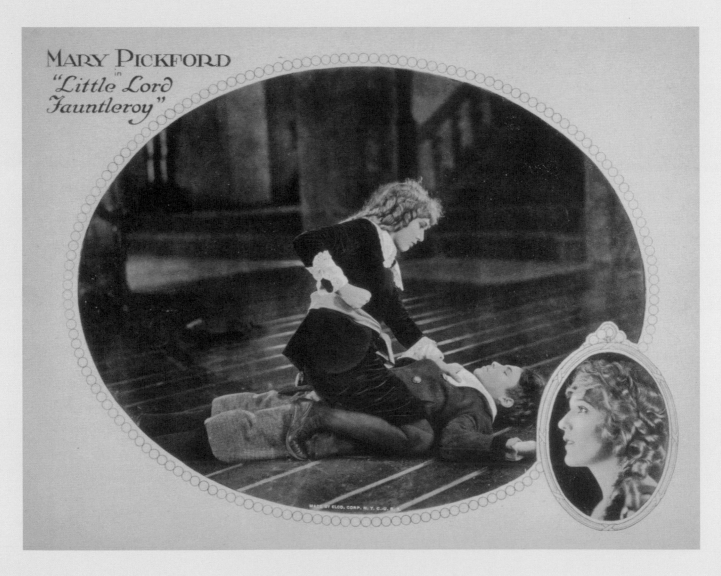

Lobby card from Little Lord Fauntleroy *(1921)*.

Rebecca of Sunnybrook Farm, for instance, shows the quick tumble of a child's emotions in its opening sequence, when Rebecca leaves her family to live with relatives. As the coach approaches, she whirls through a string of quick transitions: turning excitedly in place, giving her brothers and sisters orders, caring for a baby, nervously jumping up and down on a bed, and—alarmed at a tear in her dark stockings—rubbing some soot on her leg so the hole won't show. Elated, she finally boards the coach and, sitting alone, plays the worldly traveler, adjusting her hat with the air of a sophisticate who knows she is beautiful. Then, through the window, she sees her brother following at a run. The playacting stops: a respon-sible sister, she shoos him back, and he falls face forward in the grass. Then the weight of leave-taking overwhelms her, and in an emotional hairpin curve, the breathless, thrilled girl starts to sob. But Rebecca, above all, is resilient. In short order she arrives at her new home, climbs and falls from an apple tree, finds a best friend, and trumps the local little-girl bully in a showdown. The latter sequence involves deliberate posing, displays of clothing, upturned noses, comparisons of family, and the ominous tilting and pointing of a parasol. All these signals are as finely tuned as a scene of social insults in an Oscar Wilde play.

Scene from Rebecca of Sunnybrook Farm (1917) *with Pickford and actress Marjorie Daw.*

202-29

Sadly, for decades after the silent era, Pickford's films were rarely screened publicly (by the 1960s, they could be seen at archives by scholars). Meanwhile, publicity stills of the actress dressed as a child in frills, bows, and gingham were omnipresent. Although Pickford is correctly costumed, these images may have encouraged the impression that her work portraying children was insufferably cute. And Pickford's habit, late in life, of referring to her image as "the little girl" vastly oversimplified her career. In 1925, while trying to expand her range (which included mothers, firebrands, a cigarette girl, and Nell Gwyn), the actress asked her fans, through *Photoplay*, what kind of role they preferred. The results resoundingly favored children. Defiantly, Pickford played only one more preteen role (in *Little Annie Rooney* in 1925). Instead, she maintained her stardom by playing teenagers and grown-ups in a wide range of dramas and comic romances.

Pickford (center) portrays a preteen tomboy in Little Annie Rooney *(1925). The character, who lives in a tenement on New York's Lower East Side, is flanked by her multiethnic "gang" of friends.*

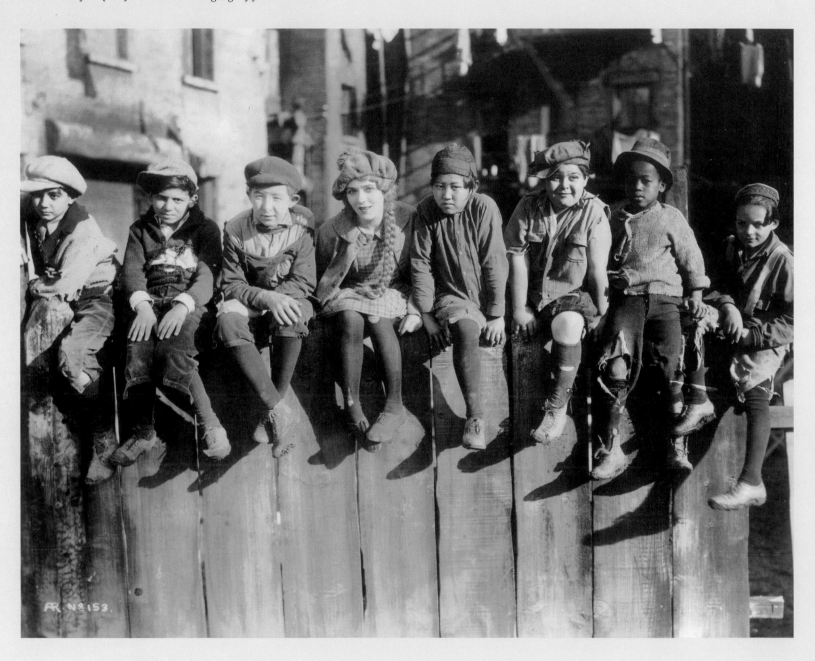

Still, *Photoplay*'s highly unscientific poll had shocked her. It seemed to reinforce her envy of stars who played glamorous women; in a low moment, she even referred to herself as "merely an actress playing children on the screen."[9] Unfortunately, many writers took her at her word. In the 1970s the image of Pickford as a rosy-cheeked girl was set in stone by the ascent of feminist film academia. Decoding movie images of women in terms of film's power to distort and trivialize female experience, this discourse is varied and decades long. But it overwhelmingly fails to evaluate Pickford's children as characters with their own agency and value. In 2003 scholar Beverly Lyon Clark observed that "[[literary]] feminist theorizing has rarely recognized, let alone addressed, the position of the child. We are so adult centered that the only child we adults can see is ourselves; we do not recognize what it means to attend to children's perspectives."[10]

Similarly, most feminist film critics cannot fathom why Pickford would choose to play children on the screen. Indeed, in her influential book *Popcorn Venus,* feminist critic Marjorie Rosen not only judges Pickford's early shorts by their titles (calling 1910's tragic *An Arcadian Maid* "a child's garden of verses") but also asserts that her choice to play children at all betrays an unnatural aversion to maturity. She calls the artistic results "an insult. In abhorring age and repressing sexuality, she had created a freak who denied—indeed, made repugnant—all that was inevitable about womanhood."[11] In fact, the actress simply believed that "the delineation of child character has a perennial interest for grownups."[12] Happily, the language of silent film gave Pickford the tools to bridge the age gap. Silent movies blend naturalistic acting with the stylized body language that the lack of audible dialogue demands. Just as a man can play a woman in Kabuki's ritualized, coded language or a ballet dancer can be cast as a juvenile, silent-film language allowed Mary Pickford to play children with truth and conviction.[13]

Advertisement for The Heart O' the Hills, *a 1919 film in which Pickford plays Mavis Hawn, a tough, justice-seeking mountain girl.*

In addition, discussion of Pickford's portrayal of children often omits her significant roles as girls who live harsh lives beyond the margins of society. Twelve-year-old Mavis, in *The Heart O' the Hills* (1919), lives in a backward patch of Appalachia and carries a rifle everywhere, determined to shoot whoever killed her father. At home, her mother regularly beats her. Finally, Mavis wrests the switch away from her, breaks it across her knee, and remarks, "I reckon that now you'll be treating me like I's growed." Holding her mother's eye, she adds, "Be my dinner ready, Mammy?" Mavis follows her frightened mother indoors and, to show that she means business, brings her gun.

Similarly, Pickford's mountain girl in *M'liss* (1918) plays a leadership role in the community, holding men who mock her at gunpoint. At home, she must parent her drunken father. But in some ways, she is still a girl, shattered when the head of her treasured doll is broken. She slips a note into the tiny doll coffin: "Buried in this yere grave lies the little gal dreams of Melissa Smith." She will need this extra step toward maturity because, a few reels later, she learns that her father has been killed.

Narratives like these speak directly to the challenge of defining childhood in the first place. Is it simply a matter of prepubescence and a reliance on grown-ups for structure and guidance? If so, how do we understand children who make adult decisions in a violent world? Roles like Mavis, M'liss, and the more conventional Gwen and Rebecca need no apology; they simply represent a complex, universal passage in the human experience and a brilliant component of Pickford's art. ॐ

Glass slide from the film M'liss *(1918).*

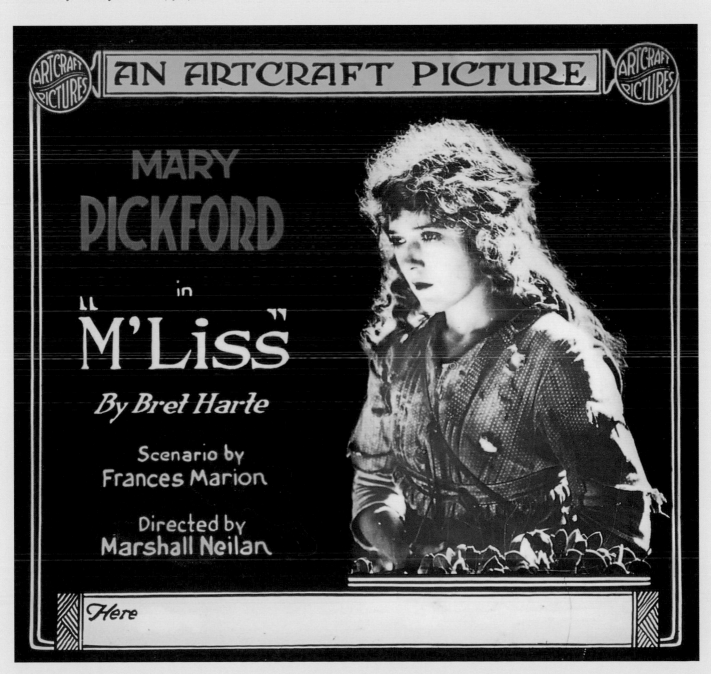

MARY PICKFORD

Passionate Producer

Kevin Brownlow

Pickford with a movie camera in 1916.

I N HIS 1923 AUTOBIOGRAPHY, independent film producer and studio founder Sam Goldwyn wrote, "There was no detail of film production which she, this girl, still in her early twenties, had not grasped more thoroughly than any man to whom I ever talked. She knew pictures not only from the standpoint of the studio, but from that of the box office. Back of those lovely brown eyes, disguised by that lyric profile, is the mind of a captain of industry."[1] He was speaking, of course, about Mary Pickford, the groundbreaking actress who, by age twenty-four, was running her own production company, the Pickford Film Corporation. Three years later, she cofounded Hollywood's first independent film distribution company. Pickford knew the industry inside and out, but its art, not its business, was her passion.

Mary Pickford grew up with movies. In 1909 the seventeen-year-old Pickford joined film director D. W. Griffith at the Biograph studio. In her seventies, she remembered, "There was something to me so sacred about that camera" and Griffith's remark that "she would do anything" for it.[2] (He once said that he "could tell her to go get up on a burning building and jump—and she would."[3]) However, the camera and her performance were not the only aspects of film that entranced her. Biograph cameraman Billy Bitzer remembered Pickford's "flexible, imaginative mind" and how it focused on things to which "none of us gave much thought."[4] Her obsession with the "ghastly and depressing" heavy movie makeup led her to reblend it and then work with Bitzer to make certain that it registered correctly under the intense lights.[5] In his autobiography he notes, it was "as if we were artists mixing colors for their canvas."[6]

Griffith recalled Pickford's "tremendous driving power ... she was thirsty for work and information."[7] She stayed at the studio long after her own scenes were shot and "was a sponge for experience."[8] Pickford acknowledged that much of her education in filmmaking was gained from working with Griffith, who is now considered one of the greatest directors in the history of cinema. Perhaps the most important thing she took from the master was the tendency to regard film, metaphorically speaking, as a religion. During the formative years of her career, she acquired his unswerving devotion to every aspect of filmmaking.

Pickford worked for Griffith for more than two and a half years, but she also had her own excellent intuition about the movies. And often, especially in the area of performance, her opinions led to conflicts. Griffith's biographer Richard Schickel writes, "There *was* mutual respect at times and certainly shrewd little Mary absorbed everything she could from the Master, the tragedy perhaps being that he refused to learn anything from a young woman whose intelligence about the medium, and especially about how to behave in front of a camera, was equal to his."[9] Pickford had a keen eye not just for how her makeup registered onscreen but also for her overall presentation. A firm believer in a natural style of acting, she rebelled when Griffith demanded otherwise. She remembered that "he was too much of the Great Master, which, of course, I never accepted. I respected him, yes. And I even had affection for him. But when he told me to do things I didn't believe in, I wouldn't do them."[10]

Pickford (seated), Billy Quirk, James Kirkwood, and Kate Bruce in They Would Elope *(1909). Kirkwood wears the ghoulish screen makeup that Pickford disliked.*

Producer Adolph Zukor, Pickford, James Kirkwood (behind Pickford), an unidentified man, and Charlotte Pickford at the New York premiere of Behind the Scenes *(1914).*

"Too intelligent and too sure of her own value," Pickford left Biograph in 1912 and eventually landed at Famous Players Film Company.[11] Her work there was guided by the studio's founder, Adolph Zukor, who had recently introduced feature films to America. Pickford, who had lost her own father at age five, saw Zukor as a father figure, and to some degree, he loved her as a daughter. Still, as she did with Griffith, she frequently shocked him with her demands for a creative voice and more money. Later, Zukor described Pickford's drive and ambition with a mix of pride and exasperation. He recalled that in their earliest days together, "she taught me a great deal. I was only an apprentice then; she was an expert workman."[12] She also "had her hand in everything, writing scripts, arguing with directors, making suggestions to other players."[13] She seemed to be interested and involved in nearly all aspects of the filmmaking process. Writer Frances Marion's first meeting with Pickford took place in the studio's cutting room, where the actress was splicing film. She gave Marion a quick lesson on film editing as "she held a ribbon of film to the light and explained how scenes had to be cut when they ran over-length and how close-ups were spliced in."[14]

Pickford was often unhappy with the directors furnished by Zukor and Famous Players. After working with the masterful Griffith for so long, it was difficult to be directed by lesser men. Five of her earliest feature films were directed by Edwin S. Porter, who had made the pioneering one-reeler *The Great Train Robbery* (1903) and owned 50 percent of Famous Players. Half a century later, Pickford still remembered his failings when directing longer films. He "knew nothing about directing. Nothing. [Porter] had none of the ideas, like close-ups, that Griffith had developed."[15] She did, however, credit Porter with convincing her to star in *Tess of the Storm Country* (1914), which became her signature role in one of the biggest successes of her career.

Pickford's instincts about Porter (who soon stopped directing) were correct, as they were about another of her early directors, Sidney Olcott. Arguably one of the dullest directors of the silent era, he worked with the actress on one of her weaker films, *Madame Butterfly* (1915). When she complained to Zukor about her directors, he chalked it up to "Mary's way of opening salary negotiations," but her motives were not mercenary.[16] Both Pickford and Zukor realized that the audience would pay to see anything she appeared in, but Pickford knew something that he did not: motion pictures did not have to be a disposable form of entertainment; nor were they simply a way to make money. The actress saw herself as an artist who was working in a burgeoning art form, something important and lasting. So it is not surprising that she wanted a greater role in creating her films, to be making decisions about director, cast, script, budget, schedule, and advertising. Pickford, in short, wanted to be her own producer—but Zukor already had that job.

At the time, the producer's main function was to hire, fire, and juggle the finances. Movie producers were businessmen who worked mostly on the East Coast and took little part in the filmmaking process. The director, working predominantly on the West Coast, was hired by the producer to make the movie. The press and the public have muddled the two jobs through the ages, but they are as different as those of a painter and his (very demanding) patron. Zukor, hoping to placate the profitable actress during contract negotiations in 1916, gave her a production company of her own. Pickford did not receive total control, but she had a voice (often the strongest one) in how her films were created. Along with a board of directors, she had a vote on selection of the script, her character, and the final cut; Pickford had the last word regarding the director, cast, and advertising. And, after starring in twenty-two features in two and a half years, she cut back to only six films a year, allowing her more time to create each production. As a result, her films improved dramatically. And, as a kind of creative insurance, Pickford the producer established a group of talented people with whom she worked regularly, including screenwriter Frances Marion, director Marshall Neilan, and later cinematographer Charles Rosher.

In 1916 Adolph Zukor bought the rights to the play *The Poor Little Rich Girl* and had to convince Pickford (who thought "it was silly for a grown-up woman to play a little girl") to produce and star in it.[17] Maurice Tourneur, who had directed Pickford's earlier production *The Pride of the Clan* (1917), handled this one with his usual flair; both movies are a showcase for his exceptional sense of composition and lighting. Though there were rumors of tension on the set (the director worked in the Griffith style, accepting no interference), Pickford did have some impact beyond her performance. She chose Marion to write the scenario, and together the two charmed Tourneur into filming at least one sequence (a mud fight) that he initially wanted "nothing to do with."[18] The director also accepted one of Pickford's suggestions on the aesthetic side. One morning she had an idea that a "baby spot," a lighting technique used in the theater to pick out a character's face or hands, might brighten a face on film to suggest that the character was extremely young. After initially refusing, Tourneur acceded to Pickford's request to shoot her close-up scenes with a special light directed at her. She recalled that the director "saw [[her]] point" after viewing the rushes, and "from then on [[they]] used it."[19]

Pickford and director Maurice Tourneur on location in Marblehead, Massachusetts, while filming The Pride of the Clan (1917).

Zukor and the other managers at Famous Players must have been waiting for an opportunity to take the strong-willed Pickford down a peg or two. After they previewed *The Poor Little Rich Girl,* they declared it a complete disaster without one "laugh in the whole picture."[20] Zukor recognized that Pickford was shocked, despondent, and willing to take the blame, so he took advantage of her mood. He sent her to the West Coast (her last few films had been made out east) to make two films, *The Little American* and *A Romance of the Redwoods* (both released in 1917) with director Cecil B. DeMille. Then, patronizing her as if she were a child, he instructed her to respect DeMille's position and "do what you're told."[21] Zukor also persuaded her—"in the deepest misery," as she put it in her memoirs—to send a telegram to DeMille in which she vowed to be "placing myself unreservedly in your most capable hands."[22] It ended "Obediently yours," words that must have been hard for her to swallow.[23]

Director Cecil B. DeMille speaking to Pickford on the set of The Little American *(1917).*

DeMille, an authoritarian on the set, objected to Pickford's having approval over nearly everything. She was uneasy about his direction and wilted under his glare. Pickford recalled "freezing up" on set if "someone is critical of me. I can't laugh or cry. I'm devastated."[24] DeMille was also on the defensive, writing to Jesse L. Lasky, Zukor's business partner in Famous Players, that they would sue the actress if she refused to perform and "stop paying her immense weekly stipend."[25] In the midst of this conflict, Pickford carried on and gave the best performance she could manage. DeMille, having won round one, treated her considerately throughout the remainder of production. And although she later claimed that "DeMille had no heart" and "wasn't a great director," both her films with him turned out extremely well.[26] Pickford disapproved of them, but it is possible that her personal experience clouded her judgment. She did regard DeMille highly as a person, and the two developed a warm friendship. He even wrote a laudatory foreword to her autobiography *Sunshine and Shadow*.

In the meantime, *The Poor Little Rich Girl* was released and, far from being the disaster the Famous Players management proclaimed, was a major critical and box-office success. Pickford was vindicated. She later joked that, as a result, "I climbed back on my high horse and rode off in all directions."[27] Back in control, she hired Neilan, her favorite director after Griffith, and writer Marion to work on her next five pictures. All were successful, with *Rebecca of Sunnybrook Farm* (1917) and *Stella Maris* (1918) among the strongest of the actress's career. Then she experienced a slump—three back-to-back pictures that did not perform up to expectations. Pickford felt that her work was slipping, and she chafed under Zukor's paternal and sometimes condescending supervision. When it came time to renegotiate her contract, she asked him for complete control. He balked. Meanwhile, First National—a group of exhibitors set up to rival Zukor's power—offered Pickford a contract that satisfied all her demands. This time, Zukor did not fight back. Believing that the move would backfire on her, a member of his family told him, "Let her go to First National, that way you'll … cure her swelled head … and she'll come back to you and behave herself."[28] She never worked for Zukor or Famous Players again.

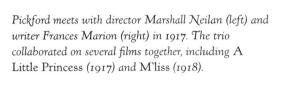

Pickford meets with director Marshall Neilan (left) and writer Frances Marion (right) in 1917. The trio collaborated on several films together, including A Little Princess (1917) and M'liss (1918).

"I wasn't goin to steal anything mister"

The Mary Pickford Company presents

Mary Pickford

In her Second Picture from her own Studios
The HOODLUM

Adapted from "BURKSES AMY" by Julie M. Lippmann   Directed by S.A.FRANKLIN

A "FIRST NATIONAL" ATTRACTION

Original poster for The Hoodlum *(1919).*

Immensely gratified at capturing Pickford, First National asked her to deliver three pictures within nine months, beginning December 1, 1918. The pictures were "to be of the same high class as to photography, acting and direction as the photoplays [she] has appeared in during the past two years."[29] I can attest to the fact that they surpassed these aims. I have seen all three, and each is superb. In fact, one of these First National films, *The Hoodlum* (1919), helped spark my excitement for American silent movies. I was astounded at the high quality of this production. The film displays such a high level of craftsmanship that *brilliant* is the only word to describe it. Some of the scenes are so realistic that it's hard to believe they were shot on a Californian back lot.

Sidney Franklin, her director on *The Hoodlum* and *The Heart O' the Hills* (1919), was a Pickford enthusiast. He remembered her as "a pro in every sense of the word; no nonsense, no temperament."[30] Their only conflict was over her extreme self-criticism while watching the day's rushes. Pickford obsessed over her performance or how she looked in a particular scene. Franklin was blunt, telling her, "They're not only looking at you, they're looking at everybody else up there, too. You've got to look at the overall effect."[31] Pickford recalled, "I see a picture and say, 'Well, Mary, you're pretty good in that scene,' and I see others and I say, 'Why, that's dreadful.' I was never satisfied."[32] After putting her heart, soul, and bank balance into her pictures, she wished she could retire as each one was released, convinced they were all terrible. But Pickford "never wanted to do anything else but make movies."[33] Or, as her husband, Douglas Fairbanks, put it, the subject "is the breath of life to her as it is to me."[34]

In March 1919 Pickford, along with Charlie Chaplin, Fairbanks, and Griffith, cofounded the film company United Artists (UA), adding to her already breathtaking level of responsibility. Actor Adolphe Menjou, who worked for Pickford's production company within UA, wrote, "Mary had her own company.... And when I say it was her company, I mean she ran the show. Everything had to pass her personal inspection."[35] Pickford was on the set "from six in the morning until nine at night"; then she stayed to "write all the checks and give the orders for the next day."[36] Director Ernst Lubitsch said, with a sense of awe, "She can dictate policies, handle finances, bargain with supporting players, attend to booking problems, and still keep her mind on acting. It is no wonder that she held her place at the top longer than any personality in motion pictures."[37]

A hard worker who expected others to work just as hard, Pickford decried the "nonsense of [[working]] nine to five" and claimed that on her set there were "no coffee break[[s]], not even a glass of water."[38] Yet there was ample evidence of her consideration for others. She was among the few who signed up for the closed-shop agreement, and in hiring she gave preferential treatment to union members.[39] Loyal Lucas, an extra on Pickford's *Rosita* (1923), said that due to a lot of night work, the actress-producer had cubicles constructed for the extras and supplied a portable stove to heat each one.[40] When she dropped actor Hugh Allan from the cast of *Little Annie Rooney* (1925), she invented a story for the press that he had broken his arm.[41] Charles Rosher remembered how smoothly Pickford handled Sidney Franklin when he balked at using Rosher for cinematography. She simply said, "If you don't like him or his photography after you've worked with him, I'll talk to you again."[42]

Pickford was straightforward. After director William Beaudine seemed uneasy about asking for retakes, she "took him aside" and said, "Bill, I am the producer, I am the star—do you want me to be the director, too? If I hadn't thought you could do it, I wouldn't have hired you."[43] She dealt similarly with Lubitsch, her director on *Rosita,* who showed too little deference during a disagreement. Meeting him in his office, Pickford said firmly, "I'm telling you that I am the Court of Last Appeal. I'm putting up the money, I am the star, and I am the one that's known. I won't embarrass you; I will never say anything before the company ... but you are not going to have the last word."[44] Lubitsch, a strong ruler himself, found it hard to bear the humiliation of submitting to the control of a woman. How often Pickford's gender was an issue for her managers, directors, or employees we may never know. She never complained about unfair treatment, but she no doubt experienced it. Maybe this is why Pickford always tried to soften her whim of iron with her Irish charm and humor.

Opposite: Pickford's powerful role as producer is behind this humorous moment with director William Beaudine on the set of Little Annie Rooney *(1925).*

Tension between director Ernst Lubitsch and Pickford was brewing below the surface during the making of Rosita *(1923).*

Pickford could be indulgent, especially when she was working with family or close friends. She hired her brother Jack to codirect two of her films, and although he had some of his sister's charm, he had none of her self-discipline. He had an antipathy to hard work, preferring to play with his drinking buddies Neilan and actor Norman Kerry. The hard-drinking Neilan was extremely amusing, and the actress-producer adored him. Sadly, the Irishman was also an alcoholic. Off on a drunk, Neilan failed to show up on the set of Pickford's *Dorothy Vernon of Haddon Hall* (1924). The film was shooting on location in San Francisco's Golden Gate Park, where they had organized a procession of horses, hundreds of extras, and a milk-white steed. Pickford, unable to locate Neilan, directed the sequence herself.[45] Apparently, no one thought this was unusual. Rosher, who worked with Pickford for twelve years, remembered the actress-producer doing "a lot of her own directing. The director would often just direct the crowd."[46]

I don't want to give the impression that Pickford was a director manqué or that she ever made complete films that were credited to others. It was a shame she didn't try, though despite her efforts, she was unable to rescue *The Love Light* (1921), a visually beautiful film directed by Marion, that even Pickford proclaimed was bad. Richard Corliss is correct when he writes that although "Pickford never took director's credit on her films she was surely their de facto auteur and probably the first major non-directorial power on the creative side."[47] Film producers, according to the history books, were not "creative" until the era of Irving Thalberg and David O. Selznick in the 1930s and 1940s, but like Corliss, I would argue that a handful were creative during the silent era—in particular, Pickford. By the early 1920s, she and husband Douglas Fairbanks were exerting more influence on American film production than anyone else.

Mary Pickford dreaded the day her acting career would end. It came, nonetheless, in 1933, when she decided to retire from the screen after making just four sound films. Remarkably, Pickford was only forty years old. She produced a few films in the late 1930s and 1940s but created nothing in the sound era that approached the standard of her work in silents. Pickford performed on radio, wrote books, and dedicated time to charitable causes, but professionally, nothing fulfilled her the way silent movies had. Over the years, she grieved deeply for the demise of her career. In a 1958 interview, she referred to the loss as a "constant ache."[48] Although people remember Fairbanks as the great love of Pickford's life, I would argue that her passion for filmmaking was her strongest and most lasting and that her abiding devotion to the art of cinema was behind her genius and power. Nearly seven decades after the end of Pickford's career, she remains one of the most remarkable and successful producers in film history. ❧

Pickford tries to instill her formula for success in her wayward brother Jack in this publicity shot from his film Garrison's Finish *(1923).*

On the set of her final film, Secrets *(1933), Pickford takes tea with costar Leslie Howard. Directly behind them are actress Mona Maris, director Frank Borzage, Douglas Fairbanks Jr., and studio executive M. C. Levee.*

FATHER OF THE FAMILY

Mary Pickford's Journey from Breadwinner to Businesswoman

Christel Schmidt

Pickford as she appeared in the
one-act play The Littlest Girl (1900).

IN MANY WAYS, it was highly unlikely that Mary Pickford (born Gladys Smith in 1892) would grow up to be a magnate in an industry boardroom. Most women of her era had little contact with finance beyond the management of household accounts, and performers were often considered too mercurial to understand business. Still, by the 1920s, Pickford was not just an international movie star but also a film producer with her own corporation. She shared and ran a studio with her husband, actor and producer Douglas Fairbanks, and was one of the original founders of United Artists, Hollywood's first distribution company for independent producers. Her financial acumen, like her talent as an actress, was innate. However, the drive to use these talents to forge one of Hollywood's greatest careers was learned in the course of Pickford's insecure childhood.

Film historians usually identify the premature death of Pickford's father, John Charles Smith, and the family's ensuing financial insecurity as the trigger for the actress's intense professional drive. In fact, Pickford traced what she called the "lure of money" to a time before he died, when she was "tormented" by a nickel caught between the keys of her mother's piano.[1] (Her grandmother stopped her before she could free it with a hammer.) She also distinctly recalled the first time her father put money (seventy-five cents) in her hands; she dutifully handed over this sorely needed income to her mother. John Charles died soon after, a trauma Pickford recounts in her memoir *Sunshine and Shadow*. Her mother, Charlotte, sat at her husband's bedside "shrieking hysterically and beating her head against the wall," her long, dark hair strewn across her face and blood from a cut on her head staining her nightgown.[2] Wild with grief, she failed to notice that her five-year-old daughter stood watching, terrified. The next day Pickford was struck "with a strange and frightening suddenness, that mother was alone, and ... I had to do something about it."[3]

The next year, Charlotte was struggling to care for her family, which included Pickford's younger siblings, Lottie and Jack, with money she earned as a dressmaker. At the same time, Pickford, acutely aware of her family's financial problems, became withdrawn, depressed, and then seriously ill. A wealthy doctor aided her recovery and then told Charlotte he wanted to adopt her daughter. Keeping the reason for the visit a secret, the widow took Pickford to the doctor's home. After giving them a tour of his house, which included a bedroom reserved for Pickford, the doctor promised the little girl anything she wished for. The child was thrilled until her mother told her she was going to be adopted. "I felt a terror clutching at my heart," Pickford remembered. When she asked her mother, "Don't you want me anymore?" Charlotte tearfully explained that she was unable to provide what the doctor could offer. Pickford answered that she didn't care; she wanted only to be with her family. Even so, the child who had once been fascinated by money now feared its absence. From that day, she recalled, "a determination was born ... that nothing could crush." She would "take her father's place and make sure that her family would never be parted."[4]

The Smith family. Pickford's parents, circa 1890: John Charles Smith (left) and Charlotte Hennessey Smith (right). Their children, Jack, Lottie, and Gladys (later Mary Pickford), are pictured below, circa 1905.

Two years after John Charles's death, a chance to help her mother fell into her lap. A stage manager for Toronto's Cummings Stock Company was renting a room nearby and asked Charlotte if Pickford and Lottie could play bit parts in the six-day run of a show called *The Silver King*. At the time, acting was considered a loose profession, and Charlotte was hesitant. However, a backstage visit to meet the cast and crew convinced her that the theater was a safe environment for her children. On January 8, 1900, the sisters made their theatrical debuts and earned thirteen dollars for the week.

Later that year, Pickford (who loved performing and was in greater demand than Lottie) appeared in *The Littlest Girl,* a one-act play on a vaudeville program that also included Elsie Janis. "Little Elsie" was about Pickford's age and made seventy-five dollars a week imitating stage stars such as Anna Held and Cissie Loftus. Janis remembered a "wide-eyed" Pickford admiring the pretty dresses in her wardrobe, but Charlotte was more impressed by her salary. Any lingering doubts Charlotte might have had about the theater vanished, and she asked Elsie's mother for advice on "preparing for so brilliant a career."[5]

As Charlotte learned the value of nurturing a young star, Pickford's own ambition grew. Another stock company in Toronto was planning to present *The Silver King,* and Charlotte hoped to secure her daughters the parts they had played in the Cummings production. Pickford, however, had a grander goal. She told the director she wished to play Cissie, the lead child role. Even though she could not read yet, Pickford was determined to memorize her lines by repeating them after her mother read them out to her. And when she was cast, the pair set to work, an effective team with a mutual purpose. Their bond became even stronger when, in 1903, all four family members were on tour in the United States. With Pickford keeping track of finances and giving her mother moral support, Charlotte and her eldest child became overseers of the family trade.

But if Pickford had dreams of instant success, they were quickly dashed. By the early 1900s, there were 21,000 American actors competing for a relatively limited number of roles. Those who did find work (even the great ones) spent most of their careers touring by rail through a grueling procession of stages and towns. Most adult performers accepted this life, but it was extremely stressful for a child. The young Pickford, working in second- and third-rate productions, virtually lived in "musty, uncomfortable trains," derelict theaters, and dingy hotels.[6] Most distressing, Pickford's mother and siblings were often cast in different productions that toured separately, causing her anxiety over the breakup of her family to come flooding back. But earning an income offered solace. In 1905, while touring with Lottie in *The Child Wife,* Pickford kept her twenty-five-dollar-a-week salary in a chamois boodle bag around her neck. "To make it seem more," she changed every five-dollar bill into singles.[7]

Professional photograph of Pickford taken on the road in Columbus, Ohio, circa 1905.

Chauncey Olcott and the Smith children (Pickford, Lottie, and Jack) in a scene from Edmund Burke, *circa 1905.*

After two years of touring in different plays, Charlotte and her three children won small roles in *Edmund Burke* starring Chauncey Olcott, a light entertainer who often played Broadway. The musical comedy was a step up the show-business ladder, giving Pickford (sick of "dirty theaters" and "unruly gallery audiences") a taste of a better theatrical life.[8] The actress feared that her work in low-end productions, with their earnest but mediocre performers, was stunting her professional growth. With Olcott, everything improved. She was linked to an established star and worked with a polished and talented cast. The *Philadelphia Inquirer* called the production of *Edmund Burke* "excellent, dignified, impressive."[9] "We were playing better theatres in better towns and before better audiences," remembered Pickford, who called the show "sumptuous."[10] Even the hotels were more upscale. Although *Edmund Burke* did not play on Broadway and the family earned only twenty dollars a week, they were able to live together from September 1905 through the following May.

At the close of *Edmund Burke*'s run, the rest of the family went back to Toronto while Pickford toured in a "wild and wooly melodrama" called *In Convict Stripes*.[11] This backslide from a more venerable theatrical level (as well as being alone on the road again) must have been a bitter pill, and after a few months, she had had enough. Now fifteen years old, she decided to take her career into her own hands, vowing to get a job on Broadway within a year or give up the theater for good. She also had a backup plan: to work in a dressmaking parlor by day while taking dress design classes at night. Whereas most young seamstresses would have dreamed of someday working in a fashionable store, Pickford aimed to own and manage an entire dress factory.

Her plan to make it on Broadway was no less ambitious. Pickford intended to meet impresario David Belasco and ask him for a role in his next production. Belasco, one of the era's great producers, was known for a fanatical adherence to realism in lighting, set design, and props. He also cultivated charismatic actresses such as Blanche Bates and Mrs. Leslie Carter. Although Pickford, like most actors, dreamed of having a star on her dressing-room door, she wanted more than wealth and status. She hoped to take her acting to another level. "I have been an actress," she later told Belasco. "I want to be a *good* actress now."[12]

Pickford considered the producer a god—but clearly, an approachable one. She spent most of the summer of 1907 sitting in his office on casting days, hoping to be noticed, but she never broke the barrier of his inner door. This infinitely persistent teen then decided to seek an introduction from Blanche Bates, who was appearing in Belasco's *The Girl of the Golden West* at Brooklyn's Majestic Theatre, where Pickford had appeared in *Edmund Burke*. With the help of Bates's maid, Pickford received permission to use the star's name when she approached Belasco. The next day Pickford stormed the great producer's office and, armed with Bates's message, caused such a fuss with the office boy that Belasco's manager, William Dean, came out to meet her. She must have impressed Dean because, within weeks, she was granted an audience with the Bishop of Broadway (Belasco's nickname due to his priestly looking garb).

Pickford was overwhelmed at first, but when Belasco asked about her urgent ambition, she recovered her nerve. "I'm the father of my family and I've got to earn all of the money I can." When he asked why she had chosen him, she was just as bold, answering, "Well, Mother always says I should aim high or not at all."[13] Her plainspoken chutzpah charmed Belasco, who cast her in a small role in his next production, *The Warrens of Virginia*. Of course, the tiny part came with a low salary, but Pickford understood the long-term value of quality work and a link to Belasco.

Throughout the run of this Civil War drama (December 3, 1907, through October 1908), Pickford was entranced by the posh Broadway audiences, later recalling their stunning evening attire and the "wave of perfume that wafted across the footlights to . . . the stage."[14] When the New York production closed, it traveled throughout North America, including Toronto, where the newspapers noted that a hometown girl had ascended to the heights of a Belasco production. Yet this success was brief; when the tour ended in the spring of 1909, the young actress was once again out of work—and at the end of the theatrical season, too.

Pickford (left) with Charlotte Walker (seated) and Richard Storey (right) in David Belasco's 1907 production of The Warrens of Virginia.

"THE WARRENS OF VIRGINIA."

Anxious that Pickford find a job, Charlotte suggested that she look for work at the American Mutoscope and Biograph Company. The flourishing studio produced one-reel movies known as "flickers," an inexpensive form of entertainment frequented mostly by the working class. Pickford, who saw herself as a Belasco actress just beginning to build a Broadway career, was horrified. Nonetheless, she was reluctant to defy her mother and headed to Biograph on East Fourteenth Street, swallowing her anger with each step. There, she was introduced to D.W. Griffith, who would arguably become silent cinema's greatest director. However, biographer Eileen Whitfield notes that even if Pickford had been aware of his importance, it would not have mattered; the actress had no interest in the "galloping tintypes." Her first impression of Griffith was that he was "pompous and insufferable."[15] When he explained that the standard salary for actors was five dollars a day, with a minimum three-day workweek, she asked for more money. It was one thing to work at a reduced rate for Olcott and Belasco, but if she was going to lower her standards by appearing in the movies, she needed proper compensation. She began a hard sell for better terms, and Griffith recalled how "her eyes fairly gleamed" when she suggested a guarantee of twenty-five dollars a week.[16] The director, who found her attractive and amusing, agreed.

Portrait of film director D. W. Griffith, circa 1910s.

Pickford spent the next year and a half falling deeply in love with film, which she came to believe was an art form. And as she blossomed in front of the camera, her brilliance, charisma, and growing popularity attracted both a fan base and the interest of other studios. In 1910 Biograph (now widely recognized for its quality movies) lost some of its best players to rival film companies promising better salaries and star publicity.[17] During this period, Pickford joined the Independent Moving Picture Company, earning $10,000 a year (nearly ten times the median salary for a worker in New York City). Yet she returned to Biograph (and took a pay cut) in 1912 because she had become dissatisfied with the quality of her films.

By 1915, Pickford was making features for producer Adolph Zukor at the Famous Players Film Company. Her fame had risen to astronomical heights, and she had negotiated a salary of $2,000 a week, an astounding income for the time. Siblings Lottie and Jack, now adults, continued to act with modest success, each earning around $300 a week. Her mother, Charlotte, still a trusted and shrewd adviser, managed her older daughter's affairs. Sitting at the top of her profession, and with her family secure, Pickford could have simply enjoyed the ride. However, she had never been content with merely showing up and doing a job for a paycheck. She wanted more.

Pickford, the determined child who was once prepared to take a hammer to her mother's piano to free a nickel, was equally resolved in her quest to get everything she wanted out of film. The struggle and shame of her indigent youth had scarred her deeply, and in all her business dealings she sought to widen the chasm between her financial past and future. She also understood that her value as a star could end at any moment. Acting has always been one of the world's most insecure professions, and Pickford, believing that an actor's career was "at best short lived," wanted to "make hay while the sun shines."[18]

With this in mind, Pickford and her mother began to renegotiate her contract in late 1915. Earlier that year, the actress had noticed that the crowds outside the Strand Theater in New York were significantly larger for her films than for those of other actors. After a little investigation, she discovered that Paramount (the distributor of Famous Players films) sold movies to theaters in a package. Block booking, as it was known, required film exhibitors to rent a group of pictures in order to obtain the ones they really wanted. In other words, theater owners who desperately wanted Pickford's highly profitable movies were forced to rent less popular films to get them. But the actress balked at the company's attempt to use her work to "sell the trashy products of a lot of unknown players who can be called stars in courtesy only."[19] Her new contract (signed June 24, 1916) stipulated that her films be distributed separately. Pickford made her position clear to Zukor, remarking, "I don't want to fly on someone else's kite and I'm not gonna have them on mine."[20]

Pickford (left) and her mother, Charlotte, seen here at the actress's Los Angeles home in 1915, were a formidable duo at the negotiating table.

Paramount agreed to distribute the actress's films through a new division of the company called Artcraft, which could not engage in block booking but would charge higher rates for rentals. Although this required only a minor adjustment to Paramount's distribution protocol, Pickford and her mother had shaken things up by "registering the first important protest against the program system of film rental." In addition, the willingness of Famous Players and Paramount to alter company policy to keep one actress within their ranks speaks to the growing power of film stars in the 1910s. As Benjamin Hampton has pointed out, a revolution had begun that shifted power from the film company to the stars, and Pickford was its undisputed leader.[21]

For compensation, Famous Players agreed to pay the actress 50 percent of the profits of her films, guaranteeing her a minimum salary of $1,040,000 over a two-year period, to be issued in weekly installments of $10,000. At the time, the standard salary for a movie star was between $1,000 and $5,000 a week. These are all remarkable figures, considering that the average American's annual income was $750. Pickford also received a $300,000 signing bonus and an extra $40,000 for the four weeks she and her mother had spent working on the agreement. Other perks included her own first-class studio in New York, a private stage for filming in Los Angeles, a parlor car for train travel to and from the West Coast, and her own press agent or secretary.

Advertisement from Moving Picture World *promoting Pickford's latest contract and her extraordinary salary.*

In a move that shocked industry insiders, the contract also gave Pickford her own production company within Famous Players. Although she did not receive total autonomy as a producer, she did gain an impressive amount of control. The Pickford Film Corporation gave her a voice regarding the selection of her directors and final approval over the cast, advertising, and marketing. The actress also had a say in the choice of her characters and stories and the film's final edit. Finally, she was required to make only six films a year (she had been making nearly twice that number) and was guaranteed a reasonable amount of time off in between.

This landmark contract changed the power and meaning of Pickford's career by allowing her to shape her own product (her art) for the market. Now she was able to work with the right people and seek continued improvement and excellence in her films. She was convinced that, in the past, Famous Players (which had made her movies carelessly, knowing that fans would turn up for any Pickford film) had provided neither. The woman who had once been embarrassed to apply for a job at Biograph now believed that "no play [[was]] too great for a picturized version," and even "the most brilliant masterpieces ... should find their way to the screen."[22]

In 1918, as her two-year contract with Famous Players neared its end, the newly formed First National Exhibitor's Circuit made an enticing offer to Pickford: $750,000 for three pictures and 50 percent of the profits (totaling an estimated $1 million to $2 million a year). There would be no block booking of any of her pictures, and most tempting of all, Pickford would have complete artistic independence. Of course, there were complications. First National had been established to challenge the dominance of Zukor, who, through such shrewd maneuvers as merging his company with Paramount, had become the leading producer and distributor of movies worldwide. He also controlled the output of most of Hollywood's great stars, and Pickford, "the magnet that drew more money to ticket windows than several other favorites combined," was his greatest asset.[23] Over the years, Pickford and Zukor had grown extremely close (she even referred to him as "Papa Zukor"), and her departure for a rival would affect them both emotionally.

Pickford watched as Charlotte, who acted as a go-between, relayed her new demands to Zukor. Unfortunately, his partners did not want to match First National's offer. They wanted to let the actress go, believing that she would learn her lesson when she ruined their rival. Zukor, desperate to keep her from working for his competitor, offered her $250,000 a year if she stopped making movies altogether. Pickford declined this unusual proposal. When Zukor refused to match his competitor's terms and the actress signed with First National, the impact of her loss to Famous Players was immediate. On the day Pickford's exit was formally announced, the company's stock fell from 85 to 22½.[24]

Daddy-Long-Legs (1919), Pickford's first independent film for First National, was still in production when rumors began to spread that the major movie companies were planning to supplant the star system by stressing stories and production values. Actors, including Pickford, feared the loss of influence, prestige, and income. An even greater threat to the actress was the rumored merger of Paramount and First National. She had gained ground after leaving Zukor's company and had no intention of ceding it to anyone. Fortuitously, a plan for a new film venture was beginning to take shape—with Pickford once again at its center.

Paramount's former general manager, B. P. Schulberg, and its ex-president, Hiram Abrams, approached Pickford and others with a brilliant scheme: she and a select group of film artists could form a distribution company to sell their independently made productions. The eventual realization of this idea was United Artists (UA), founded in 1919 by Pickford, Charlie Chaplin, Douglas Fairbanks, and Griffith. It was a risky venture. The four partners had to cover the company's start-up costs, as well as finance, oversee, and star in their own productions. With much of the industry opposed to these independent upstarts, UA might have trouble booking its films in movie theaters. But if UA were successful, the benefits of self-employment would be great. Pickford would retain creative control over her work, and although she would have to finance her own productions, she alone would receive the profits. Furthermore, as a company stockholder, the actress would share in UA's business earnings.

There were problems with UA from the start. Each partner was required to make three movies a year, but Chaplin and Griffith worked too slowly to meet the quota. Because banks considered independent films to be highly risky investments, the partners had to put up their own capital. Foreign distribution was difficult to establish, and there was growing tension among the partners. In 1924 the debt-ridden Griffith reluctantly left UA, and there were rumors that Pickford and Fairbanks (who had married in 1920) would return to Famous Players to escape the headaches of business and narrow their focus to film-making. In fact, Pickford treasured her independence, remembering it as "a heady wine [[that]] having once tasted" was impossible to put down.[25] And UA still had significant assets, including its three remaining owners, who were cinema's greatest international stars and were known for their consistently top-notch productions.

In 1924 the co-owners agreed to enlist a new partner, savvy film producer Joseph Schenck, to remedy the continual shortage of product. Schenck set up a structure to finance outside productions that UA would then distribute. With his encouragement, the partners (except for Chaplin) later entered the exhibition business through the United Artists Theater Circuit, a separate venture that purchased venues in major cities. This guaranteed a showcase for UA films in competitive markets and demonstrated to the industry that the company would not be intimidated. Indeed, the struggle to keep UA viable brought out the fighter in Pickford. The company she called her "pride and joy" would encounter and overcome a series of obstacles throughout its history, and she remained devoted to UA until 1956, when she became the last partner to sell her stock.[26]

Through all these ventures, Pickford achieved legendary status as a businesswoman. Samuel Goldwyn, who became a UA partner in 1927, thought she had the "mind of a captain of industry." Zukor believed she "could have risen to the top in United States Steel, if she had decided to." Writer Frances Marion remembered that Pickford "monitored every tributary of her vast holdings" and noted her ability to "invest and reinvest wisely, and outwit a Yankee trader." And Edward Stotsenberg, her accountant for more than two decades, often saw her outsmart a boardroom full of men "as a group or on a one-to-one basis."[27]

Yet Pickford's business acumen did not impress everyone. Chaplin, who often bumped heads with Pickford at United Artists, recalled that her business reputation thrived "in spite of her beauty."[28] In his memoirs, he recognized her knowledge of "the nomenclature: the amortizations and the deferred stocks, etc." in boardroom meetings, yet it "saddened ... more than amazed" him.[29] This reaction highlights the chauvinistic views of the day about women's involvement in business. In many circles, knowledge and expertise in commerce were considered unfeminine, as well as a threat to the notion of women's subservience to men. Moreover, Pickford's competence in business challenged the belief that a woman could find happiness only by devoting herself to a husband, house, and children. The tension underlying her remarkable success was revealed in the press's response to the unraveling of her personal and professional lives at the end of the silent era.

United Artists publicity photo of Pickford in 1927. Her combination of beauty and brains was at odds with the era's belief that business skills were unfeminine.

By the early 1930s, the arrival of the talkies had virtually killed silent film as an art form, and even the greatest silent stars had to struggle to maintain their careers. No one had more to lose than Fairbanks and Pickford, who had reigned for years as the King and Queen of Hollywood. Fairbanks simply abdicated his throne by leaving the United States and traveling abroad for nearly three years, while Pickford stayed and fought for her career. The "stage and screen … have been my life," the actress said, and "you cannot, so easily, give up your life."[30] However, that life, with all its celebrated triumphs, suddenly displeased a rabid press, which had developed a taste for tearing down the idols it had helped build up. In 1933, when the box-office receipts of her talking pictures failed to live up to her silent movie success, she stopped acting. After her separation and divorce (in 1936) from Fairbanks, the media reveled in schadenfreude.

Pickford, according to various magazines, was lonely and bereft. Her days were spent "longing for children ... mourning a husband that drifted away ... watching her fame vanish into the pathetic has-been ... [finding] little compensation in her apparently reassuring bank account."[31] *Pictorial Review* deemed the forty-two-year-old's future to be hopeless and futile. She became a cautionary tale for working women and a poster child for poor life choices. *New Movie Magazine* declared that Pickford had never even considered leaving the screen when she married Fairbanks. In contrast, actress Marguerite Clark, a former screen rival, had retired when she married because, in her view, the "man's career ... is primarily important."[32] Clark's path, accordingly, had led to domestic bliss, while Pickford's had led to an empty home.

The criticism of Pickford in *Photoplay* repeated this theme, but the basis for comparison was more painful. Lady Sylvia Ashley, an English socialite, had wed Fairbanks in 1936. The new bride, *Photoplay* reported, had no interest in a film career. Instead, she offered her husband the "masculine satisfaction" of providing for her needs.[33] Pickford, then president of UA, had signed the "death warrant" to her marriage, unaware that "no man likes to feel himself subjugated to a woman no matter what the circumstances."[34] Ironically, by all accounts, Fairbanks was never threatened by Pickford's intellect or achievements. He had shared her passion for filmmaking, created an equal business partnership with her, and sought her valuable counsel on career and financial matters.

Today, it seems that Pickford was fated from the start to hold the feminist torch—in movies and beyond. She veered from patriarchy's path for women at seven years old, when she became the family bread-winner. Over the years, she stood firm in her belief that women had the right to join the working world. In 1916, as she negotiated her stunning Famous Players contract, she told the press, "I admire most in the world the girls who earn their own living. I am proud to be one of them."[35] Later, with Fairbanks at her side, she spoke to 12,000 women at an event about female leadership in business. Pickford told the crowd that "all the pleasures of business and professional life have been reserved for men and that ... women have been sadly neglected."[36] In the 1930s she became a member of the National Women's Party and supported the equal rights amendment. And, speaking at the Women's National Press Club, she noted that "until women citizens share [in democracy] to the same extent men enjoy it, our democracy is not complete."[37]

In the face of her critics, Pickford often presented her prominent role in the industry as a "protective measure" that saved her art from corporate managers who cared only for money.[38] She, of course, cared for money too. Many creative people feel stymied by the demands of the business that provides opportunities for their creativity; few achieve the power to forge their own paths. Pickford herself acknowledged that it was rare to be skilled in both the corporate world and art. She was born with those gifts, and her childhood struggles drove her to apply them, with great success. ॐ

Pickford, a member of the National Women's Party, promotes the purchase of equal rights seals at a 1939 event celebrating the 119th anniversary of Susan B. Anthony's birth.

PICKFORD AND FAIRBANKS

A Modern Marriage

Christel Schmidt

*They were in love—beautifully, gloriously in love.
And they were equals.*

Adela Rogers St. Johns, Photoplay, *February 1927*

*Pickford and Fairbanks watch a scene
being filmed on the set of* Little Annie
Rooney *(1925).*

B Y THE TIME Mary Pickford wed actor Douglas Fairbanks in March 1920, the marriage seemed almost preordained. Each was already an international superstar, adored by fans with the passionate intensity that early cinema inspired. Each had an onscreen persona that represented American optimism, energy, and youth. Each had amassed extraordinary wealth, power, and respect within the industry. And though their courtship was fraught with complications (at the time, both were married to other people), their eventual union seemed, to the public and to their friends, the ideal match of personal and professional equals.

Just a generation earlier, middle-class men and women had usually wed for social and economic reasons, with each consigned to separate public and private realms. Breaking with that long tradition, Pickford and Fairbanks married for love and shared the domains of work and home equally.[1] Theirs was an enlightened union, a type defined by sociologists in 1924 as "companionate marriage." This marital model—which emerged during the Progressive Era (1890–1930)—"rejected patriarchal family models and instead envisioned marriage as an equal partnership" built on friendship and mutual interest.[2] In this spirit, the media portrayed the couple's bond as one of like-minded and sympathetic helpmates who had previously suffered domestic problems due to incompatible spouses. Now the pair had found true companionship and (perhaps more important for the actress) professional understanding.

"It might have been difficult for many men to be the husband of Mary Pickford," journalist Adela Rogers St. Johns observes. "Only a man who was a 'king in his own right,' as it were, would not have been overwhelmed" by it.[3] With these words, the writer acknowledges the challenges of being married to a star actress and having to play second fiddle to her career. Although women were entering the workforce in record numbers at the turn of the twentieth century, many people still believed that wives belonged at home. And although, as historian Benjamin McArthur observes, nearly all famous actresses who married continued their careers, a belief in women's subservience to men persisted, even within the performing arts.[4] As a columnist in *Photoplay* wrote on the subject of women's employment after marriage, "Many men can stand no touch of equality in their wives."[5] Pickford's first husband was just such a man.

Snapshot of Pickford and Fairbanks in Switzerland in 1924.

Opposite: The recently wed couple poses for photographers aboard the SS Lapland before setting sail on their European honeymoon in June 1920.

The actress met actor Owen Moore in 1909 at Biograph, director D.W. Griffith's film studio, where both were employed. When they married eighteen months later, Pickford's career was on the rise, and throughout their eight years as husband and wife, it continued to ascend at an astonishing speed. In her memoir, Pickford acknowledges that her fame, as well as her role as the pair's chief breadwinner, would have been hard for any man to bear. Still, Moore's resentment of his wife was toxic—especially after she met the charming and energetic Fairbanks, a man who was not threatened by her achievements but actually loved and admired her for them.

True, Fairbanks sometimes touted a conservative line on the subject of career wives, giving (as many performers did) a nod to the values of their mainstream audiences. And Fairbanks, born in the Victorian era, may have retained some shred of nineteenth-century beliefs about marriage. But he was also a modern man living in a new age, when married women in his profession not only worked but attained great success. And the actor was drawn to highly accomplished people. By all accounts, he had little if any professional jealousy and was genuinely pleased by the achievements of others. All this was reflected in his relationship with Pickford, a woman he considered a great artist and a savvy businesswoman.

When Pickford and Fairbanks wed, they forged a progressive union that not only met but surpassed companionate marriage's expectations of gender equality. In addition to domestic parity, the Pickford-Fairbanks union encompassed a professional bond: a passion for filmmaking, creative camaraderie, and a shared work ethic. In 1919, a year before their marriage, the couple—who had separately been producing their own pictures since the 1910s—formed United Artists with Griffith and comedian Charlie Chaplin, a groundbreaking operation that distributed independent productions. Three years later they started the Pickford-Fairbanks Studio on a ten-acre lot that allowed them to make their movies side by side. Their production companies remained separate, but they frequented each other's sets as often as possible, sharing creative inspiration and advice.

Fairbanks and Pickford (in costume) promote the Red Cross in 1924.

Opposite: Fairbanks and Pickford in costume for his 1926 Technicolor feature The Black Pirate. *Pickford, photographed in a gown worn by leading lady Billie Dove, stood in for the actress in a long shot for the film's romantic finale.*

This highly successful personal and professional alliance was idealized by the public and press alike. Still, journalists felt the need to temper the unconventional aspects of their union with stories about the couple's sedate home life and their grand romance, reporting that Pickford and Fairbanks shared Sunday dinners with family, kept early hours, and never spent an evening apart. Their epic love story, one journalist wrote, was as immortal as those of "Heloise and Abelard, Romeo and Juliet, [[and]] Dante and his Beatrice."[6] There was, however, no escaping the importance of art and work to the marriage when, by the start of the 1930s, sound pictures had all but replaced silent movies. At this point, the professional became personal: Pickford and Fairbanks realized that their onscreen careers were ending and that they had to reimagine their future. Unable to face the loss together, the couple drifted apart. They divorced in 1936, and each moved on to a complicated third marriage to a less accomplished spouse.[7] (Ironically, companionate marriages were also on the decline, as the optimism of the Progressive Era was extinguished by the Great Depression.)

The Pickford-Fairbanks marriage had ended, but their love and connection never entirely faded. She continued to advise him on business matters, and they spent personal time together even after he remarried. On one particular visit to Pickfair, he told his former wife that their divorce had been a "mistake."[8] The feeling of regret, at least for Fairbanks, never diminished. From his deathbed in 1939, he left Pickford this message: "by the clock," their personal code for enduring love. The legend of the Pickford-Fairbanks romance has endured. They gave Hollywood its first powerful "supercouple" and provided the world with an illustration of a successful egalitarian marriage at work. ⁂

Telegram from Fairbanks to Pickford.

Opposite: A 1925 publicity photo taken at Pickfair depicts the serene domestic life and ideal companionship of the Pickford-Fairbanks marriage.

FROM
THE CHILDREN of AMERICA
TO
THE CHILDREN of BELGIUM.

"LITTLE MARY"

Formidable Philanthropist

Alison Trope

Stop a moment, you who think of the movie stars as devoting their nights to hilarious gaiety, their only thoughts in the hours when they are not working being of vast extravagances! Picture this scene—the highest salaried woman in the entire world enduring a night of discomfort—merely because a baby cried when she took her hand away. You who have wanted to know why Mary Pickford is a great favorite and why her popularity never wanes—can you not see in this little story some clue to the mystery?

Randolph Bartlett, Photoplay, April 1920

A 1917 publicity shot of Pickford and Douglas Fairbanks holding gifts meant for children in war-torn Belgium.

UNDER THE TITLE "Mary, the Well Beloved," Bartlett's *Photoplay* article details Mary Pickford's five-year commitment to the Los Angeles Orphan Asylum. Along the way, it highlights her monetary contributions as well as her perhaps more significant gift of personal time and love. According to *Photoplay*, Pickford did not know the story was being written. An inset box (on the article's title page) emphasizes her desire for anonymity regarding her work at the orphanage. The magazine, however, claimed that her good deeds had to be made public, if for no other reason than to inspire others.[1]

Photoplay's explanation represents an unusual sidebar to what is otherwise a typical star profile, with its mix of fact and flattery. Although Pickford no doubt felt an affinity for the orphans, the article clearly weaves together her stardom and her charity toward them. It states that the orphanage inspired her to conceive the story for the 1916 film *The Foundling* and reveals that she went on to use the orphanage itself in two subsequent films, *Stella Maris* (1918) and *Daddy-Long-Legs* (1919). Conveniently, the article appeared just after the controversy surrounding her personal life had reached an apex owing to her divorce from actor Owen Moore and marriage to actor Douglas Fairbanks in the same month.

As conventional star hagiography, *Photoplay*'s portrait of Pickford seamlessly juxtaposes adulation for her offscreen life with promotion of her onscreen fare, while sidestepping any potential public relations debacles. At the same time, the portrait unwittingly underscores a tension between the actress's on- and offscreen stardom. The intertwining of these stories and interests illustrates a necessary, though complicated, balance of personal ego and the greater good. These stories, in turn, shed light on the multiple determinants at play in the act of giving, and they allow us to see the variety of meanings and gestures we can ascribe to giving—particularly beyond the concrete monetary donation.

Much has been written about Pickford as an actress, as a symbol of American innocence, and as a shrewd businesswoman. As the *Photoplay* article suggests, she also played a significant (offscreen) role as a philanthropist. Indeed, the actress's charitable endeavors and the popular discourse around them mark an important historical moment—one that signaled what has become a complex symbiotic relationship between Hollywood stardom and philanthropy. Without disparaging Pickford's pursuits or motives, it is important to put her giving in an industrial context, as well as to consider the role philanthropy can play in the creation and maintenance of star personae—issues still alive in our current celebrity landscape.

Pickford, a lifelong supporter of children's causes, visits an orphanage in the early 1920s.

In the movie The Foundling *(1916), Pickford portrays a spirited orphan who protects the institution's more vulnerable residents.*

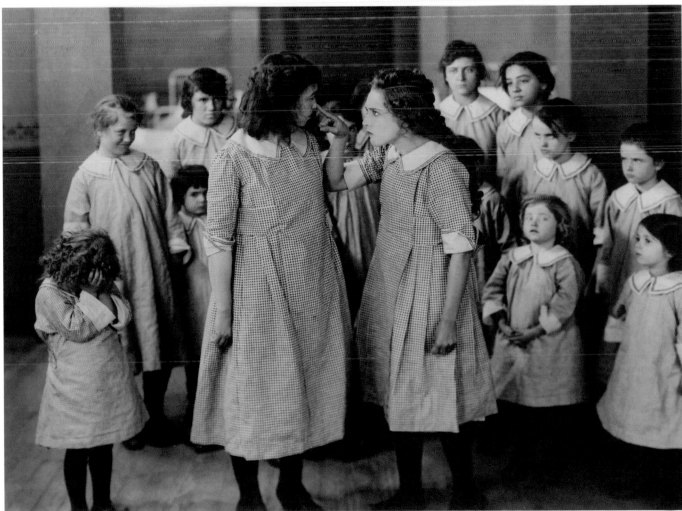

New York December 11, 1914

Miss Mary Pickford,
        Famous Players Studio,
        New York City.

Dear Miss Pickford:-

        The Board of Trustees of the Actors' Fund of

America extend to you their thanks and appreciation for

your check for $50.00 to become a Life Member of the

Fund.

        Life Membership certificate will be mailed you

in a few days.

                Sincerely yours,

                Danl Frohman.

                    President

Like so many of today's stars, Pickford's altruistic behind-the-scenes work, whether incidentally or by design, helped burnish her star image and professional status. However, as is the case with many of her philanthropic peers, the line between helping others and helping oneself can be difficult to discern. Even beyond the context of celebrity, the history of organized charity and personal philanthropy has been fraught with complications, requiring one to negotiate the lines between public service and self-promotion, anonymous giving and leading by example. Pickford's philanthropic and advocacy work (and that of stars who followed closely in her footsteps, including Jean Hersholt, Audrey Hepburn, and Jerry Lewis) set a precedent, and it offers a significant historical frame for understanding the acts of contemporary stars such as Angelina Jolie, George Clooney, and Sean Penn.

Pickford, who began her career as a child actress in 1900, likely became aware of the theater's many charitable campaigns during her youth. As early as the 1870s, benefit performances raised money for actors in need, and according to Benjamin McArthur, "actors took pride in their reputation for public service." In his book *Actors and American Culture*, McArthur shows that in the nineteenth century, an "emerging professional self-consciousness" and a widespread desire to create institutions to represent different occupations helped establish acting as an "honorable" endeavor.[2] For the actor, the promise of prestige and respectability worked to combat an ever-present stigma associated with acting and popular entertainment. This trend toward professionalism ran parallel to the Progressive Era's reform agenda, as well as a concurrent movement for organized charity.[3] Philanthropy became key to dignifying acting and the theater.

Pickford was always sensitive to both the stigmas associated with her profession and her own impoverished upbringing. Through much of the 1910s, she expressed concern for her artistry as a performer and a desire to uplift the industry and the medium that created her audience and image. It was also during this period that she began to carry out charitable work.[4] In 1914 Pickford pledged lifelong membership to the Actors' Fund, a New York organization that had been providing financial assistance to entertainers and their families since 1882. From the start of her career, then, a converging set of interests shaped the actress's values and actions: a reformist spirit and responsibility that called for giving and helping one's own, paired with a related desire to cement her craft's respectability. Through this union of public and professional service, Pickford became a unique and powerful model of philanthropic giving in Hollywood. As Conrad Nagel, fellow actor and former president of the Motion Picture Relief Fund, claimed, "Mary was one of the few great stars of that era who had a social conscience."[5]

At a Liberty Loan rally in Washington, D.C., Pickford speaks sternly to a crowd about their support for the war effort.

During World War I, when Pickford and other Hollywood stars helped the federal government sell Liberty bonds as part of the U.S. Treasury's Liberty Loan campaign, the actress began to understand her potential impact beyond the realms of entertainment and art. Her philanthropic interests dovetailed with populist concerns for the nation as a whole, particularly the education, health, and welfare of its citizens. During one of the Liberty bond drives in 1918, for instance, Pickford addressed the crowd as follows: "I have something serious to talk to you about. I know you all expect me to talk about the movies and how they are made and all those things. I'm a silent actress. I can't make a speech so I'm going to make this just a little talk from me to you. Maybe you think a blonde curly-haired girl can't be serious, but if you could see what I did in NY and if you could hear the things I've heard [from wounded soldiers] about this awful old war, you'd know just how serious I can be."[6]

Though Pickford consciously worked to sidestep her stardom (by all accounts, she was sincerely devoted to the war effort), her involvement with the Liberty Loan campaign was intimately tied to her fame. Her war work was used to promote her films through press books that linked them together, and the bond drives themselves required that she highlight her stardom and her persona as America's Sweetheart by autographing photographs, selling one of her curls for the cause, and deliberately playing to her fans with the words "if you love me, I want you to buy bonds."[7]

In April 1918 Pickford's war work helped mitigate public scrutiny of her role in the breakup of Douglas Fairbanks's marriage. An affair between the couple had long been rumored, and gossip picked up steam when, early in the tour, Fairbanks's wife announced that she was separating from her husband because he was in love with a movie star. Pickford, who was widely (and rightly) believed to be the other woman, expertly brushed off journalists' questions about Fairbanks and claimed that her focus remained on the important business of selling Liberty bonds. The media reported the brewing scandal, but they kept their coverage to a minimum because of the couple's war-related activities. In this way, the bond tour had a positive impact on the actress's career, bolstering her public image at a time when a scandal could have easily destroyed it.

It was not the last time the bond drive or Pickford's other charitable endeavors deflected attention from her relationship with Fairbanks or her divorce from Moore. Two months after the *Photoplay* piece on Pickford's work with the Los Angeles Orphan Asylum, the magazine did a follow-up story entitled "The Pickford-Fairbanks Wooing." The relationship that *Photoplay* had tactically overlooked in the April issue now took center stage. In an attempt to avoid any negative attention toward the couple, the June article dispelled the "sly eye-winking and rib-poking of the scandal monger" and offered instead a tidy narrative of their budding romance during the Liberty Loan tour.[8] Deftly denying the well-circulated tale that their affair had started long before the drive, the account painted Pickford as a victim of petty gossip, unfairly cast as a woman without morals.

During World War I, Douglas Fairbanks and Pickford—posing here with a soldier, circa 1917—frequently appeared together at home-front events.

*Pickford presents Colonel H. H. Arnold with
a service flag during a ceremony on Air Memorial Day
(May 18, 1919) in Hollywood, California.*

Despite the combination of star puffery and scandal in the popular press, Pickford had a measurable impact on the bond tour. She brought out massive crowds, even in inclement weather, and helped raise millions of dollars in Liberty bonds (as much as $14 million in a single day in Pittsburgh).[9] Along with her service for the government's Liberty Loan campaign, Pickford took an active role in her industry's work to assist in the war effort. The actress became a co–vice president of the Motion Picture War Service Association (MPWSA), an organization founded in May 1918 by leaders in the film industry for the "purpose of unifying and concentrating the patriotic work" of those in the movie business.[10] The organization, echoing rhetoric from the Liberty Loan campaign, summoned members to "put charity ahead of their professions, and their country ahead of all."[11] Membership required active participation in Liberty Loan and Red Cross drives, and the organization held numerous fund-raising events and propaganda rallies to bolster the spirits of soldiers and civilians alike. Interested in the war's impact on those closer to home, MPWSA planned to build two Motion Picture Hospitals (one in New York and one in California) and then turn them over to the U.S. government for the care and convalescence of soldiers. Once the fighting overseas had ended, the hospitals would revert back to MPWSA to aid the "aged, ailing and dependent people" of the film industry.[12]

The hospital project never got off the ground, but Pickford, who was concerned about entertainment workers who had fallen on hard times, had another idea. After the war, and with funds left over from money she had raised through MPWSA for the Red Cross Ambulance Fund, she helped found the Motion Picture Relief Fund (MPRF). Incorporated in 1921, the MPRF served as a branch of the Actors' Fund until 1924. Designed specifically to minister to the needs of members of the motion picture industry, the MPRF became the greatest beneficiary of Pickford's fund-raising efforts, influence, and time over the course of her life.

In a 1939 radio broadcast of *The Passing Parade,* host John Nesbitt and Pickford discussed the origins of the MPRF. Nesbitt began the show by telling the story of Michael Craven, an actor who had once earned $2,000 a week but, having fallen on hard times, was now relegated to selling pencils outside one of the studio gates. Following Nesbitt's setup, Pickford entered the story as a warmhearted and keenly perceptive "star who had everything [[and]] began to think about those who had nothing."[13] She bought two pencils from Craven and was subsequently inspired to develop the relief fund to serve him and others in the same predicament. As Pickford reflected:

In Hollywood there were hundreds of people who had done their work well, but were being forgotten in the first great rush of a new industry.... You see, the country was only reading about the ermine and diamonds the stars were wearing. But we who knew the heart of Hollywood knew about all the Michael Cravens and the makeup men and the grips and carpenters and bit men and all those others who had had their hour. We tried to make it like a sort of spiritual ambulance. And when the cry for help came, we tried to answer.[14]

Pickford promotes a fund-raising raffle for the Motion Picture Relief Fund.

The MPRF, in Pickford's view, not only helped those in need but also showed the world another, more serious side of the film business, one that worked against superficial assumptions about parties and riches. She clearly viewed the fund as a crucial vehicle to combat the poverty and loss to which many in the industry had succumbed. In fact, her own destitute upbringing and family struggles (and perhaps her own fear of being forgotten) likely played a role in her unswerving dedication to the cause, if not her philanthropic impulse in general.

Over the years, as the MPRF grew into a mature organization, Pickford worked tirelessly to secure financial support, ensure its stability, and make certain that it adhered to its motto: "We take care of our own." In 1932 she helped institute the Payroll Pledge Program, which asked members of all branches of the film industry who made more than $50 per week to contribute one-half of 1 percent of their earnings. In 1948, when the fund reached its lowest point, this percentage was increased to 1 percent for those earning at least $200 per week. As an expert negotiator, and with the goal of eventually eradicating these payroll deductions, Pickford maintained that the MPRF should be subsidized by a museum or some other public venue dedicated to motion pictures.[15]

Edward Arnold, Jean Hersholt, and architect William Pereira join Pickford at the ground-breaking ceremony for the Motion Picture Country House in September 1941.

Pickford signs autographs for Chinese American airmen from the Santa Ana army base at a party held at Pickfair in 1944.

Drawing on the original concept of the MPWSA, Pickford also guided the founding of the Motion Picture Country House and Hospital. As she described it on *The Passing Parade,* the Country House "will be more like a club, one with green lawns and spacious verandas and lovely gardens where the actors and actresses who have served the public well may have rest, peace and happiness when the years have passed and they have finished their work in the studios … the men and women who have made the moving picture world possible, the hundreds who have stood in the shadows while one star received the spotlight."[16] Upon its opening in 1942, the Country House promised "star treatment" to its residents. The original facility was built on a fifty-five-acre Woodland Hills estate and consisted of thirty-two single and two double bungalows. By 1948, with the completion of the Country Hospital, forty rooms were added; twenty-one more beds became available when the Country Rest Home opened in 1955, followed in 1961 by the seventy-nine-bed Pavilion.[17] On its twenty-fifth anniversary, the institution, echoing the MPRF's motto, labeled itself the only "self-serving" facility for the film industry in the United States.[18]

Pickford's involvement with the MPRF, and later the Country House and Hospital, clearly indicates a concern for her industry peers, but it also suggests that she felt a more general responsibility to her public at large. Eileen Whitfield, in her biography of Pickford, underscores the star's extreme sense of duty: "fame, in her mind, entailed obligations: to see and be seen, to spread joy simply by showing up."[19] As early as the 1920s, but especially after she retired from acting, members of the public as well as civic and industry leaders frequently solicited her support. Pickford used her social presence and celebrity to ease the way for countless projects and institutions. She supported the Academy of Motion Picture Arts and Sciences (AMPAS) and the Film Library at the Museum of Modern Art (MoMA) from their inception. At the organizational banquet for AMPAS in 1927, Pickford was introduced as "all that is fine and splendid and unselfish." She then authoritatively addressed her peers, framing their involvement as a "privilege and pleasure"—one that would help not only those who had already succeeded but also those who hoped to do so.[20]

Pickford's extraordinary success certainly afforded her the opportunity to help, and this assistance often came in the form of star power rather than monetary donations. After she married Fairbanks, the couple used Pickfair, their lavish Beverly Hills estate, to entertain their friends as well as to host events for institutions and causes they championed (and that Pickford continued to support after they divorced). Pickfair, sometimes called the other White House, served as a site to meet the public and satisfy the actress's self-imposed duty to serve it. Throughout her life, she offered her home for the weddings of family, friends, and strangers; soldiers' and veterans' parties; and benefits for various causes.

In 1935 she hosted a reception at Pickfair for MoMA's Film Library. Pickford facilitated MoMA's efforts on the West Coast, and beginning in the 1930s, she played an instrumental role in supporting numerous attempts to erect a monument to Hollywood and its history in Los Angeles. Although she encouraged other cultural institutions that sought to collect and preserve motion pictures (including the George Eastman House in Rochester, New York, and the Library of Congress in Washington, D.C.), she often publicly expressed surprise and dismay that "this important work was not undertaken long ago by the industry itself" in its own backyard—Los Angeles.[21] Given her staunch dedication to honoring and preserving motion pictures, instances of failure elicited Pickford's ire. When plans for the Motion Picture Exposition and Hall of Fame were aborted in the mid-1950s, she was quoted in many local and national papers chastising the industry for its shameful shortsightedness: "The museum would earn good will.... Millions of tourists drive down Hollywood Boulevard every year and are depressed. There's nothing for them to see. This is the country's fifth largest industry and we have no museum! Rochester, New York has a museum and a silent film theater that puts Hollywood to shame."[22] Pickford publicly threatened that unless the industry took steps to establish a museum, she would change her will and leave her multimillion-dollar collection to the three other cities that did have cinema museums. Like many fans and industry insiders, however, Pickford remained loyal to Hollywood as a site and a mythic symbol.[23]

In the late 1950s and for several years thereafter, she played a key role in the planning stages of the Hollywood Museum, including serving as chair of the Los Angeles County Motion Picture Committee. At the 1963 groundbreaking for the museum, Pickford's speech echoed sentiments from the Liberty Loan tour and the reception for MoMA's Film Library. She spoke of the museum's significance to her as an actress, to the Hollywood industry, and to the nation at large. Relating the museum project and the birth of cinema to the growth of America as a nation, Pickford declared, "The greatest tribute that I can pay to our profession is that we grew up with it. Just as our nation was taking its place upon the world's stage, so did our movies sweep to all corners of this earth and win the hearts and the imaginations of all mankind." Soliciting her peers, Pickford celebrated the museum enterprise as the "center for the actor—the star—to demonstrate his or her interest in civic responsibilities."[24] Pickford's discussion of civic responsibility and national pride was buoyed by a congratulatory telegram (also read at the event) from President Kennedy.

Hollywood Museum planners Mervyn Le Roy, Ernest E. Debs, Pickford, and Sol Lesser discuss the venture after a meeting in 1962.

Her own commitment to these matters reached far beyond Hollywood. In addition to her longtime sponsorship of the MPRF, she gave to the Salvation Army, American Cancer Society, City of Hope, Arthritis Foundation, National Foundation for Infantile Paralysis, Children's Hospital of Toronto, John Tracy Clinic, colleges and universities, youth organizations such as the YMCA and the Boys Club of America, and Los Angeles cultural institutions such as the Hollywood Bowl and the Los Angeles Philharmonic. She also regularly gave to organizations designed to help the aged, including the Jewish Home for the Aged of Los Angeles. In an interview with Arthur Friedman, Pickford discussed her (then) eighteen-year relationship with the Jewish Home and the impetus for her involvement. "I made what I thought was an intolerant remark, and it grieved me.... [As a result] I said that the next appeal from the Jewish people, I would answer."[25] Self-conscious and guilt-ridden, she devoted time and money to the Jewish Home and helped in the building of a hospital and clinic. Her attention to the elderly was recognized outside of Los Angeles as well. In 1960 she was chosen to be one of California's delegates at the White House Conference on Aging. There, Pickford addressed concerns about housing for low-income senior citizens. In a local Los Angeles newspaper, she disclosed her personal take on the issue, claiming, "Nobody likes to be referred to as old, even if they are in their 80s."[26]

Over the course of more than sixty years, Pickford gave time, money, and a public face to a range of causes. The time span attests to her commitment and generosity; her long philanthropic record also offers insight into the personal and sometimes inconsistent shifts in her interests and giving. Whitfield claims that, by the 1940s, Pickford was "known to most people as a public minded wealthy matron," but she occasionally made seemingly curious choices with regard to her charities and the amounts she gave.[27] The MPRF and the Jewish Home for the Aged remained constant beneficiaries throughout her life, but her donations to other charities could be sporadic and appear less than generous. She might give as little as $3 to an orphanage or a hospital and as much as $5,000 to the Thomas Edison Foundation or her own Mary Pickford Foundation. Pickford often divided her money among several organizations; at other times, donations were seemingly quite random. She might see a story on television or in the newspaper and be spurred to make a donation to a Sunday school class, an underprivileged child who wanted to go to summer camp, or a person whose leg braces had been stolen.

The unevenness in her donations corresponds with stories of penny-pinching discussed in Whitfield's biography.[28] These stories, framed within the larger context of Pickford's life, career, and personal relationships, do not negate her giving or her generosity. Rather, they paint a nuanced picture of philanthropy and the multiple motives and determinants that impact not only celebrities but the rest of us as well. We might label Pickford's giving inspired, heartfelt, spontaneous, capricious, measured, or even fickle. Undoubtedly, it could be all these things. Yet, as a public figure, she had to navigate a terrain complicated by the professional demands of her stardom; solicitations from the federal government, the arts, and medical and educational institutions; and her desire to satisfy her own interests and passions.

Pickford's reputation as a wealthy, public-minded matron preceded her, and decades after her last screen appearance, she was still petitioned to support many causes. As she confessed to Friedman in the late 1950s, "It's very difficult to refuse some of them, because all charity is deserving."[29] To handle the numerous requests, she formally established a charity trust in 1955, from which donations were disbursed on her behalf.[30] Over time, she gave real estate, furniture, and other personal possessions to the trust. In 1966 Pickford also set up a foundation to further apportion her possessions and shelter her estate from heavy taxation. Upon her death in 1979, Pickford's estate was estimated to be worth nearly $50 million. Much of it, including Pickfair, was earmarked for her foundation, which continues to support a range of charitable causes more than thirty years after her death. Her philanthropic legacy, therefore, remains with us today, in the MPRF and other causes to which she gave and in the spirit of her generosity. Given her lifelong and extensive involvement with charities and social causes, Pickford's persona as America's Sweetheart hardly does her justice. Likewise, celebrations of her business acumen capture only a limited picture of the actress's contributions. Pickford's philanthropy offers important insights into the balancing of stars' on- and offscreen personae, the crossover between art and industry, and the ever-increasing role of public service in the history of Hollywood. ❧

Pickford gazes benevolently at a poster promoting a local Santa Barbara charity.

Be a good
neighbor

GIVE GENEROUSLY
SANTA BARBARA
COMMUNITY CHEST
FEBRUARY 10-15

AMERICA'S SWEETHEART

Edward Wagenknecht

Photo by Marceau, 1913.

I T MUST BE VERY DIFFICULT for people today to realize what Mary Pickford meant to America when she really was America's Sweetheart—not only the undisputed queen of the movies but also, by all accounts, the most famous woman in America. The "America's Sweetheart" tag, invented by "Pop" Grauman, was sedulously cultivated by her press agents, and her career was intelligently geared and self-directed toward the success she had deliberately set for herself as a goal. Yet none of this would have sufficed without an enthusiastic public response, and nobody who lived through the years of her fame can doubt that that response was spontaneous, enthusiastic, and impassioned—the kind that cannot be manufactured or bought.[1]

In 1926 Dorothy Gish came back from England with the shocking news that a London schoolgirl, asked what "M.P." stood for, had replied, "Mary Pickford." (Actually, it stands for Member of Parliament.) More shocking—and more touching—was the story of the congressman's daughter who came home from Sunday school one day and said, "Mamma, they asked us today who we wanted to be like." "And?" queried her mother. "Oh," sighed the child, "I told them the Lord, but I meant Mary Pickford."

We all idealized Mary in those days. Reading Schiller's *Die Jungfrau von Orleans* in school, I came across Dunois's great tribute to Joan of Arc:

> If e'er truth desires
> Embodiment in form that's visible,
> Then it must wear her features as its own.
> If purity of heart, faith, innocence,
> Dwells anywhere on earth,—upon her lips,
> Within her placid eyes, there it must dwell![2]

I am willing to give the reader three guesses of whom I was immediately reminded. Nor was this a wholly idiosyncratic reaction. "There is a radiance about her," Gerald D. McDonald wrote in his review of her memoir *Sunshine and Shadow*, "and audiences never doubted that even without the make-believe she was kind, noble and true."[3] James Card added, "There is something heavenly about Mary Pickford. It is a quality, we must admit, most uncommon in motion pictures."[4]

This is an edited version of "America's Sweetheart," chapter 3 in Edward Wagenknecht's Movies in the Age of Innocence, *2nd ed. (Norman: University of Oklahoma Press, 1963).*

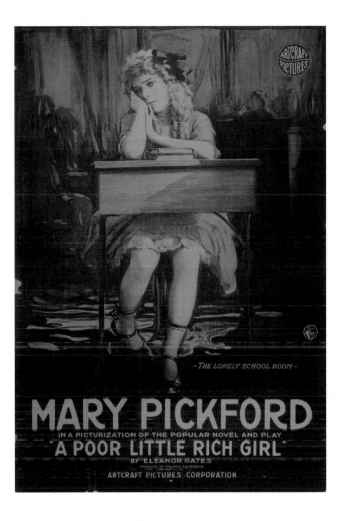

Poster from The Poor Little Rich Girl *(1917).*

Nobody has ever questioned Pickford's great skill and knowledge in all matters relating to motion picture technique, but there is a tendency among those who do not know her films well to identify her exclusively with the portrayal of children and young girls. If this were true, I should not think it necessary to apologize for it in any terms of abjectness. Most actors specialize in one thing or another; to all intents and purposes, Charlie Chaplin has played only one character, but those who disparage Pickford have not thought it necessary to remain blind to *his* great achievements. If you are going to specialize, it seems to me that children and young girls afford a very good field. I can think of highly regarded actresses who have specialized in prostitutes, and I do not believe that prostitutes are more important than young girls or that they are more varied in their motivations or more difficult to portray. "A woman of moral depravity," said stage actress Julia Marlowe, "offers the modern playwright greater scope than a good woman because her life is full of incidents that are dramatic." But, she added, rightly, "it takes a greater artist to make a good woman interesting than to make a base woman sympathetic and thrilling."[5]

As a matter of fact, it was not until after the beginning of the feature era that Pickford became definitely associated with ingénue roles, and it was not until *The Poor Little Rich Girl* (1917) that she appeared throughout a feature film as a child. Nevertheless, Pickford's children and girls were not undifferentiated; of course, there was a kind of familial relationship between them, but is this not also true of the types favored by certain other actresses? Gwen in *The Poor Little Rich Girl,* for example, is a very different girl from either Rebecca or Pollyanna—more helpless and less resourceful and considerably more wistful. She also gives the impression of being considerably younger. Her movements, her reactions are all those of a *small* child; so too is her fright when she is told by a lazy servant that she cannot be taken to her father's office because the place is full of bears. When she asks another girl, "Are you scared of bears?" she reads the line like a small child, and it is no exaggeration to speak of her "reading" such lines, even though the film is silent and we cannot hear what she says except in the mind's ear. Her tantrums are a small child's tantrums too, entirely lacking the elements of calculation and self-satisfaction of which Rebecca is capable or the sense of compulsion that sometimes possesses Pollyanna.

What I am saying, of course, is that the composite Pickford character was considerably less simple than she is generally supposed to have been. As I have already said, if she was America's Sweetheart, she was also America's—and the world's—darling child, sometimes even a problem child. But she was also the Madonna in *The Foundling* (1916) and again, briefly, in Douglas Fairbanks's production of *The Gaucho* in 1927.

She was, to be sure, generally "good," and if you do not like good women in art—or if you subscribe to the juvenile and idiotic nonsense that bad women are more "interesting"—then she is not for you; but if you reject her on this ground, I fear you will have to reject most of Shakespeare's heroines with her. What you will have to learn, however, before you can approach her intelligently, is that *good* and *saccharine* are not synonymous terms.

In *Rags* (1915), *Tess of the Storm Country* (1914), and several other films, she is a captivating and innocent young virago. What would be called outrageous conduct in anybody else is accepted as endearing in her because of the disarming air of innocence that goes along with it. In *Daddy-Long-Legs* (1919) she is a devil toward all who are in authority over her at the orphan asylum but a tower of strength to every abused younger child. In *Rags* she makes her first appearance riding on a goat. Overalls clad, she charges head-on into a gang of boys who are abusing a dog, disciplines her drunken father in a saloon, and compels him to return the money he has stolen; then she goes into a temper tantrum, culminating in free-swinging a chair about her head after one of the habitués of the place ventures to rumple her hair. In *The Pride of the Clan* (1917) she uses equally violent methods to get the fisherman into church. In *The Foundling* (1916) she feeds Mrs. Grimes's birthday cakes to the puppies, and when the dogcatcher tries to seize her own dog, she not only resists him but also unlocks the back of his wagon and sets every animal imprisoned in it loose in the streets. She also makes a statuette of the cruel Mrs. Grimes and then punishes it; probably she does not know that she is practicing witchcraft, but the impulse is there. In *Poor Little Peppina* (1916) she and her brother Beppo (Jack Pickford) attack a servant and kick him in the shins to get in to see the duchess when Peppina needs her help to avoid an unwelcome marriage. From there, they go on to more violence, culminating in Peppina's escape in Beppo's clothes. But perhaps Pickford is more vigorous in *Tess* than anywhere else. She jumps on Dan Jordan's back when he tries to put out the squatters' fire, makes impudent faces at Elias Graves and does a mocking dance step to tease him, and rushes into a tug-of-war when the warden takes a net from a fisherwoman, resulting in Tess being pulled along the ground on her bottom.

In Tess of the Storm Country *(1922), the fiery Tess (Pickford) is restrained from throwing a rock by her father (Forrest Robinson).*

In *Rags*, Pickford prepares to entertain an admirer (Marshall Neilan) at a miserable little lunch in her poor hut. She gets everything arranged to her satisfaction, but when she steps out for a moment, her drunken father and his companions come in and wolf the food. Returning she arranges the few remaining scraps on a plate and greets her suitor with a disarming, "I was so hungry I jes' couldn't wait for you." Card has rightly compared this with the famous scene in *The Gold Rush* (1925) in which Chaplin waits for the girl who never comes, and Iris Barry long ago pointed out the Chaplinesque elements in the arrangement of hat and gloves before Pickford sets out for church in *The New York Hat* (1912). These are not isolated instances, and since Pickford was doing this kind of thing before Chaplin came to the movies, there can be no question of indebtedness on her part. Unity Blake's pantomime with John Risca's coat in *Stella Maris* (1918), which culminates when she makes him put his arm about her (perhaps the best thing about Pickford's characterization of Unity is that she holds our sympathy for the girl even when she fails to keep her "place"), is Chaplin to the life. And *Rebecca of Sunnybrook Farm* (1917) is full of this kind of thing: Consider the backward dance-step movement Rebecca performs during her embarrassment while selling soap to Mr. Aladdin, or her recitations at school. Consider her battle with the divided door when she arrives at the brick house (so like Buster Keaton's never-ending war with gadgets). In closing the upper half, she knocks the bottom half open again, and when she stoops back under to remedy this, the upper half knocks her hat off. Finally, consider the wonderful running and jumping from one piece of oilcloth to another, trying not

Molly O (Pickford) scolds a crude vegetable carving of Mrs. Grimes (Maggie Weston), unaware that she is standing behind her.

to step on Aunt Miranda's carpets, culminating in a run down the final strip close to the camera and ending in a dead stop and jerk that bring her hat down over her eyes and inspire her to remark that she is sure she is going to like it here. In *Hulda from Holland* (1916) she falls through a skylight onto a young man's bed. In the way of gadgetry again, she has regular Rube Goldberg contraptions in her bed curtains and fishing tackle in *Tess,* and when she arrives in England in *Less than the Dust* (1916), she makes a floral offering to a suit of armor.

It must not be supposed that even in her feature pictures—made after she had become such a valuable theatrical property that she could do virtually nothing without considering its probable effect on millions of admirers—did she ever give the impression of having wrapped herself in cotton wool or of not understanding the world she lived in. In *Madame Butterfly* (1915) she kills herself for love (not the traditional hara-kiri method, to be sure, but more genteelly by wading out into the water). In *Hearts Adrift* (1914) she casts herself and her child into a volcano. In *Stella Maris* she commits both murder and suicide. She is a girl thief in both *Less than the Dust* and *In the Bishop's Carriage* (1913). As a messenger boy in *Poor Little Peppina,* she chokes on a cigar; in *M'liss* (1918) she picks up a five-foot snake. In *A Romance of the Redwoods* (1917) she saves Elliott Dexter, playing a reformed road agent to whom she is not married, by pretending that she is pregnant by him, using doll clothes as garments for the expected baby. The sheriff marries them on the spot, and not until after they get away does he understand that she has tricked him. *Moving Picture World* thought this situation very daring and speculated on how the public would take it, though stipulating, "It is hardly necessary to add that the acting and personality of Mary Pickford made the situation without actual offence."[6]

A movie herald for In the Bishop's Carriage *(1913) shows Pickford in several dramatic scenes.*

The curate (Arthur Johnson) confronts the pretty music hall singer (Pickford) about the sinful path she has taken in To Save Her Soul (1909). Director D. W. Griffith and the seventeen-year-old actress fought bitterly over her performance in this climactic scene but were ultimately pleased with the final take.

If the reviewer had remembered his Biographs, he might have been less shocked. Pickford has denied that she got good parts at Biograph from the beginning. "I got what no one else wanted, and I took anything that came my way because I early decided that if I could get into as many pictures as possible, I'd become known and there would be a demand for my work."[7] It is certainly true that in many of the Biographs I have seen, she is shown briefly and ineffectively. Nevertheless, Griffith gave her a wider range of roles at Biograph than she ever had again, and if she could have continued on this basis, the misunderstandings I have been opposing here would never have arisen. Look at the scene in which she "vamps" the British sentry in the otherwise comparatively ineffective "1776" or, The Hessian Renegades (1909) to see how early the fetching manners so eagerly exploited in her later films were beginning to develop. Yet there is hardly a trace of them in the many pictures in which she was cast as an Indian, and, as she says, she played mother to people who were only a few years younger than herself. When she acted Glory Quayle in To Save Her Soul (1909), Griffith's one-reel adaptation of Hall Caine's The Christian, she could not give Griffith what he wanted from her because she was too young to understand the emotions she was supposed to express.

In The Informer (1912), a Confederate belle (Pickford) fights Union soldiers surrounding her cabin

To understand Griffith's art, or Pickford's, or that of any of a number of other fine Biograph players, there is a crying need to have all the surviving Biographs printed and exhibited in chronological order.[8] I have not, of course, been able to do this. Of the Pickford Biographs that I have seen during recent years, the best are *The New York Hat, The Informer* (1912), *An Arcadian Maid* (1910), *Friends* (1912), and *A Feud in the Kentucky Hills* (1912). (I suspect that *Lena and the Geese* [1912], which the actress herself wrote, is the most Pickfordish of all the Biographs, but I have not seen it since childhood.) *The Informer* is a Civil War picture, with *The Birth of a Nation* (1915) just around the corner. The lover's (Walter Miller's) return to Pickford on the porch at the close of *The Informer* even partly anticipates the Little Colonel's return in *The Birth of a Nation* (Henry B. Walthall, this time, is not hero but villain). And in *A Feud in the Kentucky Hills* the fighting is directed with the same skill as that in *The Informer*. But there are other Biographs in which I can find better support for my argument.

In *Fate's Interception* (1912), with Pickford as a Mexican Indian girl, we have the *Madame Butterfly* situation without a mock marriage and without any imputation of innocence to the woman. Not only has she been living with her American lover without benefit of clergy, but after she is jilted, she sends her Mexican admirer to kill him; through a fluke, the Mexican is killed instead, and she goes back to the American! "Who shall blame?" asks a subtitle. One might expect there would be a good many takers.

A much better—and better known—picture of the same year, *Friends*, goes in for more ambivalence, ending with the question: "Which shall she choose?"—Walthall or Lionel Barrymore. But the amazing thing is that the girl, elegantly dressed in an 1890s gown with balloon sleeves (it had belonged to Mrs. Pickford), lives alone and receives her admirers in a room over the village tavern, where much of the action takes place. Contemporary reviews do not seem to indicate that audiences were intended to read anything into this, but it was odd, to say the least.

Finally, what shall be said of yet another 1912 film, *The Female of the Species*? Oddly enough, Griffith called it a psychological tragedy, yet it has a happy ending. Claire McDowell, her husband Charles West, her sister Pickford, and a lone girl played by Dorothy Bernard wander through a windswept desert as the sole survivors of a massacre. The husband makes a play for Bernard—what a man, to function thus under such circumstances!—and shortly thereafter dies. Although the girl is entirely innocent, the wife suspects her and treats her cruelly, and the climax comes when, for what seems an interminable time, she stands over the girl's sleeping form with a hatchet, "half mad with brooding," trying to make up her mind whether to kill her. The girl is saved when the woman is distracted by the cry of an abandoned Indian baby nearby, and reconciliation ensues. The psychological motivation here is none too clear; otherwise, *The Female of the Species* is a stark and powerful film with a grim, natural background, much like that Victor Sjöström later used in *The Wind*. But the interesting thing is that Griffith did not cast Pickford as the wronged girl and then proceed to exploit a sentimental, Little Nell kind of helplessness, as almost any late director would have done. Instead, he gave this role to Dorothy Bernard, who did not play it in anything approaching a sentimental manner, and he made Pickford the wife's bitter and abetting sister, who goes through the whole film with a frown between her eyes and a sneer on her lips, encouraging Claire McDowell's murderous desires and exuding venom toward her potential victim.

Dora (Pickford, wearing her mother's 1890s balloon-sleeved dress) beckons to her lover in the Biograph short Friends *(1912).*

Pickford, playing a malevolent woman, hands her sister (Claire McDowell) an ax with which to dispatch a female rival in The Female of the Species *(1912).*

The Female of the Species is an interesting film, and I am glad to have seen Mary in this aspect, yet I doubt very much that anybody really would have preferred her career to develop along the lines of *The Female of the Species* rather than *Tess of the Storm Country.* I well remember myself, aged twelve, coming home from *The Female of the Species* at the Victoria and announcing that I had seen a perfectly horrible picture! I even told the manager so afterward, and he agreed with me, or said he did, despite his general enthusiasm for Biograph films. All our naïveté notwithstanding, I cannot help believing that, in the larger view, the Age of Innocence did pretty well by Mary Pickford—and by us.

Make whatever qualifications and reservations you like, for us, Mary was sweetness and light, and this was more important to us than any possible characterization. If we made her up, this was all the more credit to ourselves. If there are no girls in the world like those she portrayed, then, since life imitates art quite as much as art imitates life, it was all the more important that such girls appeared on the screen, where their influence could extend farther and among more susceptible people than in any other medium. Whatever history makes of her, and whichever of her films may survive, no other generation will ever have her as we had her. If you say that you do not understand how we were able to read such ineffable meanings into her, I can only remind you of the painter and the lady who could not see the effects he had spoken of in the great painting. ("Don't you wish you could, Madame?" he asked her. "Don't you wish you could?") But none of that is very important. The important thing is that we did it. And because we did it, we shall cherish her in our hearts as long as we live, along with the memories of our own youth, and be grateful in troubled times for the joy she brought us. ॐ

Poster for The Mirror (1911).

The New York Dramatic Mirror (*December 6, 1911*).

The Motion Picture Story Magazine (*November 1913*).

Postcard for the film Caprice (1913).

An advertisement for Pickford shorts reissued by Universal in 1914.

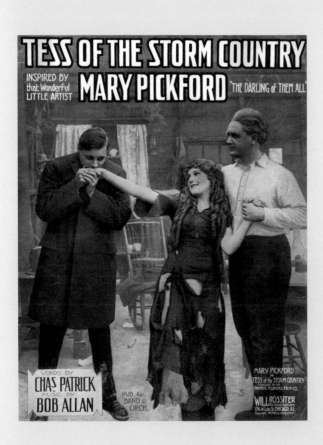

Sheet music cover from the 1914 Pickford
feature Tess of the Storm Country.

Pickford and Owen Moore on the cover
of Photoplay (January 1914).

Poster for A Good Little Devil (1914).

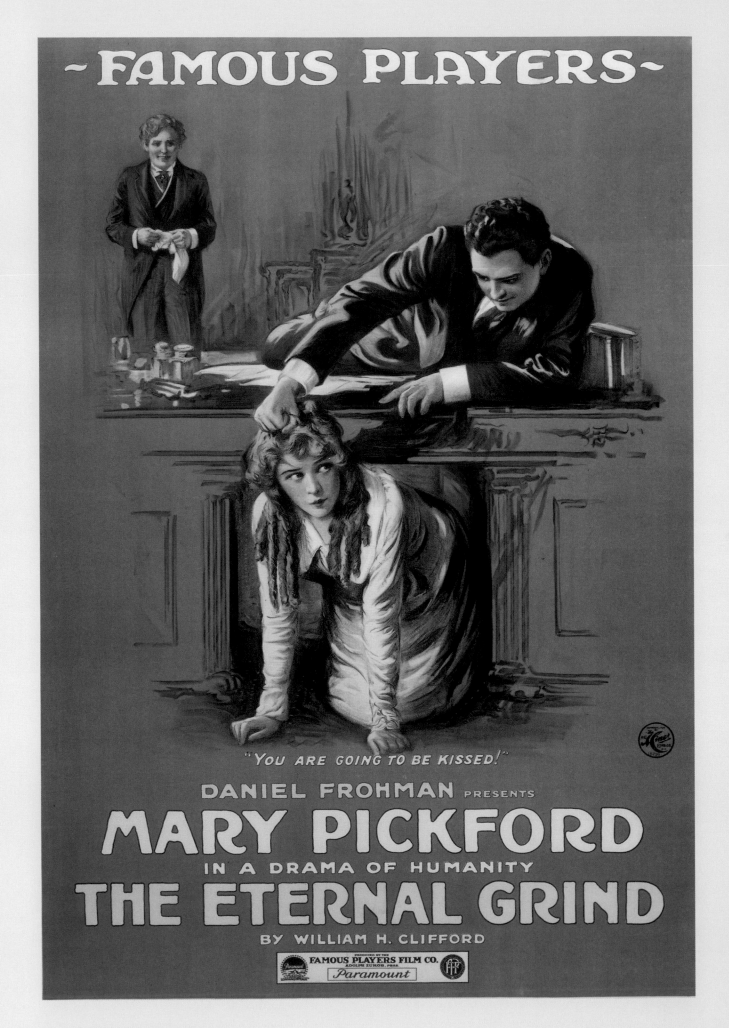

Poster for The Eternal Grind (1916).

Famous Players felt pennant for Mary Pickford (circa 1915).

A circa 1916 promotional card featuring Pickford.

Glass slide for the 1919 feature Daddy-Long-Legs.

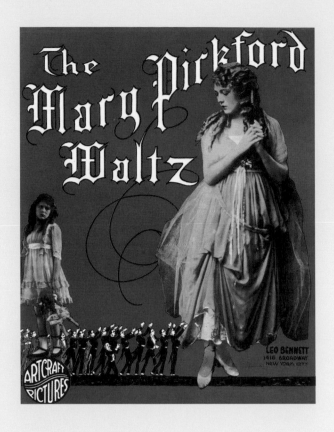

Sheet music cover, 1917.

Photo-Play Journal *(February 1917).*

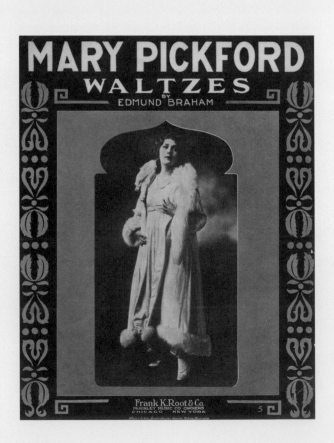

Sheet music cover, 1917.

Promotional flyer for The Hoodlum (1919).

Danish film poster by Sven Brasch for Pickford's Johanna Enlists (1918).

DRESSING THE PART

Mary Pickford's Use of Costume

Beth Werling

Pickford in Little Annie Rooney (1925).

CLOTHES MAY MAKE the man, but in the case of Mary Pickford, they definitely helped define the filmmaker. The silent film actress and producer—who had once considered a career in the fashion industry—played a pivotal role in selecting the costumes for her films. In fact, the depth of her involvement (particularly in the 1920s) highlights her brilliant producing skills as well as her realization that clothes were key to the art of storytelling.

Pickford was surrounded by costumes and dressmaking as a child. Her widowed mother, Charlotte, supported her children as a seamstress; later, when the family began to act in the theater, she cleaned and maintained their stage attire. Indeed, all actors were expected to provide and care for their own costumes, unless they required military uniforms or period fashions, which were rented from an agency. Pickford, who often toured without her mother, remembered cleaning and repairing her theatrical wardrobe during the "few hours [[she]] had for outdoor exercise."[1] She learned that all actors, whether they worked in a humble stock company or on Broadway, would be better equipped to play a greater range of roles if they maintained a vast and varied wardrobe. Some savvy performers even supplemented their income by renting out their clothing to other actors.

In 1909, when Pickford joined the New York film studio Biograph, she discovered that the operation kept a small rack of secondhand clothes for the actors. Stored in the basement near the chemicals used to develop film, the garments often reeked of fumigant. In addition, the studio wardrobe was not a good fit (literally) for Pickford's petite body. In an unusual move, director D. W. Griffith authorized the purchase of a store-bought outfit costing $10.50 for the actress's appearance in *The Lonely Villa* (1909). This seemed crazy to Pickford, who admired the fine stage clothes worn by the actors in Broadway's best productions, equating them with the art form's beauty and prestige; however, she did not think the down-market world of movies merited such an expense.

Only a few years later, Pickford's attitude had changed. The actress, by then one of the film industry's brightest stars, had become a major proponent of the cinema's relevance and artistry. She viewed even simple costumes as an integral component of a quality production and, from an actor's view, an important tool for getting into character. In 1913 she became one of the first film actors to have a contract requiring the studio to provide a proper wardrobe. The same clause was reiterated in her legendary 1916 contract with Famous Players.[2] These negotiations represented a noteworthy change. In those days, many actresses were contractually obligated to furnish their own costumes. Pickford, who preferred to save money rather than wasting it on "garments that are hung in the closets to feed the moth," had succeeded in shifting what could be a heavy financial burden from the actress to her employer.[3]

A beautifully costumed Pickford in the 1929 feature
The Taming of the Shrew. *The actress used*
a gown she wore in Dorothy Vernon of Haddon Hall
(1924) as a prop in the background (draped over the
trunk) of this bedroom scene.

By 1920, Pickford was producing and distributing her own movies. She was also spending more time and money on each film, eventually releasing one prestige picture every year. In addition, she wanted to expand her onscreen repertoire. Throughout the 1910s, she had played youthful, homespun characters (guttersnipes, immigrants, orphans, and slaveys) with increasing reluctance, finally declaring (with a sense of drama), "The sky grows cold and a chill wind springs up in my soul [when I think of portraying] another of those ragged little girls, or tattered boys, instead of doing a Pauline Frederick part in gorgeous gowns all plastered over with jewels."[4] Not surprisingly, she began to play more glamorous roles in her future productions. For these, she hired experienced costume designers and allocated generous wardrobe budgets.

During this period, the American film industry—originally based in New York City—settled in Hollywood. Unfortunately, the West lacked the costume rental agencies, department stores, and second-hand clothing shops that were plentiful in the East. In response, studios increasingly turned to fashion designers to create film apparel. Wardrobe departments with racks of clothes evolved into costume factories, complete with an in-house couturier, sketch artists, fitters, beaders, milliners, and even armorers. Pickford, an independent producer, chose a series of freelance designers to create the costumes for her films, including Adrian, Milo Anderson, Howard Greer, and Mitchell Leisen.

Pickford spent her second decade in the film industry at the highest level of power and success. Still, she was captivated by even small details involving costumes. Madge Bellamy, who costarred in *Garrison's Finish* (1923), a feature Pickford produced for her brother, Jack, recalled that the actress not only loaned her one of her own dresses for the film but also got "down on the floor herself to let [out] the hems."[5] Charlotte remained very hands-on, too; Pickford remembered her mother searching a trunk full of old costumes for material that could be used to make a mourning dress for the actress's character in *Little Annie Rooney* (1925).

During her career and after her retirement, Pickford viewed her costumes as an investment. Often, she recycled them or rented them out to others. No doubt, this practice appealed to her famously thrifty instincts. However, there was a downside. Costume rentals often entailed alterations, which, when extensive, could permanently ruin the original design. Later, when her old wardrobe was no longer in demand, Pickford stored the garments in the attic of her home. Fortunately, she also donated a selection to the Natural History Museum of Los Angeles County and the Los Angeles County Museum of Art. There, they offer visitors a tiny window into the magical world of cinema history, especially the influence of one of its most dazzling and enduring figures.

Pickford in Tess of the Storm Country *(1922).*

Tess of the Storm Country (1922)

Mary Pickford's 1914 version of *Tess of the Storm Country* was a smash hit. In addition to being a huge financial success—it saved Famous Players film studio from bankruptcy—the movie launched the already popular actress's career into the stratosphere. This was a remarkable feat for a film that was artistically and technically primitive for its time. And Pickford's Tess—a fiery, confrontational leader and problem solver guided by a strong moral compass—deeply resonated with audiences.

Tess was often promoted as the actress's masterpiece, and it became a popular reissue, playing in cinemas around the country throughout the 1910s. For a few years, each new Pickford performance was judged against it. But by the 1920s, film as an art form had grown by leaps and bounds. Pickford, who was now producing her own movies, decided that her greatest success and favorite role could benefit from the advances in modern filmmaking. Pickford chose not to update the plot—a pure Victorian melodrama with a ruthless landlord, a rich and handsome hero, a rapacious villain, a dying baby, and mistaken identities. However, she freely spent time and money on the production, including the construction of an elaborate fishing village on the banks of California's Lake Chatsworth and the creation of real snow to cover the houses.

The tattered blue and white dress worn by Pickford in the 1922 remake of *Tess of the Storm Country* is the only surviving artifact from the film. It is also the only remaining costume that documents the actress's archetypal ragamuffin heroine. One cannot help but feel the pathos when looking at this shabby dress, which stands in stark contrast to the velvets and jewels of her later costume epics and even the gingham frocks of the tenement girl in *Little Annie Rooney*.

Pickford once said, "The more ragged and dirty I look the better I can play."[6] Accordingly, her costumes for *Tess* had to reflect the character's penury. The cotton dress made for Pickford's character was deliberately torn and mended in a mosaic of tan and blue patches, most of them hand sewn with oversized stitches in dark-colored thread that would show up onscreen. Scraps of fabric dangle from the costume to create a realistic, neglected appearance.

Opposite: Dress from Tess of the Storm Country *(1922).*

Patchwork detail.

Rosita (1923)

By 1922, Pickford was keenly aware of the restrictions created by her youthful persona. It was, as she told a reporter from the *New York Tribune,* as though she was being "strangled by [her] own curls." Even though she longed "to do something ... wicked" in her next picture, she settled instead on *Dorothy Vernon of Haddon Hall,* an Elizabethan-era romance that would at least allow her "to wear smart clothes and play the lover."[7] However, Ernst Lubitsch, the famous German director Pickford had imported to make the movie, balked at its premise. As an alternative, the pair agreed to make the lavish and sophisticated *Rosita.*

Set in the Napoleonic era, *Rosita* is a Cinderella story with a hint of *Romeo and Juliet.* In the title role, Pickford portrays a cunning and seductive Spanish street singer who is desired by the king but is already in love with an impecunious nobleman. The worldly tale is a perfect showcase for the more mature Pickford. Rosita, of course, is all grown up, and the film's costumes are a key element in the transformation. Pickford's wardrobe had to be magnificent, and designer Mitchell Leisen did not disappoint. He created gowns that rivaled those worn by Norma Talmadge and Marion Davies in their costume pictures.

Pickford in costume for Rosita *(1923).*

Already known for her high standards in film production, Pickford hired artists Svend Gade and William Cameron Menzies to create the movie sets. Menzies (as well as Leisen) had recently worked for Pickford's husband, Douglas Fairbanks, on *Robin Hood* (1922). In 1920 the actor had easily transformed himself from light comedian to swashbuckler, and he was now famous for his spectacular adventure pictures. His successful transition and skill at producing on a grand scale undeniably influenced Pickford's vision of her own reinvention through historical dramas.

Leisen's only surviving creation from *Rosita* is the empire gown pictured. The gold lamé fabric is trimmed with green glass jewels and gold metallic lace. It is lined with yellow silk crepe, which prevented the metallic thread from chafing Pickford's skin. Metallic fabric was a favorite of costume designers in the 1920s because of its reflective glow onscreen. The gold gown does not appear in the existing film prints of *Rosita,* but the Natural History Museum of Los Angeles County was able to verify its use by the actress in a publicity still discovered at the Library of Congress.

MARY PICKFORD
IN
ROSITA

P. 647.

Left: Gown from Rosita.

Opposite, top: Detail of the empire waist.

Opposite, bottom: Detail of the green jeweled train.

Dorothy Vernon of Haddon Hall (1924)

After *Rosita*, Pickford returned to *Dorothy Vernon of Haddon Hall*. She had won an international bidding war for the screen rights to the popular novel by Charles Major, imagining a sixteenth-century period piece boasting spectacular sets and elaborate costumes.[8] Later, she earmarked a significant portion of the film's budget for wardrobe and again relied on the talents of designer Leisen.

The press book claims that "each costume and gown ... is a truthful design taken from the Elizabethan period."[9] In reality, the designer drew from a whole range of styles worn throughout Queen Elizabeth I's forty-five-year reign. Pickford's gowns in *Dorothy Vernon* appear to follow the cone-shaped silhouettes of Spanish fashions that were adopted in England and throughout Europe during that period. However, Leisen elected not to use hoops beneath the women's skirts, giving them a softer, looser look. He designed a ruff—based on a deeper, wide-open collar type that was popular near the end of Elizabeth's reign in the 1590s—that formed a square neckline and stood up high at the back of the neck. The sleeves combined two different styles from the 1550s and 1580s; Leisen added his own twist by cutting some of them along the straight lines of a kimono.

Like true Elizabethan gowns, the film's spectacular dresses were made of heavy fabric and weighted down with furs and elaborate ornamentation. The effect on Pickford's petite frame was so great that she began to lose weight during filming. To ease her burden and conserve her energy, Leisen carried the actress to and from the set. Ironically, it was this practice that severed their working relationship. A notoriously jealous Fairbanks saw the designer transporting his wife to her dressing room and assumed that something untoward was going on. This made Leisen so furious that he refused to work for the couple again.

Three of Leisen's creations for Pickford in *Dorothy Vernon* are featured here. The first is a stunning gown with gold metallic brocade and lace, velvet trim, pearl beading, topaz paste jewels, and tissue d'or. It also highlights some of Leisen's unconventional choices. For instance, he selected a black plush velvet fabric with a 1920s art deco motif rather than the smaller repeating pattern that would have been used by the Elizabethans. The decision to use a pattern of any kind, as well as the use of the color black, was unusual due to the way the combination would register on projected film stock. Somehow, Pickford's legendary cinematographer Charles Rosher made it work, as the gown shows up beautifully onscreen. Leisen also deserves credit for not allowing the striking pattern of the gown's fabric to overwhelm the diminutive Pickford. The dress was later repurposed, with the front panel removed and made into a separate skirt. The remaining full skirt of black and gold fabric was stretched and sewn along the side to eliminate the front gap. The reconfigured gown can be glimpsed draped over a chest in the background of her bedroom in 1929's *The Taming of the Shrew* (see the photograph at the beginning of this chapter).

Pickford dressed in a black and gold gown in Dorothy Vernon of Haddon Hall *(1924).*

Left: Black and gold beaded gown from Dorothy Vernon of Haddon Hall.

Opposite: Gold underskirt with velvet trim and pearl beading.

Below: Detail of the pearl beads arranged in a rose pattern.

The next gown of green velvet, with a matching bonnet-style head-piece, is featured prominently in *Dorothy Vernon*. This gown and head-piece are among the film's most authentic period costumes. Leisen used familiar Elizabethan design elements, including a repeating floral motif, silver and green brocade, and embroidered pearl and gemstones. The garment laces up in the back, demonstrating the wealth of the wearer, since Dorothy would require a maid's assistance to get it on and off. The headpiece is reasonably accurate, with its padded roll and an overall shape that frames the face. In its entirety, the costume presents Pickford at her regal finest. Today, a close examination reveals that the gown has been altered, possibly for use by an extra in the Pickford-Fairbanks version of *The Taming of the Shrew*.

Opposite: Pickford in the green gown from Dorothy Vernon of Haddon Hall.

Bonnet-style headpiece from Dorothy Vernon of Haddon Hall.

Backside of the headpiece.

Right: Green velvet gown from Dorothy Vernon of Haddon Hall.

Opposite: Detail of the bodice's brocade and embroidery.

The third gown shown is the only failure among Pickford's *Dorothy Vernon* costumes. The silk velvet magenta and blue gown features loose, unstructured lines that are too soft for the dashing, bold heroine. In addition, the use of silk velvet is a glaring reproach to authenticity. No noblewoman would have worn such an exquisite fabric in an informal day dress. Nor could Dorothy have worn the color magenta, as it was not invented as a fabric dye until the 1860s. In a final irony, the garment appears to be a rather humdrum gray onscreen. In fact, the gown makes Pickford look oddly colonial—more Martha Washington than Renaissance aristocrat.

The dress's lack of gems is conspicuous; it is one of the few Pickford gowns from *Dorothy Vernon* that isn't covered with them. However, there was a practical reason for it. The garment is torn in a scene in which Dorothy and her father quarrel. Multiple copies of the dress, both pristine and damaged, were needed to film this bit of action. Pickford, with an eye on expenses, may have thought it wise to forgo costly baubles on a dress that required so many duplicates.

Opposite: Pickford wearing the magenta and blue gown from Dorothy Vernon of Haddon Hall.

Magenta and blue gown from Dorothy Vernon of Haddon Hall.

Little Annie Rooney (1925)

In 1925 Pickford returned to her hugely popular "hoydenish raga-muffin" roles after *Rosita* and *Dorothy Vernon* had only modest success at the box office.[10] The story for *Little Annie Rooney,* which she wrote herself, offered a plot in the familiar setting of the lower classes.

Pickford spent much of her career playing impoverished, rough-and-tumble characters, including a cigarette girl, factory worker, laundress, lighthouse keeper, squatter, and stock girl in a five-and-dime. Such roles were suited to Pickford's spunky persona, and audiences embraced them. Gone from *Little Annie Rooney,* heralded the press book, were the "castles with their moats," the "palaces and their princes," and the "ruffled laces and bejeweled gowns" of Pickford's costume pictures. Annie Rooney lived in a tenement on New York's Lower East Side and wore checkered gingham dresses, "cotton stock-ings with runs," and "down-at-the-heel shoes."[11]

Pickford donated two of Annie Rooney's gingham dresses—both in cheerful colors—along with a wool tam. The actress liked gingham because it immediately suggested the character's social class, and she used it for her costumes in numerous films, including *Daddy-Long-Legs* (1919), *Johanna Enlists* (1918), and *Stella Maris* (1918). The clothing from *Little Annie Rooney* differs from that of most Pickford urchins, however, as it is not marred by patches, rips, or stains.

The press book claims that Pickford purchased her costumes for *Little Annie Rooney* at a discount clothing store in Los Angeles, but this seems unlikely; the surviving costumes have no labels and display no sign of alterations. Pickford's mature figure would have required a fuller cut than a child's dress accommodated. Although the square block cut of 1920s garments aided in concealing the actress's bust, additional tailoring would be necessary for a girl's dress to fall natu-rally from her shoulders. Pickford probably copied the style or pattern of the store-bought dresses for the garments she wore onscreen.

She wore the first dress pictured, and the tam, in the famous alley fight that opens the movie. Pickford wore the second dress, with its embroidered collar, in a birthday party scene and in a series of publicity shots for the movie.

Pickford and Spec O'Donnell in a scene from the fight sequence that opens Little Annie Rooney (1925).

*Gingham dress worn
by Pickford in the opening scene
of Little Annie Rooney.*

Pickford's wool tam.

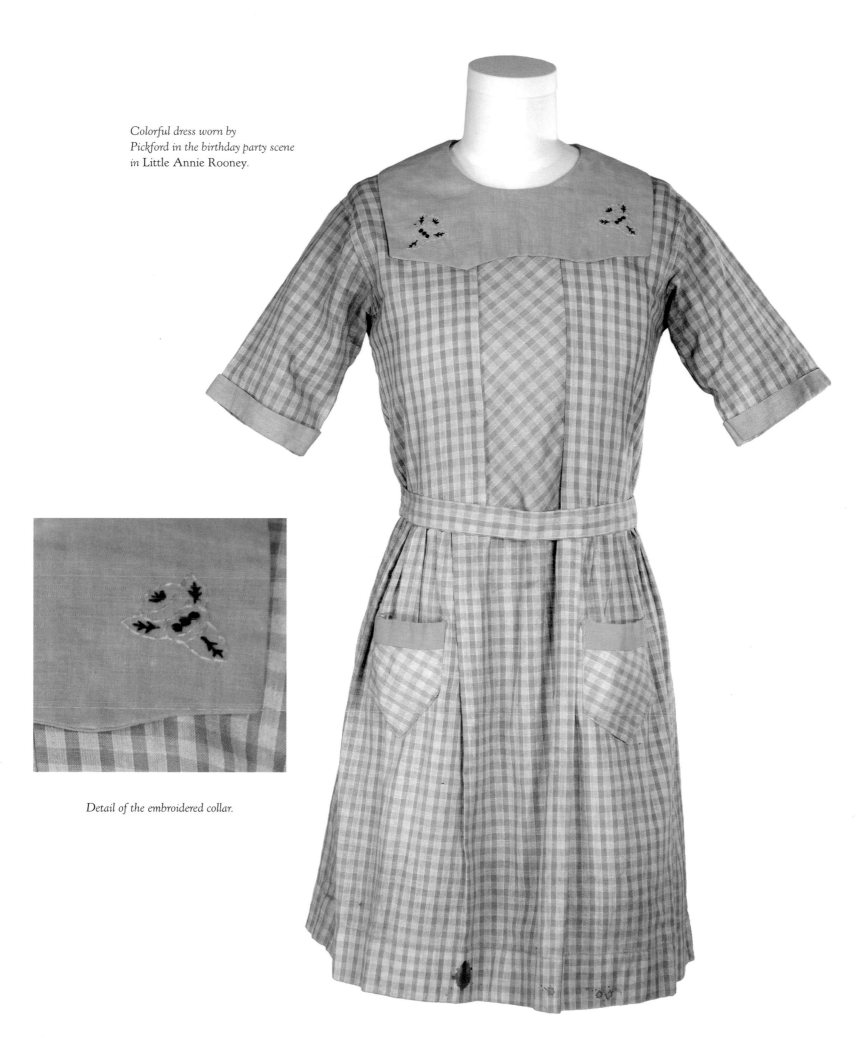

Colorful dress worn by Pickford in the birthday party scene in Little Annie Rooney.

Detail of the embroidered collar.

Coquette (1929)

In the late 1920s the arrival of talking pictures presented Pickford with several challenges. Like all actors who specialized in silent film's unique performance style, she faced a difficult transition. Almost forty years old and a familiar face onscreen for twenty years, she understood that her image needed a significant update. The actress boldly reinvented herself, trading in her famous blond curls for a fashionable bob, choosing modern (even risqué) stories, and stepping away from adolescent roles forever.

Coquette, a popular Broadway play about Norma, a Southern belle whose love for a poor man results in tragedy, seemed to be a perfect choice for Pickford's first sound feature. During the film she evolves from a carefree society girl into a strong, wise woman—echoing the actress's own shift into purely adult roles. Understanding how clothing can define a character and shape an image, Pickford hired Beverly Hills couturier Howard Greer to make her costumes. The designer had trained with Lucile (one of the early twentieth century's top fashion innovators) and had been the head of costumes at Paramount before opening his own business in 1927.

This pale pink ball gown, with its blend of girlish sweetness and adult sophistication, tells us everything we need to know about Norma at the start of the film. The form-fitting satin slip, hinting at the woman her character will become, is cinched at the waist with multicolored ribbons, and tiers of silver-edged, translucent tulle ruffles cover the lower half. Greer's costume is one of the best designed gowns Pickford ever wore onscreen and is believed to be one of only two of his extant creations for film. The actress was so pleased with the couturier's work that she acknowledged him when she accepted the Academy Award for Best Actress of 1929 for her performance in *Coquette.* ❧

Pickford's pink gown from Coquette *(1929), designed by Howard Greer.*

Left: Detail of the multicolored ribbons on the gown's waist.

Opposite: Pickford in Coquette.

Mary Pickford Memorabilia: 1920s

A Russian poster by artists Georgii and Vladimir Stenberg for the 1921 feature Little Lord Fauntleroy.
© Estate of Vladimir and Georgii Stenberg/RAO, Moscow/VAGA, New York.

Poster for the 1921 feature Through the Back Door.

Motion Picture Magazine (*March 1922*).

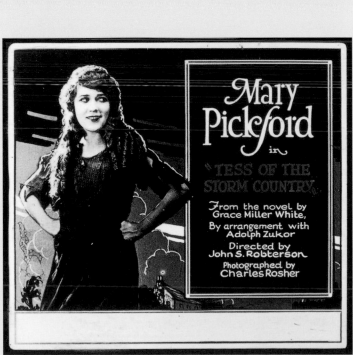

Glass slide from Pickford's 1922 remake of Tess of the Storm Country.

MARY PICKFORD AS DRAWN FROM LIFE
By NEYSA McMEIN—See Page One.

ETHEL M. DELL'S NEWEST NOVELETTE In This Issue

McCall's (March 1923).

Window card for Dorothy Vernon of Haddon Hall *(1924).*

Lobby card for Sparrows *(1926).*

Lobby card for My Best Girl *(1927), Pickford's last silent movie.*

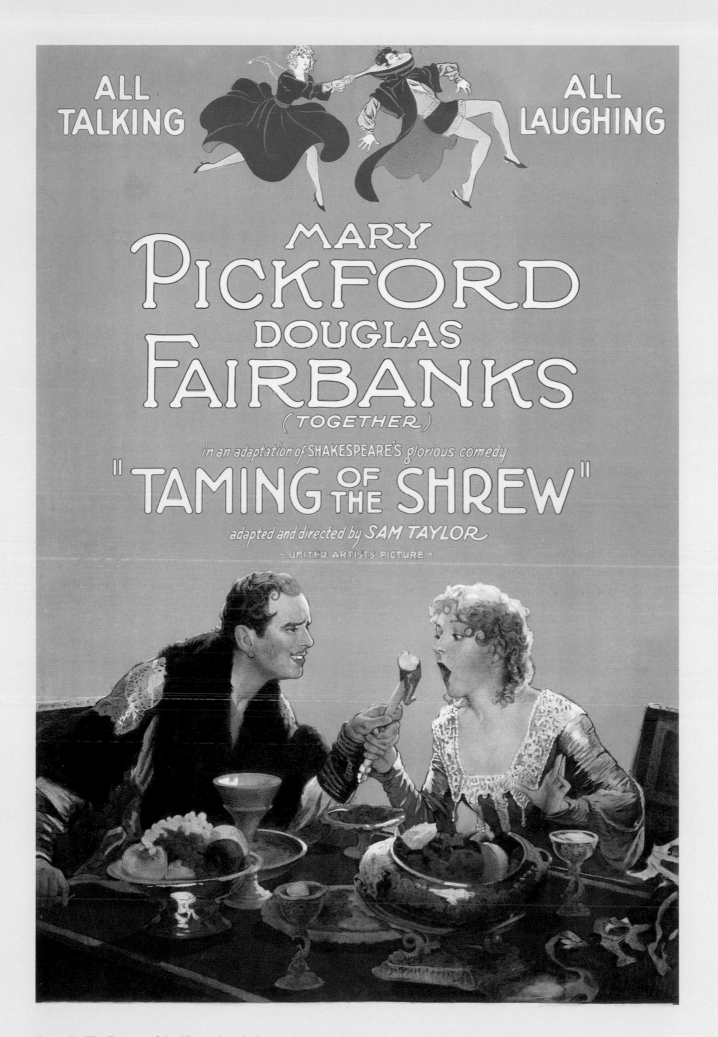

Poster for The Taming of the Shrew (1929), the only feature Pickford and Fairbanks starred in together.

A SIX DAY TAMING OF THE SHREW

FIRST

26-A—Five Column Cartoon (Mat 40c; Cut $1.50)

*Mary Pickford and Douglas Fairbanks in their first co-starring picture, the all-talking comedy **"Taming of the Shrew"**

Katherine, lovely daughter of the wealthy Baptista Menola, is the despair of her father and all the swains in Padua. A spitfire ready to burn up at the drop of the hat—anybody's, she drives off all suitors tempted by her great dowry. To make matters worse, Baptista has told the world that Katherine must be married before he will consider overtures for the hand of her fair and gentle sister, the beautiful Bianca.

Gremio and Hortensio, worshippers before Bianca's shrine, are at their wits' end to know how to dispose of the shrewish Katherine, when there comes one, the handsome, cocky and conceited Petruchio. Jestingly they tell him of the charms of the fair Katherine. The dowry clinches the matter. Even when Gremio and Hortensio, in fear and consternation, warn him as to her real self, Petruchio is unchanged. Seeking out the good Baptista, Petruchio tells him what a fine son-in-law he will make and gains the old man's consent to begin the courtship forthwith.

SECOND

26-B—Five Col. Cartoon (Mat 40c; Cut $1.50)

Petruchio concocts a scheme with Hortensio where the latter in the guise of a music master, gains access to the home of his beloved Bianca. But the plans go awry for father Baptista sends him to instruct the fair Katherine who as quickly sends him hurtling down the marble stairs of her chamber with a lute around his neck. Instead of dampening Petruchio's ardor, it is rather an incentive, for he immediately dashes up the stairs to meet his high-spirited bride-to-be. But Katherine receives him with a whip and in an attempt to use it freely finds herself pinioned in a grip of iron while her wooer whispers pretty nothings into her ears. The courtship is a madhouse. She sputters and fumes, but Petruchio is too fast for her. He beats her at her own game. Before Katherine can get well started on one of her tirades, Petruchio has her speechless with his own fireworks. Though it galls her, she agrees to marry him the following Sunday. But in spite of it all she can't help but smile when she thinks of him.

THIRD

26-C—Five Col. Cartoon (Mat 40c; Cut $1.50)

The following Sunday everything is set for the wedding. That is, all but the bridegroom. Katherine, decked out in her bridal regalia has been waiting for what seems ages. The guests have the fidgets; old Baptista is doing a St. Vitus; and Katherine herself is on the verge of tearing them all to pieces. Then comes Petruchio. Togged out in a get-up that would put a tramp in the Beau Brummel class, he appears astride a truck horse.

Katherine sees "red" but Petruchio sees nothing but amusement, as he munches contentedly on a juicy apple. There is consternation everywhere. Petruchio's friends take him aside and offer to lend him suitable apparel for the occasion. Gadzooks, fumes the bridegroom, his fair lady is not marrying him for his clothes but for himself. And so the wedding ceremony begins with the priest fumbling nervously through the pages of his missal, Katherine froathing at the mouth, and Petruchio grinning amiably between nibbles at his apple.

*Use this heading for each installment.

Page Six

A six-day installment cartoon serial from the exhibitor's campaign book for The Taming of the Shrew *(1929).*

CARTOON SERIAL FOR NEWSPAPERS

Get your local editor to run this feature well in advance of your showing. The individual drawings can also be used for ads.

FOURTH   26-D—*Five Col. Cartoon (Mat 40c; Cut $1.50)

*Mary Pickford and Douglas Fairbanks   in their first co-starring picture, the all-talking comedy   "Taming of the Shrew"

The ceremony over, Petruchio begins his taming in dead earnest. He announces to all the guests that business calls him hence and consequently they shall have to excuse him from presiding at the feast. Katherine pleads, threatens, commands; but Petruchio is unmoved. In front of the company, who are dumbstruck by this time, he packs her off to her new home on an old brokendown nag. A storm comes up and they finish the journey in driving rain. A couple of spills and a complete drenching haven't improved Katherine's disposition. But her husband is too much for her. He rages and storms about the way his servants have arranged things, finds fault with the food, throws it all over the place, rants till the rafters tremble and concludes by forbidding Katherine to eat and ordering her to retire. For the sake of quiet she submits to everything.

FIFTH   26-E—*Five Column Cartoon (Mat 40c; Cut $1.50)

While Katherine is in the bridal chamber, Petruchio returns to the banquet hall and dines heartily. In the height of good spirits he confides his plans for the "taming of the shrew" to his canine pal. Katherine, unobserved, overhears it all from the balcony. She is greatly amused by the discovery. When Petruchio returns to the bridal suite and resumes his battering tactics he finds a meek and acquiescent Katherine. If he says the moon is the sun, Katherine says the same. If he says the night is mild, Katherine, even though the wind almost blows her to the other side of the room, agrees.

Petruchio is quite amazed but he cannot help but be proud of the success of his scheme. He finds fault with the way the bed has been made up and yanks off all its covers. Katherine finds fault with the give of the springs and tosses the huge box mattress to a corner of the room. But matters reach a climax when Petruchio takes away Katherine's pillow allowing her head to knock against the wall with a considerable bang. As he walks away from her, Katherine gives vent to her feelings by hurling a well aimed stool in his direction. Petruchio slumps to the ground.

SIXTH   26-F—*Five Col. Cartoon (Mat 40c; Cut $1.50)

Thoroughly aroused, Katherine takes her whip in hand and is about to chastise Petruchio. But the onslaught is over.

Petruchio is no longer the blustering master; he has become the hurt little boy pleading for consolation. Katherine's feelings alternate between concern and amusement at this discovery. She wisely agrees with his every whim and makes her cocky husband believe his system has really effected the change in her character. At a wedding banquet sometime later, Petruchio wants to show off to the guests by demonstrating how he has tamed the shrew. He commands "Kate" to tell the other ladies present their duties toward their husbands. And Kate goes on to tell her friends that "Thy husband is thy lord, thy life, thy keeper."

All this time Petruchio beams with satisfaction. He does not see the big wink Katherine uses as an exclamation mark to her address.

*Use this heading for each installment.

Page Seven

AMERICAN IDOL

Mary Pickford, World War I, and the Making of a National Icon

Christel Schmidt

A tinted 35mm frame from the prologue
of The Little American (1917).

I N APRIL 1918 Mary Pickford stood on an outdoor stage surrounded by American flags, soldiers, and a military band. She faced an audience of thousands that, in trying to get closer to her, almost pushed through the railing between them. Using a megaphone, Pickford began a rousingly patriotic speech about the American effort in the First World War. As she spoke of Germany's military aggression, her rage spilled over. Stamping her feet and pounding her fists, she told of Germans who had crucified Belgian babies and bludgeoned Allied soldiers to death. She recounted her meeting with a brave young army man who had lost his legs to an enemy shell in France. The experience had made her want to "take a gun and go abroad [myself]."[1] The crowd responded with shrieks of approval and applause.

This was not a theatrical performance. The United States had been a combatant in World War I for a full year, and Pickford was on a mission to sell war bonds for the government. As the nation's favorite movie star, she was central to the motion picture industry's efforts to support the war and lift morale on the home front through speeches, fund-raising appeals, and propaganda films. Her onscreen persona, which linked her strongly to the national image of youth, optimism, resilience, and fair play, was easily co-opted for the cause. Now her tireless efforts on behalf of the war would transform her from film star to national symbol, representing not just the ideal woman but America itself.

In 1914, as the war engulfed Europe, the American public was engaged in a happier pursuit—a love affair with Pickford. The actress, like the movies, was a growing phenomenon. She began her film career in 1909, making one-reelers for D. W. Griffith at Biograph, when the industry was young. Her natural performance style and charisma quickly won cinemagoers' hearts, and for the next few years, both Pickford and her art form flourished. By 1914, short films had given way to new multireel features, and Pickford, who starred in two of the year's biggest blockbusters (*Hearts Adrift* and *Tess of the Storm Country*), became the focus of a fan craze that swept the country.

A 1914 *magazine advertisement for the Mary Pickford cap.*

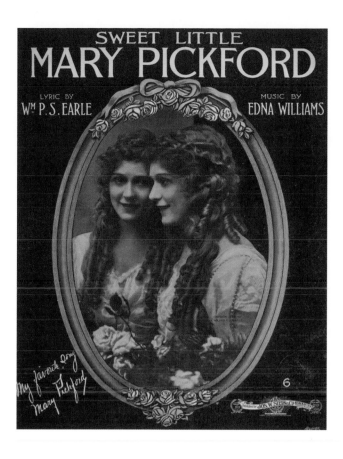

Sheet music cover for one of several songs written about the popular actress during the 1910s and 1920s

Sitting in darkened movie theaters, viewers forged a unique and intimate bond with the larger-than-life images of the stars. Silent actors, communicating heightened emotions in close-up, stirred an equally heightened devotion from fans. Pickford, the first player in the movies to ignite such unbridled passion, was loved with an intensity that was unprecedented in any medium. Her fame drove the marketing of movie fan magazines, postcards, posters, trading cards, buttons, and photographs, as well as other random items (such as a cap and a pillow) that bore her name. Songs struggled to capture her appeal, and one, a composition entitled "Sweet Little Mary Pickford," succeeded:

> There's something 'bout her that warms your heart
> You're captivated right from the start
> She's like a sun beam a breath of spring
> This maid alluring with charms enduring
> I've never met her and yet somehow
>   it seems I've known her for a long time now
> I'm in ecstasy when she smiles at me.

D. J. "Pop" Grauman, a San Francisco film exhibitor, dubbed Pickford "America's Sweetheart," and fans not only embraced the name but also wanted to know what their sweetheart thought on a range of subjects.[2] Magazine and newspaper writers obliged and tried to detail every aspect of her life. This seemingly bottomless interest led to "Daily Talks," Pickford's nationally syndicated newspaper column.[3] Published every day but Sunday, it covered far more than the conventional range of women's subjects. Although some columns did deal with the domestic realm—household economy, beauty tips, clothing, and family—there were also stories about Pickford's professional life and art. She answered readers' questions, offering a space where a twentieth-century girl could find "perfect sympathy."[4] On rare occasions she used her column to promote cultural diversity and racial understanding. Within a month of its launch, Pickford also wrote about the Great War.

On December 15, 1915, the actress published a column describing the gifts and letters she had received from the war zone. The letter that affected her most deeply was from a German woman whose daughter had died of pneumonia. But she also quoted a harrowing letter from a British soldier stationed in France: "You will excuse this dirty paper and the pencil won't you? This mud spattered in the corner was made by a bullet. They got so hot around me ... I thought I would hit the long trail before I got finished."[5] Two weeks later, Pickford's "Daily Talk" applauded women's efforts in the war zone while acknowledging her own fear of suffering and death. In the spring of 1916, she featured letters from women and girls across England who expressed their loneliness and loss. One, from a girl whose brother had been killed when the Germans sank his warship, included the young man's photograph and a letter he had started to write to the actress before he died.

At this point, Pickford refrained from expressing strong opinions about the conflict. Nevertheless, her selection of war letters from Allied soldiers and their families revealed a sympathy with the British and the French. Born in Toronto, the actress was well aware that Canada, a principal nation in the British Empire, had declared war on Germany along with Britain and had many troops in the thick of combat. She finally showed her hand in a column about the Citizens' Preparedness Parade in New York City. The parade, which occurred on May 13, 1916, was billed as "non-partisan" and an "act of constructive patriotism."[6] However, participants, which included former army chief of staff General Leonard Wood and former secretary of war and U.S. senator Elihu Root, were members of America's "preparedness movement," a grassroots campaign that had started shortly after the onset of the European conflict. Unlike President Woodrow Wilson and most Americans, the movement supported a military buildup in preparation for the nation's entry into the war. The parade sponsors wanted to show Wilson and antiwar members of Congress (for whom it was an election year) the scale of public support for increased defensive measures. The organizers also hoped the parade would inspire strong feelings of nationalism and attract more people to their cause.

Pickford's column, published a month later, confirmed that the nearly twelve-hour procession had been effective. The actress declared that, while sitting in the reviewing stands, she had been "stirred with new love" for the flag.[7] She had felt her fighting spirit awakened and now believed that, if unified and prepared, Americans could dispatch any foe. To Pickford, the event was a call to arms, and her patriotic rhetoric foreshadowed the tone she would later use when selling war bonds.

On April 6, 1917, America entered the Great War. Though the film industry had offered itself to the government as a propaganda tool as early as December 1915, President Wilson and other officials did not yet consider it essential in the fight for hearts and minds. Meanwhile, studios were making ferociously anti-German pictures that Wilson and others privately condemned. In fact, Pickford was the star of a "hate the Hun" movie that went into production less than two weeks after the United States entered the war.

The Little American (1917) tells the story of a young woman who gets caught up in the European conflict while the United States is still neutral. Producer Jesse L. Lasky, in a letter to director Cecil B. DeMille dated March 5, 1917, wrote that the film should endeavor "to arouse a patriotic spirit—the spirit of preparedness—... in American girlhood and womanhood." Pickford was the perfect star, and Lasky believed she could "portray a girl in the sort of role that feminists in the country are now interested in" and "would create a good deal of advance interest" in the picture.[8] The actress, who was her own producer and virtually controlled her own public image, thought the production would give her an "opportunity to show the world why America is really fighting."[9]

Poster for The Little American *(1917).*

"FOR FLAG AND COUNTRY"
ENLIST NOW

MARY
PICKFORD

IN A STIRRING PHOTOPLAY OF GREAT PATRIOTIC APPEAL

THE LITTLE AMERICAN

BY JEANIE MacPHERSON

PRODUCED BY **CECIL B. DeMILLE**

PRESENTED BY

ARTCRAFT PICTURES CORPORATION

Film historian Kevin Brownlow has pointed out that *The Little American,* which includes a scene based on the sinking of the *Lusitania,* "reveal[s] what Americans *thought* was happening at the front."[10] Indeed, the movie dramatizes reported (and exaggerated) German atrocities, using America's Sweetheart as an eyewitness and a near victim. Pickford plays Angela Moore, a pretty society girl from Washington, D.C., who is dispatched to the French-Belgian border to assist an aunt who is dangerously ill. En route, she narrowly escapes a watery death after a torpedo hits her ship, only to arrive and find that her aunt has died. Angela decides to stay at the aunt's château, which she opens up to care for wounded French soldiers. In due course, the Germans arrive to pillage, rape, execute the elderly, and plot their next battle. And even though Angela believes her country's neutrality will protect her, the plot drives home that she is sadly mistaken.

Pickford's Angela (who, we are told, was born on the Fourth of July) is not just a typical American but a symbol of America itself. Good, kind, and fair, she tries to remain impartial in the face of mounting horrors, until German atrocities compel her to join the war. At first she pays dearly for her new commitment. She agrees to aid the Allies by smuggling information to French authorities from her aunt's château. By her side is Karl (Jack Holt), her German American lover who has joined the German army. A spectacular example of a good man gone bad (earlier, in a drunken stupor, he tries to rape Angela, whose face he cannot see in the darkened room), Karl is rehabilitated by her love and denounces Germany. Indeed, he and Angela are convicted together as spies and soon face a firing squad. Moments before their impending death, he tries to comfort her, but it is a tiny American flag (given to Angela on her birthday and carried on her person throughout the film) that rallies her spirit of defiance. Finally, the lovers are saved by a perfectly timed French bomb that takes out the entire German firing squad. The film ends with Karl awaiting release from an internment camp so that he can return to the States with Angela.

The filmmaker's selection of a German American lover for Angela was a curious and potentially risky move. Anti-German sentiment in the United States was not as strong as it would later become. However, the choice sent a clear message to a nation of immigrants who may have felt divided loyalties. Angela (read America) is not only principled and brave; she is also forgiving of those who waver but then prove their allegiance. Still, an alternative ending was created for the film, using repurposed shots from early scenes and new intertitles.[11] Apparently, in this version, Angela never pledges herself to a man with German roots and ends the film at home, awaiting the return of a French sweetheart. There is no evidence that this revised version was shown in the United States, but it may have been used in foreign markets. According to Brownlow, no version of the film was distributed in France until 1926, when it was panned by *Cinémagazine* as "puerile."[12]

Angela (Pickford) and Karl (Jack Holt) barely survive a German firing squad and a French bomb attack in The Little American *(1917).*

In late May 1917, a month before *The Little American* opened, Pickford made news by participating in the government's first Liberty Loan drive, purchasing $100,000 worth of bonds and giving a statement of support to California's Twelfth Federal Reserve publicity committee. "It is not about duty but absolute necessity for every man, woman, and child in the nation to put their shoulder to the wheel in this great hour of need," she declared. "Considering that thousands of our boys will give their lives for the country, surely the least we can do is to furnish them with food, clothes and ammunition … I myself am placing all my available cash in the Liberty loan."[13] Whether Pickford was asked for her comments or simply offered them is unknown, but her passionate feelings and incredible influence with the public probably led the committee to invite her to attend a bond rally in San Francisco on June 13, 1917.[14]

This was Pickford's first appearance for the loan drive. She spoke to a capacity crowd of 12,000 in the Civic Auditorium and was credited with aiding the sale of $2 million worth of bonds. The *San Francisco Chronicle* said Pickford's efforts were "a serious matter," for she "thinks, sleeps, dreams … Liberty bonds."[15] Indeed, Pickford tackled these fund-raising events with the same resolve she used to build her career and her fortune. Alongside actors Charlie Chaplin, Douglas Fairbanks, Elsie Janis, Marguerite Clark, and countless others, she worked to raise morale on the home front, promote recruitment, and obtain funds for the government and the Red Cross. Her efforts for the national cause were reported in newspapers, fan magazines, and industry journals—sometimes in connection with *The Little American*. In fact, the studio's campaign to promote the feature began almost simultaneously with her advocacy for the Liberty Loan. And although there is no evidence that the actress discussed the release of the movie at any war-related function or financial appeal, the film was often promoted as an extension of her "moral, mental, and physical support of the flag."[16] Reportedly, Pickford believed it would be her most important effort for the national cause.

Still, no one knew how audiences would react to *The Little American* when it was released. According to historian Robert Birchard, it was "one of the first films to seriously deal with American involvement in the conflict."[17] There was a real chance that many Americans, still grappling with their country's entry into the war, would stay away.[18] Instead, the film was praised by most critics, played to packed houses, and was used as propaganda to encourage recruitment. In hindsight, considering the public's enthusiastic response to Pickford's offscreen patriotic endeavors and the skillful way *The Little American* connected to them, it seems unlikely that moviegoers would have rejected the film. In fact, the nation seemed virtually incapable of resisting any of the star's almost nonstop appeals for the war effort.

Pickford serves ice cream to her "adopted" soldiers from the 143rd Field Artillery at Camp Kearny, circa 1918.

On December 13, 1917, Pickford led a marine band down San Francisco's Market Street to encourage enlistment in the U.S. Navy.

Over the next several months, Pickford started her own Red Cross fund and adopted a battalion of soldiers and a squadron of aviators (whom she supplied with tobacco and other comforts). She also appeared in Liberty Loan films and would later write the scenario for her most notable war bond short, 1918's *One Hundred Percent American*.[19] Pickford proved to be almost magically successful at attracting crowds and bringing in money at war-related events. At the end of 1917 the star led two parades in San Francisco—one for the navy, in which she wore a skirted variation of a military uniform, and the other for the Red Cross. Afterward, she attended teas and parties where she danced with soldiers and met local society. At an evening rally, she appeared in a tableau as a Red Cross nurse caring for a wounded soldier on the battlefield. Miss Columbia, standing behind her, held a laurel wreath of victory over Pickford's head. A large American flag fell to close the scene and was then drawn away, revealing the actress and fifty army nurses lined up onstage in the form of a cross. The exuberant audience, now standing on its feet, joined Pickford in the national anthem.

ROOMS 300-1-3
SPRECKELS BUILDING
SAN FRANCISCO, CAL.
TEL. SUTTER 2394

OFFICE OF

RECRUITING INSPECTOR
WESTERN DIVISION

U. S. NAVY

REFER TO NO._____

December 13, 1917.

Miss Mary Pickford,
C/O St. Francis Hotel,
San Francisco, California.

My dear Miss Pickford:

In behalf of the United States
Recruiting Service in general and of the Western Division in particular, I wish to thank you and express our
appreciation of the important part you played this date
by leading the Marine Band down Market Street of this
city in an effort to stimulate recruiting for the U.S.
Navy and to correct the mistaken impression held by
most people that no registered men would be permitted
to enlist in the Navy after December 15, 1917.

I can assure you that your connection with the parade will be the medium through
which the Navy will obtain many enlistments, which otherwise would not have been the case.

Again thanking you and expressing to
you the good wishes of the Navy Recruiting Service, and
wishing you the compliments of the season, I am

Very sincerely,

M. C. Gorgas
Lieut-Commander, U.S. Navy,
Recruiting Inspector.

The success of Pickford and other stars at these patriotic assemblies did not go unnoticed by the federal government—especially the U.S. Treasury, which organized the Liberty Loan campaign. In July 1917 President Wilson and his colleagues set aside their qualms about employing the motion picture industry in war propaganda. Wilson agreed to appear alongside actors in short films for Liberty Loans, and the government invited film and stage performers to home-front events. Yet it was not until March 1918—when Treasury Secretary William McAdoo summoned Pickford, Chaplin, Fairbanks, and a few other movie stars to assist in a national tour for the third Liberty Loan drive— that the government selected actors to be its official speakers. This elevated performers to the status held by members of Congress, prominent political and religious leaders, military officers, and influential businessmen—a landmark achievement, as actors had previously been considered too bohemian for privileged society. Now they were viewed as opinion leaders with a passport to America's most powerful circles.[20] Pickford, who still felt the sting of boardinghouse signs that, ten years earlier, had banned both dogs and actors, was honored. She readily set aside her professional and personal obligations for the loan drive and paid her own expenses for the one-month national tour. To top it off, before leaving Hollywood, she also bought another $100,000 worth of bonds to help launch the drive in her own community.

Opposite: Letter from the U.S. Navy thanking Pickford for her participation in the military parade.

Publicity photo of Douglas Fairbanks, Pickford, and Charlie Chaplin before they set out on the third Liberty Loan tour for the U.S. Treasury.

Pickford, it was said, was McAdoo's first choice when he sought a group of actors to assist the Treasury. In addition to being loved across the nation, she was a true believer in the cause. Still, the government was not prepared for the "monster crowd" that turned out in Washington, D.C., to see Pickford, Chaplin, Fairbanks, and Marie Dressler kick off the drive on April 6, 1918.[21] The date had been chosen to coincide with the first anniversary of America's entry into the war, but what really drew the masses of men, women, and children was the chance to glimpse, touch, or meet their favorite movie star. Plans for the actors to autograph bond receipts were temporarily derailed when their booths were surrounded by swarms of people before they even arrived. When the celebrities were finally in place, only a few who had pledged to buy bonds ever managed to reach them. Even the press was starstruck. The *Los Angeles Times* reported that while appearing at the National Press Club, Pickford, Chaplin, and Fairbanks had to be "guarded in a private room" to escape the overly enthusiastic audience.[22]

Despite the chaos, $3.5 million in bonds were sold, and Pickford—the crowd favorite—spent hours signing receipts worth over $1.5 million. From Washington, the actress traveled to Baltimore and then joined Chaplin and Fairbanks in Philadelphia. She was alone again for an event in New York City on April 11 when the scandalous news broke that she was the woman behind the breakup of Fairbanks's marriage. The story must have rattled her; after wrapping up her New York appearances, Pickford retired from the public eye for a week.[23] She then returned to the tour for drives in Chicago, Pittsburgh, and St. Louis, working tirelessly from morning until late in the evening, giving speeches, signing autographs, and shaking hands with average citizens. Pickford could attract not only the "fifty-dollar man" the government wanted her to reach but also the wealthy and well connected. She sold one of her curls for a $5,000 bond and convinced Marshall Field & Company to invest $800,000. By the end of the tour she was exhausted, but she had raised millions of dollars for the war effort.

A large crowd gathers at the Capitol to see Chaplin, Marie Dressler, Fairbanks, and Pickford promote war bonds on April 6, 1918.

The actors were lauded in the press for their war work—sometimes excessively. One writer referred to Pickford as a "modern Joan of Arc," while another claimed the actress had done more for the national cause than "soldier, king, poet or prophet."[24] Still, the group had its detractors. Most notably, former treasury secretary Leslie Shaw thought the movie star campaigns, which sometimes had an element of the circus, were "sacrilegious in view of the seriousness of the war."[25] (For instance, in Chicago, Pickford christened a baby elephant with a bottle of champagne.) There were also skeptics in Congress who suggested that the stars (especially Pickford, Chaplin, and Fairbanks) were profiting from "conditions created by the war"; in addition, cynical citizens believed their participation in the bond drive was a publicity stunt.[26] Wisely, Pickford stayed above the fray and sustained an almost boundless energy for the war effort. Even after the armistice, she continued to give time and money to the Victory Loan, a campaign that helped the government pay down the war debt. By the summer of 1919, Pickford held a staggering $600,000 in U.S. war bonds, $100,000 in Canadian war notes, and $25,000 in British Victory Loans.[27]

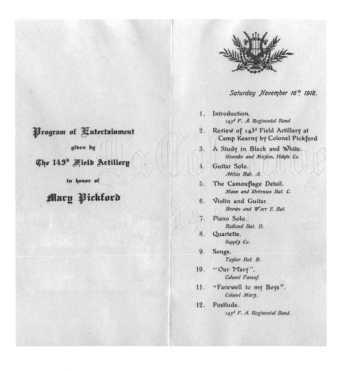

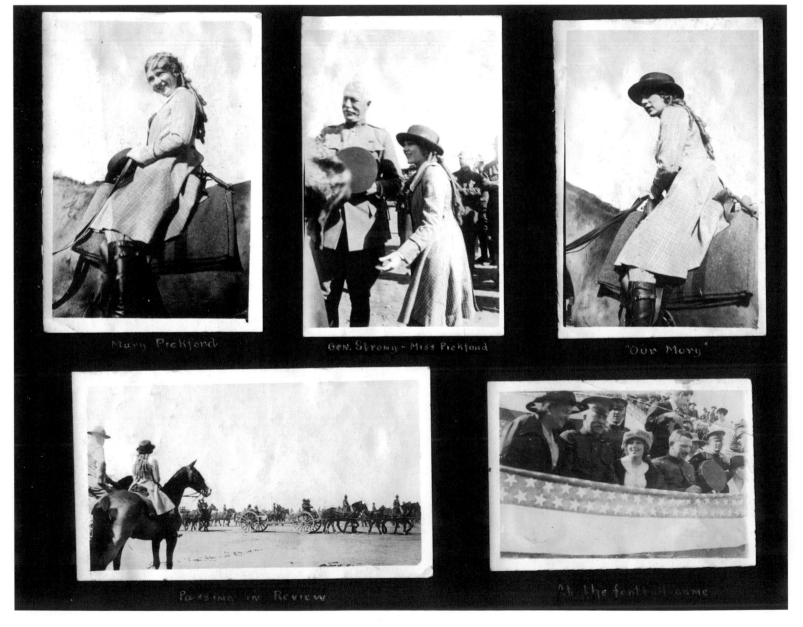

In the postwar years, Pickford's popularity and influence continued to grow. In Europe, where the war had decimated the film industry, American movies and stars now dominated. When Pickford and Fairbanks honeymooned on the war-weary Continent in the summer of 1920 (the first of several visits that decade), they were met by massive crowds similar to those they had attracted during the third Liberty Loan tour. Now, however, they were greeted not simply as movie stars but also as representatives of the United States and its culture and ideals. In Paris, the newspaper *Lanterne* referred to the couple as "true ambassadors," capable of bringing people together more than the official ones.[28] And in England—where they caused near riots during their travels—it was noted that their frenzied admirers came from all levels of the rigid British class system. Alabama's *Montgomery Advertiser* added a little levity (and perspective) when it facetiously reported that after fostering goodwill in Great Britain, Pickford and Fairbanks were expected to successfully broker the Irish problem.[29]

In Germany, Pickford and Fairbanks celebrated the Fourth of July with an American occupation force stationed in Koblenz. The arrival of the stars created chaos in the city as thousands of soldiers and German civilians gathered to get a glimpse of them. Of course, the official festivities were patriotic. The couple, backed by two military bands, kicked off the event by singing "The Star-Spangled Banner" as servicemen stood at attention and German civilians removed their hats. At the song's close, Fairbanks leaped into the air and rallied the audience into a roaring chant of three cheers for America that lasted for five minutes.

Back in the States, Pickford returned to her hectic work schedule and a social life full of obligations. However, she remained committed to patriotic causes throughout her life, participating in local and national campaigns to aid the government, active-duty soldiers, and veterans. Most notable was her work during World War II, when she headed the film industry's Red Cross fund-raising effort. Although she had long since retired from movie acting, Pickford was still popular at war bond drives. Her volunteerism was so great that she even enlisted her pet German shepherd in the Dogs for Defense program, which supplied canines to the U.S. Army. She also hosted a weekly party for servicemen at her mansion, Pickfair. These gatherings, sponsored by the United Service Organizations (USO), offered enlisted men an opportunity to dance, play games, sunbathe, and swim for an afternoon. The get-togethers, which began in March 1942, lasted for the duration of the war.

In 1953, as the Korean War was winding down and the Cold War was heating up, Pickford accepted an invitation from the U.S. Treasury to become the associate national chair of a "vital" defense bond campaign (first lady Mamie Eisenhower was honorary chair).[30] On March 30—thirty years after she helped launch the third Liberty Loan tour in Washington, D.C.—she was standing on the steps of the Capitol starting a new bond drive, an event that intentionally recalled her work for the Treasury during World War I. After Washington, Pickford, now sixty years old, embarked on a two-month nationwide tour to twenty-five cities in fourteen states. She relished her assignment as "Uncle Sam's Saleslady," working seven days a week from early morning to past midnight.[31] Meanwhile, she doubled her commitments, adding meetings with various groups (lawyers, bankers, politicians, homemakers, women's clubs). Via radio and television, she reached an audience in the hundreds of thousands. She visited state legislatures in California, Iowa, Massachusetts, and Minnesota, persuading government officials and their staffs to invest in savings bonds. As a result, the Treasury honored Pickford on May 12, 1953, with a distinguished service citation. Six weeks later, Congressman Donald L. Jackson, speaking on the House floor, hailed Pickford's work and called the actress a "great American." Although she was no longer a famous movie star (her last film had been released two decades earlier), Pickford remained an enduring symbol of America. ঌ

On tour in the spring of 1953, Pickford speaks to an attentive audience about defense bonds.

LAWS OF ATTRACTION

Mary Pickford, Movies, and the Evolution of Fame

Eileen Whitfield

The first of the great film stars, Mary's rise had been sensational—and more than a little frightening. While preaching a glowing future for motion pictures, I had never prophesied anything like this.

Adolph Zukor, The Public Is Never Wrong, 1953

Fairbanks carries Pickford on his shoulders as fans surround them at a garden party in London during their 1920 honeymoon.

Mary Pickford - Paul Whiteman - Leonore Hughes - Maurice - Morris Guest - John Barrymore - H. L. Mencken - Mary Garden - Ignacio Zuloaga - Alfred Lunt - Lynn Fontaine - Cecil B. de Mille.

THE PIONEERS of silent cinema had no idea that the advent of movies would not only reshape entertainment but also spark the transformation of fame itself. Producer Adolph Zukor, whose company made Pickford's early silent features, first thought that leading theatrical players such as Minnie Maddern Fiske and Sarah Bernhardt would claim screen stardom for their own. But watching live actors is an arm's-length relationship. The experience of watching silent film is different: the medium is trancelike, ethereal, and fluid. The performer's image is everywhere and nowhere, a nebulous presence made of shadow and light. Viewers sit immersed in the glow of an actor who, if the chemistry is right, can seem both intimate and mythic.

Pickford triggered this charismatic bond within a few months of her start in one-reelers. The power of her acting, combined with the newness of film itself, produced a love and wonder that could happen in the medium only once. "From gay to grave," confessed a critic, "the quick flash of her eyes transports us."[1] And audiences became addicted. A stage star is confined to one venue, one play at a time, once or twice a day, each theatrical season. Pickford could leave her imprint on millions around the world, over and over, nearly every day, in the guise of many characters. Her bond with fans reached an almost mystical transcendence in 1914 when *Hearts Adrift* and *Tess of the Storm Country* were released. Pickford's work as (respectively) a castaway and an "expressive-eyed tatterdemalion" touched the public so deeply that some thought she must possess special, unearthly insight.[2] Rapturous reporters called her an avatar of "tender human sympathy," incapable of affectation, falsehood, or ego.[3] By the mid-1910s, the actress reigned as "the nearest thing to a universally recognized holy icon," the ideal daughter, sister, sweetheart, and angel of the filmgoing world.[4]

During World War I, Pickford's work selling Liberty bonds took this numinous image and wrapped it in the Stars and Stripes. By Armistice Day, she represented a shining brand of can-do America to her fans around the globe. So did Douglas Fairbanks, a star whose acrobatic, carefree films had made him a symbol of virility and hope. When he and Pickford married in 1920, the couple became "living proof of America's chronic belief in happy endings."[5] And, as it turned out, the rest of the world believed the dream as well.

The newlyweds honeymooned in Europe, which responded with euphoria. In London, Pickford leaned from a window at the Ritz to greet their fans, "thousands and thousands of them, waiting day and night in the streets below."[6] Their presence routinely brought traffic to a standstill. The couple often met with politicians and bluebloods, who (in a nice reversal of the class system) sought their company and asked them for photos and autographs. Such meetings were safer than those in public, where fans showed a "grim determination to pet and fondle [Pickford] or die in the attempt."[7] At a garden party, the actress was swarmed and almost trampled by fans who tried to pull her from an open car. As police tried in vain to control the mob, the groom staggered forward with his wife on his shoulders; still, strangers nearly dragged them to the ground. Fearing for Pickford's safety, the couple decided it would be wise to leave England. But almost everywhere in Europe they met similar reactions. In Paris, for instance, a riot erupted in an open market when Pickford was besieged by fans. This time, a quick-witted butcher saved her by locking her in a meat cage for her own protection.

Poster for the now lost 1914 film Hearts Adrift.

Opposite: In 1920 Pickford soared above the most celebrated figures of the day, including opera singer Mary Garden, director Cecil B. DeMille, musician Paul Whiteman, and writer H. L. Mencken, in this 1938 caricature by Miguel Covarrubias. © Estate of Miguel Covarrubias.

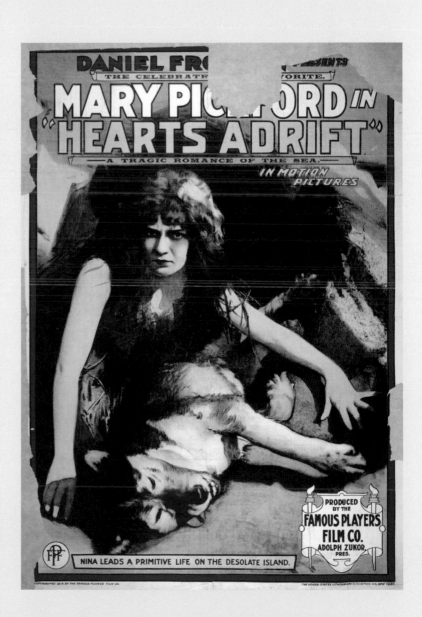

And so it went, from nation to nation, as the press watched and analyzed. Some journalists fretted that, "after all, there were more important and wonderful people in the world than the Fairbankses."[8] This was true. But the honeymoon showed that the nature and rules of fame had changed. In London, the *Times* observed that renown had once been awarded to legendary figures after decades of accomplishment. Now, "by the alchemy of a [camera], centuries have been shortened into days and nights."[9] Movies had the potential to lift an actor from obscurity to stardom overnight, based solely on sex appeal, charm, or the impact of a certain performance on the audience's mood. The actor's screen self then became an icon of character and beauty in a virtually worldwide collective dream. In Pickford's case, the public fervor was magnified by the roles she had played to vast acclaim since the first years of film. In the *Pall Mall Gazette,* an editorial asked readers to "imagine if at the heyday of Charles Dickens's popularity, when an eager public waited impatiently for each installment of his stories, it had suddenly been announced that all the humble heroines of his creation had suddenly come to town. Well, that is what has happened now."[10] Pickford, once an intangible being, was briefly available in the flesh, and her fans were driven to see, hear, and touch her for themselves. "With the new world comes new values," groused the *Aberdeen Press.*[11] Indeed, through the stardom of Mary Pickford, fame found its modern incarnation. It was up to the actress, its accidental pioneer, to navigate this powerful, unknown sphere.

Four weeks after their arrival in Europe, the world's favorite couple returned to Pickfair, their stately manse atop a mountain in Beverly Hills. Throughout the decade, it became the nation's second White House and the crossroads of the world for bold-face names. The nonstop retinue of guests included Albert Einstein, the Queen of Siam, Amelia Earhart, H. G. Wells, Lord and Lady Mountbatten, King Alfonso VIII of Spain, and Babe Ruth. Still more visits occurred at the studio, with Pickford and Fairbanks taking breaks from filming to chat with Helen Keller, her teacher Anne Sullivan, Anna Pavlova, and Tolstoy.

These interactions confirmed that Pickford and Fairbanks were American royals, a position that involved endless obligations. As artists, they starred in first-class films they produced themselves, enchanting the audience and advancing cinema's technical standards. As industry mascots, they cut ribbons, led parades, gave speeches, attended sports events, and counteracted Hollywood scandal by promoting sobriety, good humor, and health. They also spread these concepts abroad during seven expeditions to destinations such as Asia, Africa, Greece, and Russia. "We were ambassadors, not only of the motion picture industry but of our own country," wrote Pickford, who knew that she and Fairbanks were the flash point of the world's infatuation with postwar America. "The cheering crowds … were not for me but for the American motion picture and the world of make-believe."[12] In the history of film, no performer (or married couple) has approached this level of celebrity influence and goodwill.

Then it vanished. After twenty years, the arrival of talkies destroyed silent film's hypnotic spell. Pickford was prepared for her fall from grace. She had once described the world's ovations as "a splendid stimulant" to vanity, "except that Douglas and I had long since analyzed the personal element out of these receptions. Ovations … are seldom or never accorded to persons, but to ideas."[13] Still, to her credit, she honored the idea the world assigned her, living up (not down) to its idealized love. Today, we are accustomed to the interaction between the public and the stars who shape our ambitions, dreams, and values. It is a game that Pickford never sought to play. But with gallantry and spirit, she played it well. ❧

Opposite: Lord and Lady Mountbatten (right, circa 1923), seen here in a playful pose with Pickford and Fairbanks, were frequent guests at Pickfair.

Left: Publicity photo of Fairbanks and Pickford promoting their upcoming world tour in 1929.

CROWN OF GLORY

The Rise and Fall
of the Mary Pickford Curls

Christel Schmidt

Cover illustration of The Theatre (January 1915).

I T IS NO EXAGGERATION to say that Mary Pickford had one of history's most famous heads of hair. During the early twentieth century, the eighteen honey-golden ringlets that beautifully framed her face enraptured filmgoers and became a key element in her meteoric rise to stardom. Over time, her tresses—the most admired, coveted, and copied in America during the 1910s—came to symbolize the era. It is not surprising, then, that her hair became a focal point during the cultural shifts and major battles over women's hairstyles, dress, and behavior that marked the 1920s.

When Pickford first started appearing in movies in 1909, the names of film actors were not publicly available. Companies did not want to pay more to performers who might become popular, and players did not want their names associated with what was then regarded as low-end entertainment. Nonetheless, fans selected their favorites. Players were most often identified with the companies they worked for—Florence Lawrence, for example, was the Biograph Girl, and Florence Turner was the Vitagraph Girl. Pickford, who inherited Lawrence's title after her predecessor left Biograph in the summer of 1909, also had more personal nicknames, such as Little Mary, which referred to her small stature. But her hair, the actress's most striking feature, sparked the greatest number of pet names, including Goldilocks and the Girl with the Curls.

Of course, Pickford, considered the first great movie star, did not ascend to fame and fortune's highest ranks because she had gorgeous hair. Anyone watching her films today will see a remarkably gifted actress with effortless charm and charisma. However, Pickford's ethereal beauty—which softened or belied the frequently hoydenish antics of her onscreen personae—and in particular her hair, played an important role in shaping her career and her image. "In the early days," Pickford remembered, "I have no doubt [my hair] impressed people from whom I sought work."[1] She may have been referring to her first film director, D. W. Griffith, who hired her when she was just sixteen years old. (Griffith was professionally and personally attracted to angelic-looking young women.) Clearly, Pickford understood that her hair was alluring to male potential employers. Smart, ambitious, and still young enough to wear her tresses down (adult women kept their hair pinned up), she probably showed them off at every audition. Yet at Biograph, the onscreen appearance of what became known as the "Mary Pickford curls" was never guaranteed. It always depended on the type of role the actress was playing.

Hair helped define, among other things, a character's age, class, ethnicity, race, and social status. A wealthy young woman in the Confederate South would certainly dress and style her hair differently from a rural laundress or a Native American bride. In the Biograph one-reelers, Pickford's locks were often pulled back, pinned up, or hidden under a dark wig, a hat, or a bandanna. Still, they were prominently featured in numerous early shorts, particularly those from 1912, including *The Mender of the Nets, The Inner Circle, Just Like a Woman, So Near, Yet so Far,* and *Won by a Fish.* In fact, these films and others from this period helped establish Pickford's trademark tresses.

The Pickford curls on display in
Just Like a Woman (1912).

By 1914, Pickford was not just a popular actress; she was a cultural phenomenon. Her image appeared on magazine covers, postcards, and product advertisements, and she was the subject of countless magazine and newspaper articles. Pickford had captured America's heart with her onscreen antics and "saucy ways," and the public's adoring eyes fixated on her physical appearance: her petite frame, pouting mouth, baby stare, and, particularly, long golden curls.[2] Her natural, dangling locks were an inspiration to women seeking an alternative to the elaborate, bulky pompadour that was fashionable in the twentieth century's first decade. The heavy, elevated coiffure—popularized by that era's feminine ideal, the Gibson girl—required intricate structural support from hair attachments and accessories. The style was not just an effort to achieve but also difficult to maintain. Pickford's more down-to-earth coiffure brought relief to increasingly weary female heads.

Of course, the Pickford look was not totally new. Sausage curls (large, tight coils of hair), similar to Pickford's but arranged differently, had been in vogue in America during the nineteenth century, particularly during the 1860s and 1870s, although they were never as popular as the chignon. Beginning in the late 1880s, the corkscrew locks became trendy for children, reportedly due to the popularity of the title character in the novel Little Lord Fauntleroy (1886), a curly-headed boy—and a character Pickford would play in a 1921 film.

So identified was Little Mary with her golden ringlets that when she donned a dark, heavy wig in films such as *Hearts Adrift* (1914), *Little Pal* (1915), and *Madame Butterfly* (1915), writers and critics took note with more than a hint of disappointment. Seeing the Pickford curls was an important part of the program. The "public admired Mary's versatility," producer Adolph Zukor later recalled, but people wanted to see her with curls.[3] In fact, the female audience did more than gaze at the star's hair; they adopted her look for themselves. "All the women in the world are trying to make themselves over into Mary Pickford," or so it appeared to Dame Fashion in 1915.[4] Previously, Paris designers had been the arbiters of U.S. fashion. Now Pickford became one personification of a new fashion trend: Americans began to copy the "look" of actors or members of royalty and the illustrations in magazines and books (such as *Little Lord Fauntleroy*). One of the foremost trendsetters, Pickford was a harbinger of things to come as Hollywood, and America's consumer culture, blossomed.

The actress's advice and opinions on fashion, hair care, and makeup became recurrent topics in "Daily Talks," her national newspaper column launched in late 1915 as a feature of the women's section. Pickford, not a "flashy girl" (a type she once decried in the column), promoted a simple, natural look. She favored proper skin care over makeup and believed that a brush, when properly used, was the key to radiant-looking hair. The star deemed brilliantine, hair dyes, and curling irons to be unnecessary or harmful. And she frowned on eccentric coiffures, especially those accessorized with glitzy barrettes or combs.

Pickford's opinions on fashion, as well as her personal style, echoed her screen persona as a down-to-earth, innately good American girl. And the understated look she championed was surely easier for young women to achieve (and afford) than the look of such exotic film beauties as Alla Nazimova and Gloria Swanson. Moreover, Pickford's movies tied her curls closely to themes of dedication and hard work. The star's resilient working-class heroines—with their diamond-in-the-rough allure—overcome life's obstacles dressed in tattered apparel, with little makeup and unkempt hair. By exhibiting strength and virtue in the face of adversity (and with the help of a rich benefactor), these characters *earn* their Cinderella-like transformations, including exquisitely styled tresses.

Pickford's hair certainly had always been central to the public's perception of her most cherished qualities—beauty and innocence. These aspects of her persona were captured and perpetuated in luminous publicity photos (particularly those taken by Fred Hartsook and Moody Studios, New York) and in her many coming-of-age characters. Then, in 1917, Pickford caused a sensation when she played the title characters (all under age thirteen) in *The Poor Little Rich Girl, Rebecca of Sunnybrook Farm,* and *A Little Princess*. These realistic portrayals immortalized her as a symbol of youth, and her ringlets—extensively showcased in these movies—became an even larger component of her fame.

PAUL GOOLD

AT THE HAIRDRESSER'S
" PLEASE ARRANGE MY HAIR LIKE MARY PICKFORD'S "

Illustration by Paul Goold published in the May 25, 1916, issue of Life *magazine.*

Opposite: Portrait by Moody NY, circa 1914.

Thereafter, Pickford was the film industry's model for ingénues. Movie critics, Zukor remembered, were writing about a "Mary Pickford role" even when she was not in the picture.[5] Young actresses, hoping to replicate Pickford's success, wore their hair in long, tight coils. In fact, there were so many curly-headed female players in the summer of 1917 that a writer for *Moving Picture World* complained of their becoming a "regular thing . . . no matter what the role or mood." The star's look was evidently easier to emulate than her talent and personality, for although the writer thought Pickford "charming and consistent," he found her "copies inane."[6]

Indeed, some critics were already tired of the Pickford type—a "poor little neglected ingénue in curls who wears a pretty frock in the last act."[7] Still, Pickford remained so popular with fans that even Alla Nazimova and Norma Talmadge, both known for their onscreen glamour, starred in Pickfordesque material.[8] This was jarring indeed; previously, the silent cinema's sexy sirens—known for their sophisticated, even risqué, wardrobes—wouldn't have been caught dead wearing rags or coiled locks, and their expertly coiffed hair was almost never blond. Yet in 1919, even Theda Bara, silent film's most notorious vamp, donned Pickford-like curls and a tattered dress to play a sweet Irish lass in *Kathleen Mavourneen.* Bara, weary of being cast as a seductress, was thrilled to star as a respectable girl. Ironically, at about the same time, Pickford was chafing against her wholesome image and yearned for a wicked role. In 1916 she confided this to a friend, who responded with a troublesome question: "What would you do with your curls?"[9]

Pickford sometimes altered her appearance, using wigs or slicking down her hair to play a range of roles. Still, audiences preferred her as an upstanding girl topped with golden ringlets—an image that she, herself, had carefully molded, with advice from her mother and Zukor. Like the Gibson girl before her, she had come to symbolize the ideal young woman of the era.

However, Pickford was not the only model of a modern ingénue. Australian swimmer Annette Kellerman exemplified the era's athletic girl, and Irene Castle, a sleek-figured dancer, embodied the carefree all-American girl. Both, like Pickford, created a stir in women's fashion, but it was Castle who became a trendsetter, causing a sensation in 1914 when she appeared on Broadway with short hair—a highly unusual style for women at that time. Some bohemians or feminists might clip their tresses, but the average woman did not want to lose what was widely perceived as a key element of her beauty. (Attractive women had power, especially over men, who otherwise ruled every aspect of society.) Yet the "Castle bob," as it was known, found acceptance in some circles, signaling that many women were open to the unconventional style.

Irene Castle sporting her stylish bobbed hair, circa 1915.

Bobbed hair, a daring alternative to the Pickford curls, gained converts throughout the mid to late 1910s and particularly during World War I, when it was adopted by many of the women who served as ambulance drivers, nurses, and munitions workers. For them, cutting their hair was a sensible, safe, and hygienic alternative to long, unwieldy tresses. When the conflict ended, some of these women were unwilling to grow their hair out again. The younger generation of girls, just coming of age at the end of the decade, had also started to embrace the bob. Scarred by a devastating war that had killed millions and a flu pandemic that had killed millions more, they sought ways to rebel against the status quo, shocking their elders not just by cutting their hair but also by donning short skirts, rolling their stockings, and wearing heavy makeup. These modern girls were called flappers, and Pickford, long viewed as an "example of modesty and simplicity of dress," was soon out of step with them.[10]

Although the bob was born in New York City, it was Hollywood that promoted and perpetuated bobbed hair and the flapper lifestyle, just as it had once done with the Pickford curls. In 1919 several actresses, including Nazimova, Constance Talmadge, and Viola Dana, joined the ranks of the bobbed. The following year, Metro Pictures released *The Flapper* starring Olive Thomas. Despite the title, Thomas spends most of her screen time in simple but fashionable clothes and wears her hair in long curls. When she tries to act and dress in a worldlier manner, the result is comic failure. The same studio released *Are All Men Alike?* (1920) with a bobbed-haired May Allison playing a "rich young woman possessed with the idea of living her life in her own way," seeking "adventures in the Bohemian quarter of New York."[11]

As these two different film portrayals of the modern girl appeared in theaters, Pickford, now twenty-eight years old, was starring as a child in *Pollyanna* and as an unattractive cockney laundress in *Suds* (both released in 1920). Each film made money, but it was *Pollyanna*—which prominently showcases Pickford's beauty and curls—that became a huge financial success. Since she was now the producer and distributor of her own movies, as well as a cofounder of United Artists, it was crucial that her films be highly profitable. And Pickford strongly believed that it was her duty to please her fans, as well as the theater owners who relied on her box-office revenue. In 1920 she easily achieved these goals. More than a decade into her career, she was still the Queen of the Movies (a title given to her by the press in 1913), the most popular and powerful actress of the era. Her marriage to actor Douglas Fairbanks in March of that year increased her influence and fame as the pair became Hollywood's first supercouple. Yet some Pickford fans were growing restive.

Pickford portrays a homely laundress in Suds *(1920).*

In early 1920 an article in a Kentucky newspaper noted that the younger generation of girls did not find Pickford's look "admirable," even if boys did.[12] Many of these young women (and a growing number of older ones, too) saw the changing fashions of the 1920s as part of a long-desired emancipation from restrictive clothing and laborious hairstyles. For them, this was a logical extension of the struggle for women's rights (which scored a major postwar victory when the Nineteenth Amendment, allowing women to vote, was ratified in August 1920). Others simply wanted styles that were carefree and fun.

Over the next two years, the craze for bobbed hair reached epic proportions, and Hollywood got much of the credit—or blame. Traditionalists thought the style was mannish, undignified, and even freakish. Across the country, department stores, factories, hospitals, offices, restaurants, schools, and major companies such as Aetna Life Insurance, American Railway Express, and Marshall Field's banned short hair on their female workers. Ministers claimed that the Bible forbade short hair on females; they quoted Saint Paul, who told the Corinthians that long hair was a woman's "glory" and a "covering." Doctors thought flappers with bobs, rouged lips, and rolled hosiery spread vice and disease. Husbands beat their daughters and abused or divorced their wives if they cut their locks. High school boys in Chicago and Denver pledged not to date girls with short hair. And young men in Mosquero, New Mexico, started an organization whose members vowed not to marry modern girls.

Portrait by White Studios, circa 1915.

The bob also had detractors in the arts. In 1921 film director and producer George Fitzmaurice was said to be seeking a long-haired actress for his next movie because "short hair lacks the finishing touch that one demands in a beautiful face."[13] The same year, Broadway impresario Florenz Ziegfeld, known for his extravaganzas with scantily clad showgirls, banned women with bobs from his latest show, claiming that "audiences do not like to see girls that way."[14] And illustrator Haskell Collins, whose work graced the covers of some of the country's best-selling magazines, refused (initially) to use short-haired models.

Nevertheless, many women continued to embrace the bob and never turned back; others, daunted by disapproval, wrestled Hamlet-like with the question: "to bob or not to bob."[15] Those over the age of thirty faced accusations of succumbing to vanity and making an undignified effort to be young again. Yet the biggest obstacle may have been the emotional attachment some women had for hair painstakingly grown and cared for since childhood. Moreover, it was constantly reported that the craze for bobbed hair was fading—an unpleasant reminder that it would take years for sheared tresses to grow back to "normalcy."[16]

Portrait by Campbell Studios, circa 1922.

Newspapers and magazines considered short hair and short skirts (worn at the knee or just below it) a passing fad from the beginning. The press reported the impending death of this revolution in women's hair and clothing throughout the 1920s, particularly between 1921 and 1923. Paris fashion houses reintroduced the long skirt for the 1921 fall season, and it was commonly believed that short hair did not look good with long skirts. (French models sporting the long fashions wore their abundant hair pulled back in a bun or piled on top of their heads.) So far, nothing had curbed the craze for bobbed locks and short skirts, but the dictates of fashion would surely put an end to the madness. As the press pronounced the "old-fashioned girl" the victor in a theoretical war between the "bobs and longs," all eyes turned to the Hollywood trendsetters to see what they would do.[17]

Pickford, though nearly thirty and a generation ahead of the flapper, remained influential on matters of fashion. Her personal style was still admired by young women around the country. (The first Miss America, the long-haired, sixteen-year-old Margaret Gorman, crowned in 1921, bore a striking resemblance to Pickford.) Yet in 1920, when "everybody seems to be wearing short skirts," the actress continued to opt for long ones, claiming that her husband (Fairbanks) preferred them.[18] She found the display of bare knees "shocking" and thought that most women's legs were not worth showing off. It was "a question of beauty not morality," she claimed.[19] And although Pickford stood up for the modern girl and praised her bobbed locks as "clean" and "comfortable," she chastised "shop and school girls" for wearing clothes made from "cheap and tawdry material," and she disapproved of high heels, low-necked dresses, and one-piece bathing suits.[20] This rigid stance was reported by the press, most notably in a 1921 article that juxtaposed Pickford's conservative position with the liberal view of forty-seven-year old opera singer Mary Garden. (Six years later, the two would be counterpoints in a magazine piece about the bob.)

When Pickford embraced the long skirts introduced in Paris (five inches or less from the ground), she unleashed a firestorm of speculation about the future of women's fashion. Her popularity and influence were such that it was assumed the "younger set" would follow her lead.[21] The flapper style would be replaced, and a new type of girl would emerge, one who would define the modern era. But Pickford was a twice-married woman with a successful career. No longer the girl with the curls, she appeared regal in candid and promotional photographs. She wore her hair up, and her clothing was elegant. Yet it would be the end of the decade before she portrayed this kind of 1920s woman onscreen.

Other Hollywood stars, including Bebe Daniels, Pola Negri, and Gloria Swanson, also adopted the more sophisticated French styles (Swanson even pronounced the flapper "passé").[22] But contrary to predictions, it was clear by late 1922 that American women were going to keep their short skirts and bobbed tresses. In fact, short hairstyles became more diversified, complementing a range of facial shapes; as a result, women young and old relinquished their locks to join the modern era. Although the battle over women's choices continued, short hair had triumphed by 1924. The *Los Angeles Times* pronounced long hair a "relic of the past," as the bobbed style dominated in urban areas across the country.[23] Even Pickford's mother, Charlotte, cut her own hair that summer while the family vacationed in France.

Despite this revolution in fashion, Pickford held on to her tresses and opted to portray modern girls of other eras in two period movies, *Rosita* (1923) and *Dorothy Vernon of Haddon Hall* (1924). These films allowed her to adopt adult sophistication outside a Jazz Age setting, sidestepping controversial issues and pleasing a wide range of female viewers. Although these historical features received favorable reviews and earned healthy receipts at the box office, they failed to capture the star's most steadfast followers. These devotees, according to a 1925 article in *Photoplay*, wanted the actress to "return to the lovable character of youth which she rendered a classic."[24] They wanted, in other words, the girl with the curls. Pickford felt trapped, but she was not alone.

Pickford in Dorothy Vernon of Haddon Hall *(1924). Her sister, Lottie, who plays a maid, can be seen standing in the shadows (right).*

MARY PICKFORD
IN
"COQUETTE"

UNITED ARTISTS PICTURE

Many stars who specialized in ingénue roles, including Lois Moran, Jobyna Ralston, and Norma Shearer, kept their hair long. They, like Pickford, were reluctant to lose their locks for fear of alienating their fan bases. Moran believed the "audience had [[her]] securely fastened to long hair, long skirts and unsophistication."[25] Yet Hollywood had already declared these old-fashion girls passé and embraced bobbed actresses who epitomized the flapper, such as Colleen Moore, Clara Bow, and Joan Crawford. To survive in the new order, female players had to adopt short hair. By 1927, the Pickford type had toppled; nearly all the film industry's long-haired holdouts had succumbed to the barber's shears. The career of the actress who had started it all was already in decline, as box-office numbers and fan polls revealed that other stars were now more popular. Pickford, the woman who had set trends both on- and offscreen, would have to follow the lead of a younger generation if she was going to remain relevant.

For many women, short hair was a symbol of female emancipation and progress, and cutting their tresses was a liberating experience. For Pickford, it was the stuff of nightmares. She was haunted by the thought of "cold shears on the back of [[her]] neck," reducing her curls to "useless, lifeless things."[26] Even worse, she feared that once shorn, her power (like Samson's) would be lost. She certainly had reason to be afraid: newspapers predicted that the cost of cutting her hair would be a "million or more of her most ardent and adoring fans."[27] The mere rumor of a snipping brought Pickford a "deluge of criticism … from mild reproof to violent denunciation."[28] Even her two closest advisers, her husband and her mother, opposed the idea.

In June 1928, despite the "terrifying unanimity of disapproval," Pickford had her hair bobbed.[29] The event was reported around the world and made the front page of the *New York Times.* Distraught fans responded with "letters of protest, grief, even … rage."[30] "You would have thought I murdered someone," the actress later recalled, "and perhaps I had, but only to give her successor a chance to live."[31] The intensity of the backlash stunned her, but she moved forward with a new picture, a "talkie" in which she played a flapper.

In *Coquette* (1929), Pickford's onscreen persona—cultivated by the actress for two decades—was completely transformed. Gone were her trademark curls, and with them the illusion of youth they had helped create. Her stylish new bob revealed a mature woman, now in her late thirties, who suddenly seemed too old to play the modern girl. Gingham frocks and tattered dresses were replaced by strappy silk gowns that exposed her bare shoulders and knee-length skirts that revealed her shapely legs. She even adopted a flirtatious manner, batting her heavily made-up eyes.

The dramatic changes to Pickford's image were a serious challenge for her fans, and the addition of sound complicated matters. *Coquette,* the actress's first talking picture, introduced her voice, which was small and had a reprimanding tone, making the star seem even more unfamiliar. Still, the film had an immense curiosity factor and became her biggest box-office success. Pickford won the Academy Award for Best Actress for her performance in *Coquette*—an honor that likely recognized her career achievements more than her work in the film itself.

Apparently, Pickford's career had survived the loss of her iconic curls. She went on to star alongside Fairbanks in *The Taming of the Shrew* (1929), the first talking feature to tackle Shakespeare. The film, which opened two days after the 1929 stock market crash, made a healthy million dollars despite the turmoil. Still, the zeitgeist had changed, seemingly overnight. Hollywood, still reeling from the transition to sound, soon embraced gritty tales, dark themes, and flawed heroines. Chorus girls, gold diggers, fallen women, and gangster's molls replaced flappers, vamps, and virtuous ingénues. New stars embodied these roles, and old favorites struggled to adapt.

For her next role, Pickford chose to play the title character in *Kiki* (1931), a gold-digging chorus girl with short, tight curls reminiscent of Harpo Marx. Two years later, she reinvented herself again as a pioneer in *Secrets* (1933), a drama in the still-popular western genre. Both titles failed to find an audience and became the only Pickford vehicles to lose money. It seemed that the public's taste had changed so much that there was no longer a cultural place for Pickford, with or without her curls. In response, she took a break from acting—a break that ultimately became permanent. ❧

Portrait by George Hurrell, circa 1932. Pickford presented a sexy and mature image in her early 1930s publicity photos. © Estate of George Hurrell.

BLOOD AND SYMPATHY

Race and the Films of Mary Pickford

Elizabeth Binggeli

Pickford as the tragic Cho-Cho San in Madame
Butterfly *(1915). The actress played numerous nonwhite
characters during her early film career.*

Frame enlargement from a Technicolor test of Pickford dressed as the Virgin Mary for The Gaucho *(1927).*

I N THE OPENING of the 1927 Douglas Fairbanks film *The Gaucho,* audiences are given a treat: a brief, unbilled appearance by Mary Pickford as the Virgin Mary, a miraculous vision in two-strip Technicolor. She materializes magically from a rock wall, a blond, rosy-cheeked shock of color in an otherwise black-and-white world; her large eyes brim with compassion for the Argentine shepherd girl who has fallen from a cliff and whose broken body lies motionless next to a spring. A single loving glance from the Madonna heals the rapturous girl and dazzles a gathering throng of pampas folk. *The Gaucho*'s Technicolor Virgin is neatly emblematic of the star persona Pickford had honed over many years: her radiant sympathy for the suffering seems to transcend the mortal realm.

The casting of his wife as feminine purity incarnate was a cheeky move for Fairbanks, who was widely rumored to be having an affair with his *Gaucho* costar, the "Mexican Spitfire" Lupe Vélez. Early in her career, Pickford might have played the fiery Vélez role or, indeed, the native shepherdess role. Although best remembered today for her fair skin and brilliantly back-lit halo of golden curls, the actress portrayed many characters of non-European descent, including Native Americans, Mexicans, Filipinos, Japanese, and a Native Alaskan. Unlike many actors (including rival actress Marguerite Clark), Pickford never appeared in blackface makeup, but she did play these roles in a kind of "brownface" by darkening her hair and complexion.[1] Curiously, these nonwhite characters abruptly disappeared from her repertoire after 1916. Pickford is often described as an "everywoman" with "universal" appeal, but only seven years into her twenty-four-year film career, her "universality" became unambiguously white.[2] Why?

It would be easy enough to argue that as her star ascended, audiences wanted Pickford to look like Pickford. But this answer only begs the question: whatever her natural skin tone, why did "looking like Pickford," after 1916, mean looking indisputably white? Other actresses at the height of their popularity, including Norma Talmadge and Colleen Moore, were allowed considerably more leeway in their racial appearance onscreen; they were "exoticized" with dark makeup, and their star personae were not threatened. And if familiarity were the sole issue, why did so many of Pickford's own roles glory in her ability to metamorphose, sometimes unrecognizably, into little girls (*The Poor Little Rich Girl* [1917], *A Little Princess* [1917]), little boys (*Little Lord Fauntleroy* [1921]), or homely women (*Stella Maris* [1918], *Suds* [1920]). With these roles, the actress could display her virtuosity by casting aside her maturity, her femininity, or her charisma. But after 1916, Pickford did not cast aside her whiteness.

To portray a white character is not a choice to play racially "blank" or neutral. Regardless of an actor's motives, playing white involves investing that skin tone with the attributes the culture designates as "white." Whiteness in Western culture, critic Richard Dyer argues, "reproduces itself regardless of intention, power differences and good-will, and overwhelmingly because it is not seen as whiteness, but as normal."[3] To the extent that white people are portrayed as unraced, or as grounded in a "spirit" that is more essential than the body encasing that spirit, nonwhite people are conversely portrayed as encumbered and indelibly defined by their bodies. Dyer contends that "what makes whites different, and at times uneasily locatable in terms of race, is . . . their spirit of mastery over their and other bodies, in short their potential to transcend their raced bodies."[4]

Idealized white masculinity is often expressed in terms of noble mastery over base bodily desires, including lust, greed, and violence. The idealized white woman, in contrast, is patterned after the Virgin Mary herself; she is a pure "vessel for the spirit," wholly without bodily desire.[5] This is not to say that all white characters are virtuous and pure, but rather that their virtue or corruption is measured by the degree to which they conform to the cultural expectations of whiteness implied by their skin color.

But there is a reason that Pickford's Virgin Mary appears only briefly in *The Gaucho*: after hovering and beaming, what else can she do? An idealized white female character offers a spectacular locus for spiritual virtue but a problematic locus for desire, the engine of narrative. In a sense, the "whiter" Pickford plays, the less she can do as a character, and this restriction creates significant narrative challenges for her films. I suspect that many of the defining characteristics of Pickford's characters—juvenescence, virginity, righteousness, feistiness— are themselves different strategies for managing the narrative problem of her hyperbolic white femininity.

In other words, rather than accepting whiteness as an incidental characteristic of the Pickford persona, we might do better to consider it the primary characteristic from which the persona springs. Clearly, she was not the only actress of the silent era whose public image was shaped by cultural attitudes about white identity, but both the magnitude of her popularity and the profound degree of personal control she exerted over her image fostered an extremely conservative approach to the management of her career. In the public's eye, over the course of her career, Pickford became an ever more highly refined distillation of "herself."

To understand the role race played in this distillation of the Pickford image, it is useful to first consider her range of racialized roles before 1916, the year of the "white turn" in her career.

Pickford as the homely Unity Blake in Stella Maris *(1918).*

Blood and Sex: The Butterfly Type

According to the wife of director D. W. Griffith, her husband "thought Mary [Pickford] had a good face for Indians on account of her high cheek bones, and usually cast her for the red-skinned maid or the young squaw. A smear of brown grease paint over her fair face and a wig of coarse straight black hair made a picturesque little Indian girl of 'our Mary.'"[6] When she uses the expression "our Mary," who does the word *our* suggest? Lest we be tempted to answer Americans or, more generously, all humanity, it should be noted that the black audience did not always agree. Christel Schmidt has shown that the black press heralded African American actress Edna Morton, star of several Reol melodramas, as "our Mary Pickford," and a publicity still featuring Morton is remarkably similar to a contemporaneous Pickford publicity still for *Rosita* (1923).[7] These images suggest that "our Mary" is the imagined possession of a white collective—a point not lost on African Americans, who sought their own Pickford in Morton.

Pickford's Native American, Mexican, and Filipino roles occur exclusively in Biograph or Independent Moving Picture Company (IMP) one-reel or two-reel shorts released from 1909 through 1912. Pickford plays a Native American character in *The Indian Runner's Romance* (1909), *Ramona* (1910), *The Song of the Wildwood Flute* (1910), *A Pueblo Legend* (1912), and *Iola's Promise* (1912). She is Mexican in *The Two Brothers* (1910), *Fate's Interception* (1912), and *A Lodging for the Night* (1912) and Filipino in *A Manly Man* (1911). Pickford did not portray nonwhite characters again until 1915, when, in a pair of Famous Players features, she played a Native Alaskan in *Little Pal* and the Japanese title character in *Madame Butterfly*.[8] During the production of *Madame Butterfly,* Pickford wrote, "I have been studying the Japanese women very carefully lately and I sincerely believe that [John Luther] Long knew whereof he spoke when he endowed Cho-Cho-San with her wonderful faculty for silent suffering."[9]

In 1898 American writer John Luther Long published his story of the doomed geisha who commits suicide after she is loved, used, and cast aside by a white naval officer, providing the twentieth century with its most enduring miscegenation tragedy. In 1900 Long collaborated with theatrical producer David Belasco on a stage adaptation; Puccini's 1904 opera is largely based on the Belasco play. Belasco was also the man who would later give Gladys Smith her first major role on Broadway and the stage name "Mary Pickford." At heart, the Butterfly story is a cautionary tale about the consequences of interracial sex. Audience members may despise the faithless officer and pity the naive Butterfly, but the story encourages us to read these characters against a backdrop of immutable racial law, presenting the plot of the tantalizing interracial romance within the confines of tragedy.

The "silent suffering" of the Butterfly character hovers over many Pickford films. *Ramona* tells of a Scottish–Native American girl in a doomed romance with a Native American shepherd. *Iola's Promise* is the story of a Native American girl in a doomed romance with a white prospector. In *Little Pal,* Pickford plays a half-breed Eskimo girl in a doomed romance with a white miner. *A Manly Man,* also known as *His Gratitude,* seems at first glance to be an exception to the tragic

Snapshot of Pickford (left) in costume for her role as a Native American in the 1910 Biograph short The Song of the Wildwood Flute.

The actress played a Mexican in the 1912 short Fate's Interception.

Butterfly plot: it tells the story of Lola, a poor Filipino woman who nurses a white man back to health and falls in love with him.[10] When her lover's white fiancée appears on the scene, he stays true to Lola. The film does not offer an unqualified happy ending, however; presumably, the hero's self-sacrificing gesture is prompted less by love than by "his gratitude," which is what makes him such a "manly man." The tragedy, in this case, is his.

Variety lauded Pickford's portrayal in *Madame Butterfly* of "the simple-minded, simpering, giggling little Japanese girl" and promised that if Cho-Cho San's fate "doesn't raise a lump in your respective throats … nothing will."[11] According to Adolph Zukor, for *Madame Butterfly*, Pickford "made up (she applied her own make-up in those days) to seem more like a Japanese than the director [Sidney Olcott] desired … she fastened the skin of the outer corners of each eye back and achieved the long and slant eyes of the Oriental. The director finally got her to agree to a make-up somewhere nearer the Caucasian."[12]

The conflict over makeup suggests a narrative tension at work. In order to wring the tragedy the *Variety* reviewer so admired from the Butterfly plot, Cho-Cho San had to be unambiguously racialized as nonwhite: her tragedy functions only if the audience accepts race and racial taboos as fixed categories. But the more Mary became "ours"— a figure of (white) audience identification—the more problematic these tragedies were. The spunky white Pickford was able to triumph over anything; the nonwhite Pickford was trapped.

Pickford's turn toward white roles was probably less a function of audience desire for a visually familiar Mary than a desire for a triumphant one—one who could conquer tragedy with innate feistiness. Rather than being encumbered by an immutable bodily tragedy, like Butterfly, the feisty Mary's obstacles became those that could be conquered with her indomitable white spirit. Her perpetually victorious white characters guaranteed audiences a kind of predictable pleasure, but they drastically confined the range of her film plots.

Blood and Soap: The Washable Butterfly Type

Without the racialized doom of the Butterfly plot, how could Pickford's films revel in romantic melodrama? One strategy was to make the taint of the forbidden match superficial and surmountable, unlike the permanence of racial identity. Pickford's "washable Butterfly" type suffers for her star-crossed match, but only temporarily. Often, all the heroine needs for success is a felicitous encounter with a bar of soap.

The old minstrel stage gag of soap failing to turn black skin white appears in a handful of Pickford films. In *Rebecca of Sunnybrook Farm* (1917), her character attempts to scrub a black boy white; in the short *The School Teacher and the Waif* (1912), Pickford's character is shocked when a black man (really a white man in blackface) is able to wash his color away. These bits play off a well-known biblical passage: "Can the Ethiopian change his skin, or the leopard his spots?"[13] Although the jokes are mere funny business in Pickford's films, the same biblical passage is evoked in the title of the racist screed *The Leopard's Spots*, part of Thomas Dixon's Ku Klux Klan trilogy that inspired Griffith's *The Birth of a Nation* (1915). Lest the comparison seem a strained one, we should remember that Pickford's own *Heart O' the Hills* (1919) explicitly echoes *Birth of a Nation*'s charge of KKK riders when Kentucky mountain girl Mavis leads a posse of night riders against a group of white "furriners." Mavis's charge domesticates (and feminizes) the brutal Griffith scene: led by the spirited young white girl, the night riders seem pure and righteous in their cause. So while the racist jokes and references in Pickford's films seem benign compared with the viciousness of *Birth of a Nation*, one might wonder whether, in their pigtailed and wide-eyed benignity, these racist asides are even more influential.

After many trials, Molly O (Pickford), the dirty and disheveled orphan in The Foundling *(1916), is reunited with her wealthy father.*

The film *Less than the Dust* (1916) sets its racialized romance in British colonial India. Pickford plays Rahda, an East Indian girl who falls in love with a white officer. But Rahda is no suicidal Butterfly. When a British woman sees her and declares, "I can't bear these native children; their clothes are so dirty," Rahda has the gumption to make herself clean "English" clothes. Her desire to learn to read English shows that her purification process is more than exterior. And fortunately, any chance of a Butterfly tragedy is averted when it is revealed that Rahda is, unbeknownst to herself, English! The revelation has her literally rubbing the brownness from her dirty arm in disbelief. The comedy in the film—which later gives us Rahda kneeling before a suit of armor and mistaking a bathtub for a "sacred pool"—comes from the relief that her backwardness is merely a product of acculturation and dirt, not a problem of blood. *Less than the Dust* is, in a sense, the racial hinge in Pickford's career; she begins the film as a seemingly nonwhite character, but by the end, her white star persona has taken over.

Pickford's famous portrayal of the title character in *Tess of the Storm Country* (1922) also offers us something of a washable Butterfly.[14] Tess is white, but because she lives in poverty among a "filthy lot" of fishermen—whose stink literally drives the wealthy from their terraces—she is portrayed as unfit for the wealthy landowner's son. When reminded that "cleanliness is next to godliness," Tess decides to undergo a miraculous transformation by soap. "She'd be a darn pretty kid if she were cleaned up," we're promised, and so it proves: a quick dunk in soapy water magically turns Tess's tangled hair into the star's familiar ringlets. Like Rahda, Tess's cleanup is interior as well; her washed body, hair, and clothes are accompanied by a wholehearted immersion in the Bible.

A charmingly begrimed Pickford made for popular publicity stills: a coal chute in *The Hoodlum* (1919) and a backstreet brawl in *Little Annie Rooney* (1925) blacken just enough of her fair face to underscore that whatever the superficial taint, the true (and white) Pickford is just below the surface. Rahda and Tess triumph because their inherent worthiness is ultimately unveiled to themselves and to the audience, and this worthiness is emblematic in their clean, white skin.

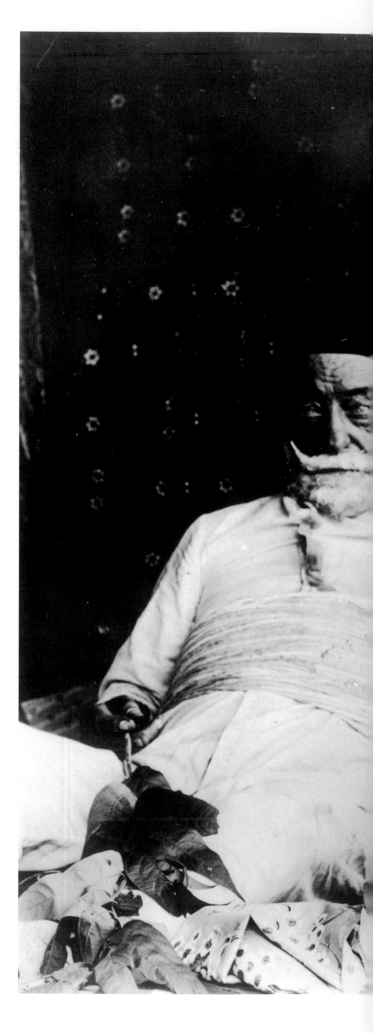

Pickford as Rahda, a Hindu girl in Less than the Dust *(1916).*

Blood and Inheritance: The Fauntleroy Type

Frances Hodgson Burnett's 1886 novel *Little Lord Fauntleroy* tells the story of an American boy who unexpectedly becomes a British lord and heir to a vast estate. Though raised among common folk, Cedric proves his worth to his grandfather, the earl, by displaying sympathy for everyone. A coarse Italian American boy pretends to be the rightful heir, but his scheme is thwarted by friends loyal to Cedric.

In addition to the Fauntleroy role itself, Pickford played many characters of the Fauntleroy type. Her Sara Crewe in *A Little Princess* is a privileged child who loses her wealth when her father dies, and she must work as a slavey in the boarding-school kitchen until her fortune is restored. In *Such a Little Queen* (1914) Pickford stars as the exiled queen of Herzegovina temporarily living in poverty in Harlem—mashing potatoes with her scepter!—until her true station can be restored. *The Foundling* (1916) has Pickford's young Molly O toiling as a servant in a boardinghouse until her long-lost father surfaces, bringing her status and wealth.

Rather than rags-to-riches stories, Fauntleroy plots are riches-to-rags-to-riches stories: protagonists lose status temporarily, "slum it" in another country or with another class, and then demonstrate through exemplary behavior that their nobility is inherent—in the blood—rather than a product of acculturation. Sara is pathetic in her miserable garret precisely because we understand how little she belongs there; Cedric clearly deserves the title of "Lord Fauntleroy" because it is in his blood. Fauntleroy plots work to quell anxieties about the worthiness of those with inherited wealth by having the hero or heroine prove through trial that their blood is "blue." Moreover, these plots give audiences aristocrats whose blue blood has been saved from Old World inbreeding and the dissipation of idleness by wholesome, authentic experience with "folk," with land, and with labor.[15]

The word alone *on this poster for* Rags *and on a publicity still for* Little Pal *(see next page) describes a girl's isolation in a poor mining town. One is white and one is Inuit, but each longs for the companionship of the white hero.*

But the rusticated child who inherits wealth is not the only figure who has a dramatic change of class in *Little Lord Fauntleroy*. In addition to playing Cedric, Pickford takes on the role of Dearest, Cedric's commoner American mother, who challenges class mores by marrying a British nobleman. Just as her son must demonstrate that his blood is worthy of his inheritance, Dearest must demonstrate that her blood is of the right sort to mix with the noble line she has married into. She is one of many Pickford heroines of lesser station who must prove that they are fit to wed (and, by implication, reproduce with) wealthier men. In *Caprice* (1913), for instance, Pickford plays a mountain girl who must be trained to be an acceptable wife for a wealthy man. In *Daddy-Long-Legs* (1919) the orphaned Judy initially refuses to marry her beloved because he "comes from a family full of ancestors." The title character in *Rags* (1915) must leave her rough mining camp home to be educated as a lady so that she might be fit to marry the banker's nephew.

While one might read these plots as examples of progressive class mobility, they are more conservative than they seem. Each "marrying up" Pickford character may be charming in her rusticity, but she must also prove that she can shed what is lowly in her identity and leave it behind—a Butterfly whose taint of class can be washed off like Rahda's East Indian tan. In the end, mining camp resident Rags is able to slough off her lowliness in a way that mining camp resident Little Pal cannot because Rags is white and Little Pal is not. In other words, while Fauntleroy plots seem to rely on class transformation alone, these transformations are predicated on a biologically inherent worthiness.

A still from Little Pal *(1915).*

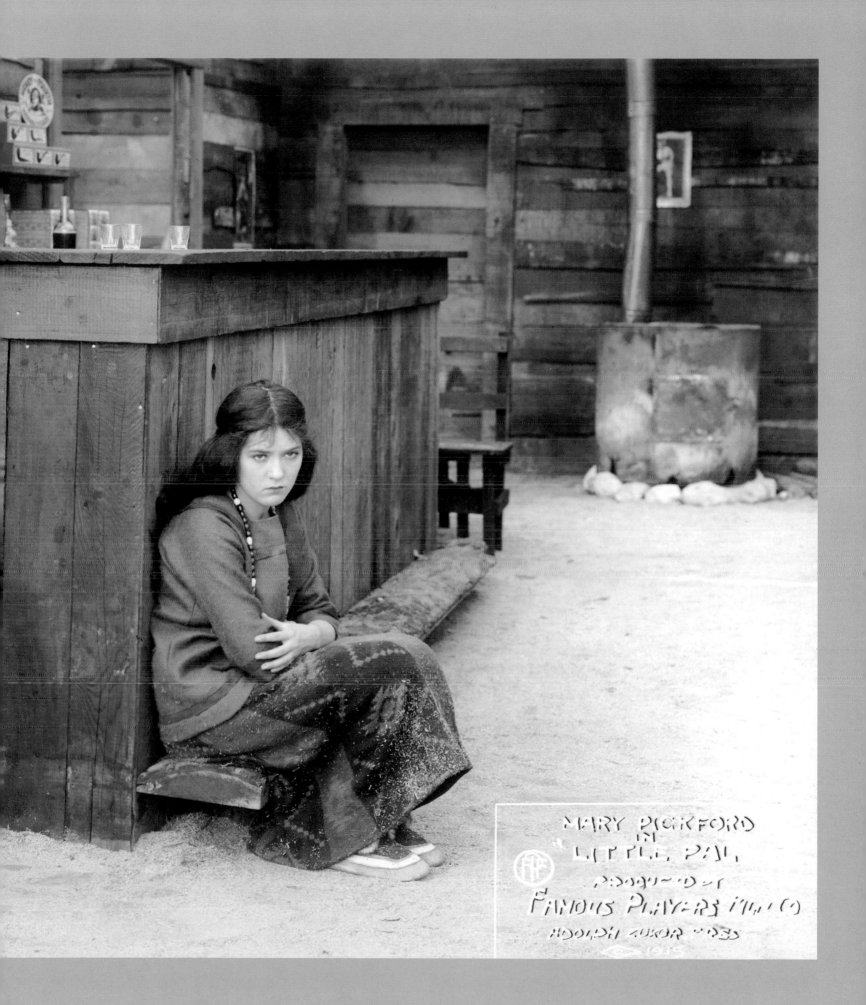

Blood and Mother Love: The Eva Type

In 1901, while working in a local theatrical stock company, nine-year-old Pickford appeared on a Toronto stage as the most influential heroine of her day: Eva St. Clare, the white, ringleted girl in Harriet Beecher Stowe's 1852 abolitionist novel *Uncle Tom's Cabin*.[16] Eva had an unparalleled influence on theatrical and silent film ingénues. In the novel and in the phenomenally popular stage adaptations, audience pity for the tortured slave Uncle Tom found expression in the saintly figure of Eva, who, wiser than her years and seemingly unstained by the prejudices of the plantation, was a model for Christian charity and devotion to all. Eva provided predominantly white audiences with a nonthreatening way to channel their sympathy for black suffering, much as Pickford herself provided in her newspaper column when she wrote, "What was going to be the fate of thousands of these little ones without their mothers' sheltering care on the one hand and stoned by their white playmates on the other hand because they were 'niggers.'"[17]

While Butterflies suffer permanently, and washable Butterflies and Fauntleroys suffer temporarily, Evas suffer for someone else. Like the Virgin Mary with her Argentine shepherd girl from *The Gaucho,* Pickford's white Eva characters are often placed in close proximity to nonwhite characters so that they have narrative opportunities to demonstrate their Eva-like tolerance and sympathy for the downtrodden. A late-career Eva type—albeit a brick-wielding one—appears in *Little Annie Rooney,* which was based on a story that Pickford wrote herself. The actress plays twelve-year-old Irish American Annie, the scrappy ringleader of a child gang that includes boys who are Jewish, African American, Greek, Mexican, and Chinese. Motherless herself, Annie acts as a mother not only to her gang but also to her elder brother and father, whom she gently reminds to pray before the evening meal. Throughout the film, Annie's gang battles with the all-white Kid Kelly gang, while her policeman father carefully brokers the peace in the fractious working-class ghetto. Both Annie and her father are presented as color-blind advocates for their nonwhite neighbors. Later, Annie's spiritualized sympathy for others becomes Christ-like when she donates blood to a young man she adores. By the final reel, Annie's maturation is linked to her movement away from a childish relationship with her nonwhite gang and toward an adult relationship with her white suitor, with whom she has literally mixed her blood.

Annie Rooney (Pickford) is the leader of a spirited gang of boys from different ethnic and racial backgrounds.

Pickford's Eva type reaches its purest expression in *Sparrows* (1926), a film about a group of white orphans imprisoned on a southern "baby farm." Although nearly every critic of *Sparrows* characterizes the film as "Dickensian," presumably linking the plot to *Oliver Twist,* they miss a much more apt narrative inspiration closer to home: the American slave narrative in general and *Uncle Tom's Cabin* in particular. The *Sparrows* children occupy the narrative position of black slaves in an abolitionist text: they are exploited as farm laborers, fed little and punished for stealing additional food, dressed in rags, and ruthlessly sold when the opportunity arises. When Stowe's Uncle Tom is sold away from his family, he paraphrases the same passage from the Bible that Pickford's film title cites: "Yer ought ter look up to the Lord above—he's above all—thar don't a sparrow fall without him."[18] Just as Eva reads the Bible to Uncle Tom so that he might know Christ, Pickford's character, "Mama" Molly, reads to her charges from a tattered book of Bible stories so that they, too, will know that salvation is coming. Just as Eva ascends from her deathbed to "a beautiful world, where Jesus is," the film gives us a small child who dies in Molly's arms and is delivered up to heaven by Christ himself.[19] *Sparrows* even culminates with its own flight to freedom. Like Stowe's slave Eliza, who flees a pursuing dog across a frozen river while carrying her son, Pickford's Molly flees a pursuing dog through an alligator-infested swamp, a cherubic child clinging to her neck.

Uncle Tom's Cabin and the figure of Eva can help explain why Pickford was more often cast as a "little mother," a child or adolescent girl who takes care of children, rather than as an actual mother who has physically borne a child. Pickford's Evas become little mothers through sympathy rather than sex; they are little mothers for the same reason that Eva St. Clare dies in childhood: with her indiscriminate love for others, if Eva were allowed to grow up and be sexualized, she might become a Butterfly, guilty of miscegenation.

Mama Molly (Pickford) comforts the orphans with stories from the Bible in Sparrows *(1926).*

*   *   *   *   *   *   *   *

Pickford's films, both before and after the white turn in her career, use race in complicated and contradictory ways. Race elicits sympathy, dread, or identification; it stirs indignation or evokes laughter. It is a crude narrative shorthand meant to quickly mark the wicked and the virtuous, the American and the imposter. Her *Gaucho* appearance is so effective because the Virgin Mary character is so in keeping with her star persona: Mary Pickford, like no other public figure, seems to *feel* for the orphans, the persecuted black children, the silently suffering Japanese women, the world's oppressed. In terms of the *Gaucho* scene, the white turn in Pickford's career can be described as a step away from the pitiful native shepherdess role and toward the celestial white goddess role: a shift from a role of suffering to a role of sympathy. Perhaps with Kentucky night rider Mavis and the Virgin Mary we define the poles of Pickford's white star persona: the tiny crusader who patrols the boundaries of the pure, and the infinitely sympathetic icon who is purity incarnate. ঌ

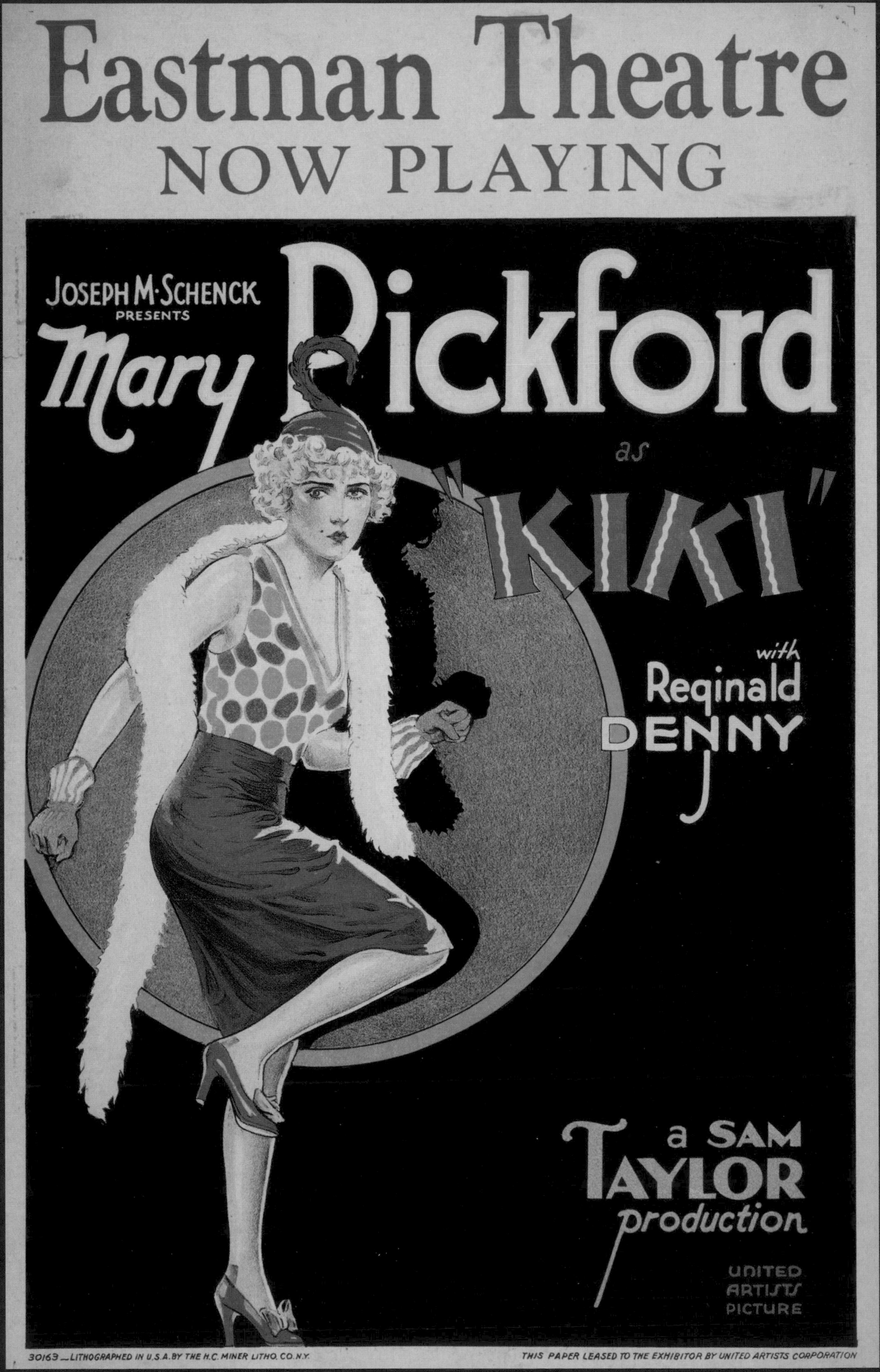
Eastman Theatre
NOW PLAYING
JOSEPH M·SCHENCK
PRESENTS
Mary Pickford
as
"KIKI"
with
Reginald
DENNY
a SAM
TAYLOR
production
UNITED
ARTISTS
PICTURE
30163 _ LITHOGRAPHED IN U.S.A. BY THE H.C. MINER LITHO. CO. N.Y.
THIS PAPER LEASED TO THE EXHIBITOR BY UNITED ARTISTS CORPORATION

THE FILMS OF
MARY PICKFORD

James Card

Poster for the Pickford comedy Kiki (1931)
from the Eastman Theatre in Rochester, New York.

"THE TWO GREATEST NAMES in the cinema are, I beg to reiterate, Mary Pickford and Charlie Chaplin.... Theirs are the greatest names in the cinema and from an historical point of view they always will be great." The quotation is from Iris Barry's *Let's Go to the Movies,* originally published in 1926. Further on in the same book, Miss Barry adds the name of Douglas Fairbanks and observes: "Fairbanks, his wife and Chaplin are, and behave like, serious artists: in that is their great strength ... they are, largely, the history of the cinema."[1]

Certainly, no one writing film history has ever neglected the work of Chaplin. And Fairbanks, along with receiving generous treatment in the pages of most film histories, has even enjoyed the undivided attention of Alistair Cooke in a monograph. But one may search in vain for a serious discussion and analysis of the work of Mary Pickford. In Arthur Knight's *The Liveliest Art—A Panoramic History of the Movies,* reference is made to only one Fairbanks film (*Robin Hood*) and to only three of Pickford's pictures; one of the three (*The Little American*) is cited as a DeMille production, with no mention at all of Pickford.

The nearest approach any recent writer has made to the Pickford contribution occurs in Richard Griffith's text to his 1957 picture book *The Movies.* Observing that she was the "undisputed queen of the screen" for twenty-three years and "for fourteen of these years she was the most popular woman in the world," Griffith asks himself, "Why? It becomes increasingly difficult to answer the question ... the answer can only be a guess."[2]

The same question asked forty-one years earlier was no less difficult. It was stated by the reviewer of the Pickford film *Poor Little Peppina,* which appeared in 1916. Writing in the *New York Dramatic Mirror* (March 4, 1916), the reviewer complained:

To analyze the acting of Mary Pickford is about as satisfactory as trying to draw a definite conclusion from a metaphysical premise. After much circumlocution, after the use of many words and the expenditure of much grey matter one is forced to the inevitable conclusion that Mary Pickford is Mary Pickford. She has a charm, a manner, an expression that is all her own. She seems to have the happy faculty of becoming for the time being the character she is portraying. At no time does one gather the impression that Mary Pickford is acting. She is the epitome of naturalness. But why go on? The sum and substance of it all is that Mary Pickford is unique, and irrespective of the strength or weakness of any picture in which she appears, the fact that Mary Pickford appears in it makes it a good picture.

This is an edited version of an article first published in Image: The Journal of the George Eastman House of Photography, *December 1959.*

A 1917 publicity photo of silent cinema's three greatest stars: Charlie Chaplin, Pickford (in costume), and Douglas Fairbanks.

Before dismissing this little rhapsody with a feeling of present-day superiority over a naïve enthusiasm of forty-three years ago, consider these words of theoretician Paul Rotha, who was never baffled by a Dreyer, Pudovkin, Pabst, or Murnau. In words reminiscent of those of Iris Barry, Rotha wrote: "Both Mr. and Mrs. Douglas Fairbanks are extremely serious about this film business.... They are both of extreme importance to the cinema. With Chaplin, Stroheim, and, to a lesser extent, Griffith, they are the outstanding figures of the American cinema." Rotha devoted five pages of his *Film Till Now* to the work of Fairbanks. But when it came to Pickford, he faltered. "Of Mrs. Douglas Fairbanks I find difficulty in writing, for there is a consciousness of vagueness, an indefinable emotion as to her precise degree of accomplishment."[3] Rotha, writing in 1930, was having the same trouble as the reviewer in 1916.

Perhaps it required the perception of a poet to solve the mystery of Mary Pickford's gifts. Vachel Lindsay had no doubts about her, and in 1915 he gladly shared his discovery: "Why do the people love Mary? Because of a certain aspect of her face in her highest mood. Botticelli painted her portrait many centuries ago when by some necromancy she appeared to him in this phase of herself.... The people are hungry for this fine and spiritual thing that Botticelli painted in the faces of his Muses and heavenly creatures. Because the mob catch the very glimpse of it in Mary's face, they follow her night after night in the films."[4]

Without the certain vision of poets, most writers now, in assessing Pickford's place in history, confine their observations to the spectacular if not particularly revealing details of her financial triumphs. They generally affix on her (much more so than on Chaplin) the implied opprobrium of having firmly established the star system to the detriment of the whole course of motion picture history. Such materialistic evasion fails to probe any of the reasons that Pickford's films were so successful that she could challenge the fiscal supremacy of Chaplin.

One of the basic reasons for the historians' remarkably inarticulate understanding of the Pickford genius is that few of them ever looked at her pictures. Most of the Chaplin films have been repeatedly reissued over the years. Fairbanks's *Robin Hood* was still available for rental in the United Artists' exchanges as late as 1933. And two years later the Museum of Modern Art Film Library undertook the circulation of various classics of the cinema, but none of the Pickford features was among them.

The disappearance of the Pickford films was no accident. In a *Photoplay* interview with Ruth Biery that appeared in May 1931, Pickford dispensed a ghastly piece of news: "I am adding a codicil to my will. It says that when I go, my films go with me. They are to be destroyed. I am buying all my old films for this purpose. I would rather be a beautiful illusion in the minds of people than a horrible example on celluloid. I pleased my own generation. That is all that matters."[5]

Luckily for the history of motion pictures, she later reconsidered the cruel destruction of her own shadows and made a gift of her collected films to the Library of Congress. In 1952 Pickford also granted the George Eastman House permission to assist in saving her films. Now, thanks to that wise and enlightened decision, so happily at variance with her original intention of wiping out forever the vision she had created, both the George Eastman House and the Library of Congress have preserved on long-lived acetate film the majority of Pickford's most important movies—the lasting contributions of her unparalleled career that extended from 1909 to 1933.[6]

At last, the films of the third member of "the presiding deities of the cinema," as Barry called Chaplin, Pickford, and Fairbanks, are available for the study of any historian or writer who is seriously interested in the history of motion pictures. And looking at these films, one is immediately struck by the enormity of the gap in all written film history that now exists, the void in all works that have failed to consider these missing links in the vast pattern provided by that exceptional triumvirate.

Whether one ponders the Chaplin-Pickford-Fairbanks films for their intrinsic accomplishments or for their great success throughout the world, it becomes startlingly clear after repeated screenings that although they represent the work of three unique artists, they are all animated by a curiously related esprit de corps; there is a kind of family resemblance that becomes quite marked in the years between 1915 and 1925. If, in her chases, in her grotesqueries as gamin, urchin, or enfant terrible, Pickford quite often seems to be doing Chaplin routines, we should remember that it is just as likely to be the other way around. Chaplin, when he clowns by suddenly becoming mock-heroic in the midst of slapstick, enacts Fairbanks, with head held high and romantic valor flashing from his eyes. And Fairbanks, along with all his own lyrical movements, can, on occasion, shrug and skip away au Charlot, to underline his indifference to the odds against him.

Fairbanks and Chaplin were close, intimate friends. After Mary and Doug married in 1920, the three of them spent much of their free time at Pickfair. Together they screened their own and one another's films, discussing their results, their plans, and their hopes. Pickford wrote: "the three of us became almost inseparable ... we had become virtually one family."[7] It is not surprising that their film work bears both visible and intangible kinship.

But of the three, there was no question about who had seniority of experience. When Chaplin began work on the first film of his career at the end of 1913, Pickford was already an international celebrity and the first great star of motion pictures, with four years, more than 125 short dramas, and three full-length features behind her. Fairbanks made his first picture in 1915 (The Lamb), at a time when Pickford was about to demand (and receive) the unheard of salary (at the time) of $10,000 a week.

The past absence of Pickford films from the programs of film societies and the showings of institutions devoted to film history led to the unchallenged growth of a total misconception of what her films were like. Among the writers who have tended to sidetrack this creative talent that was so basic to the development of the silent film, the notion prevails that all Pickford vehicles are rather trivial variants of the Cinderella theme. Either out of respect for Pickford's unassailable position as one of the cinema greats or out of praiseworthy caution owing to their not having seen her films, many writers only circuitously imply that Pickford's performances are the epitome of saccharine banality, sweetness, and light and permeated with the philosophy of Pollyanna.

While it is true that Pickford confessed to a penchant for tearful scenes involving the demise of an infant, a beloved parent or guardian, and occasionally herself, the idea that the prevailing note of Pickford films is one of sentimentality is totally wrong. If Pickford portrayed many versions of Cinderella, her slavey character was no feckless, weak-willed, or dispirited heroine pining away for rescue at the hands of a fairy godmother or Prince Charming. Those of her films devoted to the rags-to-riches story invariably present the ragged one as a battling hellcat, morally and physically committed to all-out attack against the forces of evil, bigotry, or malicious snobbery that seek to frustrate the proper denouement of a triumphant, lovely girl appropriately presented in stunning close-up, her incomparable curls backlighted and the Botticelli smile shimmering through the last glittering remnants of any leftover teardrops.

Lobby card from M'liss *(1918). M'liss (Pickford) confronts the men responsible for the murder of her father.*

MARY PICKFORD IN "M'LISS"

"YOU'RE A-LYIN'!"

ARTCRAFT PICTURES

In the whole gallery of her roles, she has presented us with dozens of rough-and-ready young ladies of action—action that, in many cases, is so rugged as to raise the eyebrows of present-day viewers, whom one might suppose had seen their share of cinematic horrors. Pickford has been a night rider, meting out summary mountain justice in the robe of the Ku Klux Klan (in *Heart O' the Hills*), and she has done battle royal in a frontier saloon to bring out her drunken father (in *Rags*), whereas some writers have depicted her as more the type to sing "Father Dear Father" in a white nightgown. She has shown us her fiancé hesitating at the entrance to a brothel (in *Amarilly of Clothesline Alley*), and in *Stella Maris* we have seen her leading man married to one of the screen's most convincing alcoholics, played with memorable distinction by Marcia Manon. The villains of *M'liss* are lynched with everyone else's hearty approval. In the swampland baby farm of *Sparrows*, Pickford's character succeeds in preventing Mr. Grimes from tossing a kidnapped infant into quicksand, fights him off with a pitchfork, and leads her young charges in flight through a nightmare morass of terror, compounded by the slavering jaws of a pursuing mastiff and lurking alligators.

None of these roles is remotely redolent of Sunnybrook Farm or Frances Hodgson Burnett. They are part of the wonderful variety of screen performances by the gifted Mary Pickford throughout a total of fifty-two full-length feature films. In them, she has molded a screen character that may be considered, on a feminine plane, an achievement comparable to the creation of Chaplin's tramp.

There is a scene in *Rags*, made in 1915, that points up an essential difference between these two equally lovable personages. Pickford, as Rags, lives in a broken-down miner's shack with her father, who is the town drunk. She is tattered and dirty, abjectly poverty stricken. But romance has come to her in the person of a handsome young miner, Mickey Neilan. Rags invites him to lunch at her tumbledown home; she makes loving preparations, fixing a meal and setting the table with flowers in a scene that inevitably brings to mind the famous Chaplin party sequence in *The Gold Rush*. It is equally touching, the situation is much the same, and, of course, Pickford's version preceded Chaplin's by ten years. Rags steps out of her shack to fetch something to complete the decor. She is gone just long enough for her father to come lurching in with a drunken companion. They eat most of the food, mess up the rest, and leave her pretty table in a shambles. Rags returns to see the destruction and then beholds her sweetheart on his way up the path for their first date. In *The Gold Rush* Chaplin effectively wrenches our hearts with his agony of disappointment and chagrin when the loved one fails to show up. In *Rags,* instead of feeling sorry for herself and breaking down in tearful frustration, Pickford slams the door shut and goes to work. With lightning efficiency, she cleans the mess and distributes the few remaining crumbs on her guest's plate, then opens the door to him. When he looks at his fantastically sparse meal and at her empty plate, she smiles at him and says, "I was so hungry I just couldn't wait for you."

In Rags (1915), Pickford plays a spunky teenager who lives in a mining town with her alcoholic father.

DANIEL FROHMAN
PRESENTS
MARY PICKFORD
IN
"RAGS"
PRODUCED BY
FAMOUS PLAYERS FILM CO.
ADOLPH ZUKOR, PRES.

In The Foundling *(1916), Molly O (Pickford) glares disapprovingly at her dog after she discovers that it has had puppies. Popular with family audiences, animals were often used for comedy or pathos in Pickford features.*

Pickford, as the East Indian girl Rahda, with actor David Powell in a scene from Less than the Dust *(1916).*

There is no doubt that, most of the time, Pickford had her sights trained on the American women, young children, and families who made a ritual of attending the neighborhood movie theater one or two nights a week. This was the audience that demonstrated quite clearly (at the box office) that it wanted Mary Pickford to play little-girl roles. She had to remain the Little Mary they had first discovered playing in the Biograph films when she was fifteen.[8]

To please her family audience, she used whole menageries of cute performing animals. There were kittens and puppies, shaggy dogs and goats, donkeys, pigs and piglets, performing geese, waltzing ponies, and tipsy ducks. And she ranged quite thoroughly over the popular heroines of the younger set in those days: there was Rebecca of Sunnybrook Farm, Sara Crewe, and Pollyanna, too. But she also gave us Madame Butterfly, the East Indian of *Less than the Dust*, the ugly drudge of *Suds*, the cigar-puffing messenger boy of *Poor Little Peppina*, the mature DeMille heroine of *The Little American*, and the tragic protector of an enemy soldier in *The Love Light*.

The fact that Mary Pickford was discovered not by a talent scout, not by a producer or director, but by the public itself is a tribute to the power of her personality and her beauty. The dramatic story of how she came to work for the Biograph Company and D. W. Griffith in 1909 has now become legend. But the lost part of the story is that, earlier, she had tried to get work at Biograph and failed. When she was in Chicago with David Belasco's *Warrens of Virginia* company, she tried for a film job with Essanay, where, years later, Gloria Swanson and Chaplin would both make comedies. But Essanay, too, had the historic distinction of refusing to hire Mary Pickford. Not until the spring of 1909, with *The Warrens of Virginia* closed and Pickford back in New York, did she try Biograph for the second time. And for the second time, the office had no work for her. She was on her way out when she met Griffith, who asked if she had any stage experience. She was able to tell him, proudly, "Ten years" (although she was only sixteen). When Griffith learned that two of those years had been spent in a Belasco production, Pickford was in.

About fourteen years later, Griffith was glad to point out that Pickford had won her spurs in his early Biograph one-reel dramas and to suggest that he had given her the best parts in these films. But Pickford has denied such a claim. Looking at many of the 1909 and 1910 Biographs tends to bear out her version; she plays many bit parts and secondary roles, and not until 1911 and 1912 does she seem to be carrying a reasonably large share of the leading parts.

How she could have counted on "becom[ing] known" through the Biograph films of 1909 to 1912 is a mystery. The players were anonymous then, and, contrary to later claims, close-ups of actors were not used, not even by Griffith, until late in 1912. With the harsh, flat lighting of naked sunlight for the exteriors and mercury vapor lights in the studios, and with the camera fixed in position to shoot only medium long shots, differentiating one person from another from film to film was quite an achievement.

Pickford and Broadway producer David Belasco
share a laugh in 1913. The actress and her art form
would soon surpass the theater in popularity.

Nevertheless, Pickford did stand out, even in the crowded sets of the Biograph one-reelers. In her first year she started getting notices. In the August 21, 1909, issue of the *New York Dramatic Mirror*, she is singled out in the review of the Biograph film *They Would Elope*: "This delicious little comedy introduces again an ingénue whose work in Biograph pictures is attracting attention." Her work attracted such attention that she supplanted Florence Lawrence as the public-invented Biograph Girl. And in England, lacking an official name, she was given one by the British: Dorothy Nicholson. After Carl Laemmle temporarily lured her away from Biograph and gave publicity to the Pickford name, the secret was out, and reviewers could place credit with confidence, as this one did in writing of *The Italian Barber* in *Motion Picture News* (January 28, 1911): "*The Italian Barber*, also a Biograph, was most interesting because it contained 'Little Mary.' I guess Carl didn't get some 'scoop' when he secured this talented little lady. Can a duck swim?" In *Moving Picture World* (November 2, 1912), *The One She Loved* is reviewed: "In it, once again the Biograph producer, whom everybody knows is Mr. Griffith, has succeeded in picturing something that seems to be finer and sweeter than words. The best scenes of it are also a great personal triumph for Little Mary."

In 1913 Mary Pickford left Biograph, Griffith, and filmmaking for good—or so she thought at the time. She had decided to return permanently to the theater, and the title role in Belasco's *A Good Little Devil* provided her with the opportunity she hoped for. But one evening when the play was on its pre-Broadway tryout run, a prophetic incident occurred. Pickford described it as "the first real intimation that I had that the films were making for themselves vast audiences.... On Christmas Day, in Baltimore, Ernest Lawford, who was one of the cast, knocked on my dressing room door and called: 'There are hundreds of people waiting in the alley to see Little Mary, Queen of the Movies, leave the theater!'" Perhaps it was those hundreds who saw her leave the theater that Christmas Day who helped Pickford change her mind. She left the theater forever at the end of the play's successful Broadway run and returned to the cinema. And it is scarcely an exaggeration to say that she took most of the Belasco audiences right along with her.

Pickford, with actors Iva Merlin and
William Morris, at the top level of a two-tiered
set (Henry Stanford is below), in the 1913
Broadway production of A Good Little Devil.

The Striking Action Poses in the Play at the Republic Theatre

Pickford and the cast of David Belasco's play
A Good Little Devil are caricatured in the
New York Morning Telegraph, *February 9, 1913.*

In the spring of 1913 the movie version of *A Good Little Devil* was filmed in New York City by Adolph Zukor's Famous Players Company. This picture, almost a straight reproduction of the play, with most of its original cast, became the first of Pickford's fifty-two feature films.[9] Thirty-one of these pictures can now be screened at Eastman House by anyone who feels impelled to rewrite the history of the cinema and to begin filling in a major, almost unknown continent on the map of motion picture achievement.[10]

Whoever studies these films will no longer have to wonder why Mary Pickford's success was so phenomenal. Her courage, her will, her determination, her love, and her faith are the life-giving elements in each of her great screen roles, just as they are the facts of her own life. Sometimes it seems that these qualities have gone out of fashion on the contemporary screen—perhaps they are disappearing from our electronic-brained life. Whether this is true or not, Mary Pickford has had no successor on the screen.

The best part of the rediscovery of the Pickford films is that the measure of their greatness does not depend on the isolated opinions of a few connoisseurs or, worse, on the cherished preciousness of the cultist's infatuation. Pickford's pictures are shown repeatedly to the public in the Dryden Theatre of Eastman House, and in these continuing encounters, her art stays wonderfully alive. The kids still giggle and squeal over her antics. It is not unusual to hear women become engulfed in sobs when Mary's tears begin to glisten. She still charms, and she always will. The poet, too, was right—there is something heavenly about Mary Pickford. It is a quality, we must admit, most uncommon in motion pictures. ❧

MARY PICKFORD AND THE ARCHIVAL FILM MOVEMENT

Christel Schmidt

*What a wonderful thing it is to think that when we actors and
actresses who appear in moving picture productions are dead
and gone, our likeness will still be preserved and our actions
and characteristics shown on to generation after generation.*

Mary Pickford, 1914

*Pickford cuts a ribbon of film at the opening of the George
Eastman House Museum of Photography on November 9, 1949.
She is joined by the museum's director, Oscar Solbert (left),
and the president of Eastman Kodak, Thomas J. Hargrave (right).*

NINETEENTH-CENTURY stage star Lawrence Barrett once said that acting a role was like "carving a statue out of snow."[1] Indeed, before the invention of cinema, all that remained of an actor's performance was a memory in the viewer's mind. The silent film camera, designed to record only images, could fully capture the work of movie actors whose voices were not a part of their art. Mary Pickford, like many of her colleagues, marveled at the thought of screen immortality. However, as early as 1921, she felt a growing concern that the technical simplicity of her early films would earn audience ridicule.[2] This was one of the reasons she purchased her Biograph films (made between 1909 and 1912) from producer Nathan Hirsh in 1921 and remade her great 1914 success *Tess of the Storm Country* in 1922.[3] Seven years later, the arrival of talking pictures dealt silent film a fatal blow; the world's leading form of entertainment for nearly three decades had become obsolete, seemingly overnight. The immediate acceptance of the new medium and the ease with which the old art form was discarded only exacerbated the actress's insecurities.

Pickford, the silents' most enduring star, fell out of fashion; the press, which had once cheered her, now seemed to relish her failure. Her response was alarming. She announced that she planned to add a codicil to her will, requiring that all her films be destroyed, "except in the imagination of future generations."[4] Apparently, Pickford shared the views of a 1906 article in *Munsey's Magazine* that stated, without a lasting record of an actor's work, her reputation enters into legend, "whatever the changes of critical theory and whatever the vagaries of public opinion." The verdict of her contemporaries "is final and posterity has no court of appeal."[5]

But privately, Pickford was conflicted. She later credited her change of mind to the public's negative reaction and to Lillian Gish's firm opinion that silent pictures would be valued in the future. By the mid-1930s, Pickford not only sought a permanent archival home for her vast private movie collection but also became a strong advocate for the archival film movement.

In 1935, when the Film Library at the Museum of Modern Art (MoMA) opened in New York, Pickford was an early and avid supporter.[6] The first major cinema archive in the United States, the Film Library began with a mission to collect, preserve, and exhibit selected films that form a "record of the motion-picture as an industry" by choosing "examples of the motion picture as an artistic creation." Pickford championed the cause in the press, saying, "As one of the pioneers of the industry, I ... believe in the preservation of significant and outstanding films to be of great historic and educational value."[7] The actress also became a donor, offering the new archive ten Biograph titles from her personal collection.

The relationship between Pickford and MoMA's Film Library deteriorated following a July 9, 1937, fire at a storage facility in Little Ferry, New Jersey, which burned a portion of the museum's nitrate film collection. Pickford had provided three of the ten promised Biograph one-reelers to the museum prior to the blaze. These camera negatives—*The Violin Maker of Cremona* (1909), *Lena and the Geese* (1912), and *The New York Hat* (1912)—were apparently lost. Sadly, the star had experienced the loss of her work before. In 1915 a fire at the Famous

Players studio in New York had destroyed several film negatives, including an unreleased Pickford feature called *The Foundling* (it was promptly refilmed). Although she may have sympathized with MoMA (she later claimed that she and the archive had a falling out over the exhibition of her films), her involvement with the museum ended.[8]

Pickford might have been finished with MoMA, but she was still devoted to film archiving. On May 6, 1938, she visited the National Archives in Washington, D.C., to discuss the preservation of American films and to urge the institution to assist in saving the nation's movie heritage. In direct contrast to MoMA's narrow selection policy, Pickford told the archives' staff that *all* films "should be preserved for the use of universities and researchers."[9] She was given a tour of the film vaults, where the government stored two million feet of historic footage relating to the United States. Later that fall, the National Archives accepted Pickford's donation of a 35mm print of her 1912 short *The New York Hat*, but it was unable to further support her cause because the institution had no mandate to collect and preserve nondocumentary film.

Pickford meets with staff from the National Archives to discuss the state of American film preservation. John C. Bradley (second from the left), head of motion pictures at the archives, later worked at the Library of Congress and was instrumental in its acquisition of the Pickford film collection.

Opposite: One of eighteen rare movie stills from the 1915 version of The Foundling. *The film's negative was destroyed in a fire just two weeks after these photographs—the only known to survive—were submitted for copyright. Actors Frank Mills (left) and Gibson Gowland (right) appear with Pickford.*

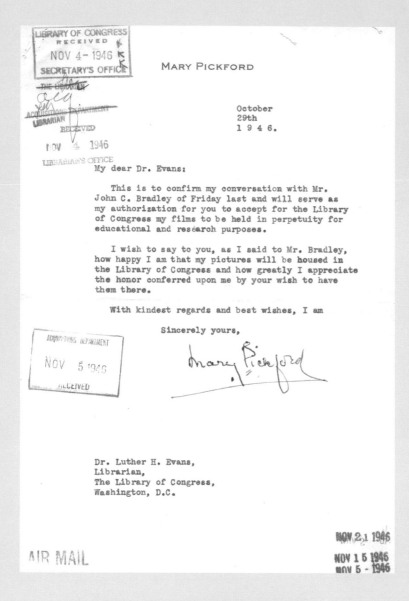

MARY PICKFORD

October
29th
1 9 4 6.

My dear Dr. Evans:

This is to confirm my conversation with Mr.
John C. Bradley of Friday last and will serve as
my authorization for you to accept for the Library
of Congress my films to be held in perpetuity for
educational and research purposes.

I wish to say to you, as I said to Mr. Bradley,
how happy I am that my pictures will be housed in
the Library of Congress and how greatly I appreciate
the honor conferred upon me by your wish to have
them there.

With kindest regards and best wishes, I am

Sincerely yours,

Mary Pickford

Dr. Luther H. Evans,
Librarian,
The Library of Congress,
Washington, D.C.

AIR MAIL

*Letter, dated October 29, 1946, from Pickford to the
Librarian of Congress, Dr. Luther H. Evans, confirming the
donation of her film collection to the Library of Congress.*

The National Archives' inability to aid in movie preservation most likely left Pickford feeling discouraged. However, her efforts led another institution, one that was just developing plans for a film archive, to contact her. In 1942 Archibald MacLeish, the Librarian of Congress, became interested in creating a Motion Picture Division. The Library of Congress already had some moving image materials (mostly paper rolls dating from 1894 to 1915), but it was now ready to actually start collecting and preserving motion pictures. MacLeish approached Pickford in 1943 with a request for her film collection, which she readily approved. Her enthusiasm led to further discussions about her assisting with funds for an in-house movie theater; giving the Library her collection of photographs, scripts, and other movie memorabilia; and facilitating relationships in Hollywood. Unfortunately, the Library's progress on these ventures was slow. It was late 1946—three and a half years after the original request—when the Pickford Collection was officially received by the institution. Six months later, Congress cut funding for the fledgling Motion Picture Division, effectively dismantling it. Naturally, Pickford was frustrated and angry. Two years later, she turned to a promising new institution.

In November 1949 the George Eastman House opened in Rochester, New York. It began as primarily a still photography museum, but the founders acknowledged the importance of the moving image by asking Pickford to speak there on opening day. Her appearance in Rochester added an air of celebrity glamour to the festivities and gave the actress an opportunity to publicly discuss the history and value of motion pictures. It was also the beginning of a long and happy association with Eastman House. Pickford later worked with museum director Oscar Solbert and film curator James Card to preserve her film collection, and both the Library of Congress and Eastman House received copies.[10] In 1955 and 1957 she returned to Rochester to accept (with twenty-four of her peers) the museum's George Award, given to the pioneers of silent cinema. In 1958 she sat down at Pickfair for a recorded interview with George Pratt, who worked with Card as assistant film curator; she later kept up a friendly correspondence with them both. She also ardently supported the screenings of her films at the museum's Dryden Theater.

Though pleased with the East Coast's preservation efforts, Pickford wanted to see film history collected, preserved, and honored in Los Angeles, the industry's hometown.[11] Committed to the cause, she even flirted with the idea of making Pickfair into a museum.[12] Then, in the early 1960s, plans to build one elsewhere picked up steam. The Hollywood Museum, which had had Pickford's support since the late 1950s, would not only collect film and memorabilia but also have an exhibition hall, graduate school, sound stage, and more. As she had for MoMA, the Library of Congress, and Eastman House, the actress offered the Hollywood Museum material from her movie collection. But this time, she also searched European film archives and private collections, hoping to turn up additional titles. She offered Pickfair, rarely opened for such events, to the project founders and their guests. The seventy-one-year-old actress also attended public hearings and events, including a January 1964 trip to Washington, D.C., where the Hollywood Museum sponsored a luncheon in honor of the Library of Congress.[13] According to the *Washington Post*, Pickford "dazzled most in the spotlight" as she stole the show from the other guests, including singer Nat King Cole, producer George Stevens Jr., and the daughter of Thomas Edison.

The actress's passion for the Hollywood Museum project waned when plans started to unravel. In April 1965 the *Los Angeles Times* revealed a host of problems facing the museum's organizers, including a "headstrong" leader (producer Sol Lesser), loss of staff and supporters, and a building design that many considered economically impractical. These and many other factors were all part of the museum's slow, disorganized demise in the mid-1960s.[14] Pickford, like several others, had given up on the project months before. In 1965 she focused on a request from another institution. The Cinémathèque Française in Paris was hosting a major retrospective of her work and wanted to buy twenty film titles for its permanent collection. Pickford gladly agreed to the purchase.

After the retrospective in France, Pickford retired from public life, which included abandoning the push for a film museum in Los Angeles. She had always feared that she would not live long enough to see one. Happily, one of that city's most important film archives, at the University of California–Los Angeles, began operations during her lifetime.[15] Today, the facility is known as the UCLA Film and Television Archive. In the end, Pickford chose the Library of Congress, already the major repository for her movies, to receive her remaining film collection at her death. ༄

Pickford shakes hands with cinematographer George Folsey at the George Eastman House in 1957. The museum honored her and twenty-four of her peers for their work in the silent film industry.

California senator Thomas H. Kuchel (center) greets Pickford and Librarian of Congress L. Quincy Mumford at a luncheon in the Library's honor in January 1964.

The Mary Pickford Film Collection at the Library of Congress

Christel Schmidt

Scenes from four movies in the Mary Pickford film collection at the Library of Congress: Henry B. Walthall and Pickford in The One She Loved *(1912); a dramatic moment from* Sparrows *(1926); Pickford watching a scene from* Little Annie Rooney *(1925) during filming; and the actress in period costume for* Rags *(1915).*

THE LIBRARY OF CONGRESS Packard Campus for Audio Visual Conservation (PCAVC), a state-of-the-art facility for storing and preserving audiovisual materials, is home to the largest archival collection of motion pictures starring Mary Pickford. Currently, the Library retains moving image materials representing 156 Pickford titles out of the estimated 210 she made between 1909 and 1933. (Sadly, 36 films are considered lost.) Over the past century, a number of films have been acquired through copyright deposits, through repatriations from European archives, and from movie collectors. However, the Library received most of the films from the actress herself, who made a gift of her collection in the 1940s. This donation—which covers her entire career—provides not only a comprehensive record of the work of one of cinema's great artists but also a unique and sweeping view of Hollywood's pioneering era, from the days of one-reelers to the early years of sound. As such, it is one of the PCAVC's most important collections. It is also one of the first major gifts of moving image materials the Library received in its long quest to establish a motion picture archive. The Pickford Collection's often complex history at the Library of Congress reflects both the struggle and the tremendous strides made by the institution and in the field of film preservation.

In 1943 the Library's management drew up a plan to create a Motion Picture Division that would collect and preserve American cinema and make it accessible to the public. For its first major acquisition, Librarian of Congress Archibald MacLeish sought a high-profile donor with strong Hollywood connections as well as an extensive film collection. Pickford, who had retired from acting a decade earlier, was still a respected and powerful figure in the industry, and she was a strong proponent of film preservation. As producer and distributor of many of her features, she often owned the early release copies, foreign and domestic camera negatives, and work prints. She had also acquired half of her earliest Paramount films (made before she had producing credit), as well as most of her one-reel Biograph shorts. In the summer of 1943 MacLeish wrote to Pickford, offering to make the Library of Congress the "ultimate repository" for her vast film collection. She agreed.

In late 1946, after preparations had been made for storage, the Library formally accepted the actress's donation.[1] But shortly after preservation began, Congress cut funding for the Motion Picture Division, effectively dismantling it. The process of copying the unstable nitrate films in the Pickford Collection to safety stock was halted, leaving the material in limbo. Without preservation, her life's work was in danger of being permanently lost, and relations between the Library and Pickford became strained.

Luckily, Oscar Solbert and James Card, director and film curator at the George Eastman House, respectively,

intervened. In 1956 they convinced the star to pay for the preservation of her collection and to give the Library of Congress and Eastman House a print of each of the preserved films. To save on costs, Pickford's original 35mm materials were copied onto 16mm stock, even though it was considered an inadequate form of preservation. Once the work was finished, the Library returned the nitrate films to the actress.

By the 1960s, the Library of Congress had created a Motion Picture Section within the Prints and Photographs Division and began to work with the newly formed American Film Institute (AFI) to acquire and preserve the nation's movie heritage. With the relationship between Pickford and the Library much improved, she agreed to donate fifty Biograph camera negatives (the majority directed by D. W. Griffith) to the AFI for eventual inclusion in the Library's collection. This new Pickford gift included such notable titles as *To Save Her Soul* (1909), *Ramona* (1910), and *A Beast at Bay* (1912). Along with the negatives, the actress donated nitrate release prints of some Biograph titles, including *Her First Biscuits* (1909), *The Smoker* (1910), *A Decree of Destiny* (1911), and *Friends* (1912). After preserving the camera negatives on 35mm film, the AFI transferred them to the Library of Congress. There were subsequent discussions between the AFI and Pickford about more donations, but questions raised by Pickford's staff about the AFI's handling of the material

brought an end to their relationship. In the future, the Library of Congress would have to work directly with Pickford and her associates to obtain more of her collection.

The Library built a strong relationship with the actress during the late 1960s and early 1970s. At Pickford's request, the institution repatriated a rare tinted nitrate print of *Cinderella* (1914) from Holland and promised to preserve her films on 35mm. However, the Library was also working on a plan to expand its ability to collect and preserve the nation's cinematic heritage, as well as to reestablish a division devoted to motion pictures (aligning them with broadcasting and recorded sound). Opened on July 31, 1978, the Motion Picture, Broadcasting, and Recorded Sound (MBRS) Division was a giant step in this vital preservation initiative. Unfortunately, organizing the new division necessitated a slowdown of preservation projects. When Mary Pickford died on May 29, 1979, at age eighty-seven, the Library had not yet undertaken additional work on the actress's film collection.

Almost immediately, Librarian Daniel J. Boorstin contacted those in control of the Pickford estate, expressing his wish to "keep [the actress's] name and achievements alive at the Library." His ideas included a movie theater named in her honor (an idea he had broached with Pickford in 1976). The Pickford Theater opened in the Library's James Madison Memorial Building in 1983. It was funded by half

a million dollars from Pickford's foundation, which also contributed to other MBRS Division projects. Pickford herself had already given the Library a remarkable final gift when she donated the bulk of her film collection to the institution in her will.

Thanks to Pickford's bequest, the Library has received motion picture material from her estate over the past thirty years, including nineteen Biograph camera negatives, five complete nitrate features, and miscellaneous footage such as outtakes, home movies, and newsreel clips. The institution has preserved much of this material, including the shorts *Simple Charity* (1910) and *The Female of the Species* (1912); her first sound film, *Coquette* (1929); test shots from the never-completed *Forever Yours* (1930); and behind-the-scenes shots from *Little Annie Rooney* (1925). In the past five years, the Library restored *Sparrows* (1926) and a number of her Biograph shorts. In 2013 the film laboratory at the PCAVC is slated to complete the restoration of two Pickford features, *Rags* (1915) and *The Pride of the Clan* (1917). Since the division's inception, MBRS curators have also procured additional Pickford materials from sources other than the actress and her estate. Most recently, it acquired prints of the rare titles *Little Red Riding Hood* (1911) and *The Dawn of a Tomorrow* (1915). All these projects are part of the Library's continuing commitment to the preservation of Pickford's unique film legacy. ☙

The Mary Pickford Photograph Collection at the Academy of Motion Picture Arts and Sciences' Margaret Herrick Library

Robert Cushman

This is an edited version of a piece originally published in Kevin Brownlow, Mary Pickford Rediscovered: Rare Pictures of a Hollywood Legend (New York: Harry N. Abrams, 1999).

Shortly after I began working at the Margaret Herrick Library in 1972, I contacted silent film actress Mary Pickford about the possibility of her donating her collection of still photographs and papers to the institution. She responded that, although she didn't have very much left, she would eventually give us what remained. When the Academy held the grand opening of its new Wilshire Boulevard building in 1975, we decided to feature a huge Pickford exhibit (on two floors) to commemorate the event. In addition to being one of the great figures of film history and a founder of the Academy of Motion Picture Arts and Sciences, it is widely believed that the original concept for the organization was hers.

The Herrick Library already had a respectable number of Pickford photos. But, hoping to make the exhibit as spectacular as possible, I asked for permission to borrow stills from Pickford's private collection, which we would copy for inclusion in the exhibit. She immediately gave her consent, and I went to Pickfair to see what she had. Her husband, Buddy Rogers, led me to a basement area and into a small furnace room. There, on shelves along one wall, sat a huge array of photo albums filled with film stills. He turned me loose and even found me a pair of pliers and a screwdriver so that I could take the books apart to access individual prints. At the end of the day, I borrowed more than 600 prints, some for inclusion in the exhibit, but most to be copied for the library's files.

We realized that Pickford had much more material than she knew; meanwhile, there was no further word regarding the collection coming to the Academy. When Pickford died in 1979, her will made no mention of her photographs, papers, and other memorabilia. It was up to Rogers to decide what would happen to them. When I reminded him of her letter about the material going to the Academy, he immediately agreed that it should.

There was no progress for over a year, as we awaited the sale of Pickfair. When it was sold in 1980, the premises had to be emptied of all contents, and off I went to round up the collection. This process took several days, as we discovered there was material scattered throughout the massive house: in various basement areas, in closets, in Pickford's room, in the attic, in her secretary's office, in storage areas next to the porte cochère and under the guest wing, and in the enormous garage. There, amidst piles of cast-off furniture and every other imaginable sort of flotsam, were several crates containing even more stills and—incredibly—several thousand original eight-by-ten nitrate photo negatives from Pickford's film productions, some dating back to 1918. Even though they had been there for decades with no temperature and humidity control, they were nearly all in perfect condition. This was an unexpected bonanza. We later preserved these negatives, and prints made from them now reside in the Pickford Collection at the Herrick Library.

I combed every room, closet, and piece of furniture from basement to attic—all the while witnessing the entire contents of Pickfair being dismantled and removed—an eerie, disheartening, and somewhat depressing experience. The material I was able to claim for the Academy—photos, papers, scrapbooks, clippings, and so forth—was removed in scores of boxes, the contents of each box constituting one piece of a gigantic jigsaw puzzle. It became our job at the library to organize the collection so that it formed a comprehensive picture of Pickford's career. However, the albums of film stills I had gone through in 1975 were nowhere to be found. Later, to my dismay, I discovered that during the dismantling of Pickfair, someone had managed to spirit them away and had sold them to various memorabilia dealers around town. Luckily, we had already copied hundreds of the best photos, and later, I personally bought several hundred more from one of the dealers.

I had long been interested in Pickford's career and had collected more than 3,000 Pickford stills over the previous fifteen years. I decided that these should join the Academy's Pickford Collection, but I was in no financial position to make an outright gift of them. Fortunately, the Pickford Foundation gave the Academy a grant to purchase my photos and add them to the Herrick Library's collection. My photographs covered all of Pickford's 1913–1918 feature films very well; her holdings for the same years had been sparse. Thus, the amalgamation of the two collections was a happy and appropriate one.

Then more material came from Buddy Rogers and his wife, Beverly. They had retained a large quantity of Pickford memorabilia and gave the Academy nearly all of it. Around the same time, Pickford Foundation trustee Edward G. Stotsenberg also donated Mary's financial and accounting records, which he had maintained in his office.

The Academy's Pickford Collection covers photographically Mary's 52 feature films (1913–1933) and most of her 108 Biograph shorts (1909–1912). Also included are more than 80 scrapbooks, script and story property material, and other papers. Unfortunately, written materials are scant for the years during which she produced and appeared in her own films. Her production and correspondence files for these years are conspicuously absent. Could they have been inadvertently disposed of without her knowledge? Were the files destroyed, or are they still lying dormant in some unknown location? We can only hope that someday they will surface.

I close, however, with the comforting thought that the photographs in the Mary Pickford Collection at the Margaret Herrick Library are unprecedented in their comprehensiveness and volume and are unequaled by any other archive in the world. ॐ

A Pickford portrait (circa 1935) from her photograph collection at the Academy of Motion Picture Arts and Sciences.

The Mary Pickford Costume and Ephemera Collection at the Natural History Museum of Los Angeles County

Beth Werling

AMONG THE ESTIMATED 35 million artifacts and specimens that reside at the Natural History Museum of Los Angeles County (NHMLAC) is a collection of fifty objects that document Mary Pickford's role as Hollywood's first movie star and female film mogul. Postcards displaying scenes from the actress's now-lost first features, a pair of badges bearing her photograph from the Motion Picture Exhibitors' Ball in 1914, costumes from the 1920s, and her iconic blond curls are some of the items that make up Pickford's extraordinary donation to the museum.

Why did Pickford decide to give her career-defining collection to the NHMLAC? The answer is deceptively simple; the institution's name does not reflect its origins or its mission. Although associated primarily with dinosaurs and other scientific specimens, the NHMLAC's History Department has a mandate to collect and preserve artifacts from an array of Los Angeles–based industries.[1] Since 1930, the museum has solicited items from people and organizations in the movie business, including studios, moguls, inventors, animators, cameramen, and actors. Today the institution is home to the world's foremost collection of artifacts from early motion pictures, including scenarios, costumes, animation cels, cameras, set models, mercury vapor lights, editing equipment, sound effects devices, and more.

In 1932 Pickford, who was starting to take a serious interest in the preservation of Hollywood history, responded to the museum's request for cinema-related donations. She gave a variety of materials from all aspects of her career as an actress, producer, movie star, and international celebrity. Pickford was not merely cleaning out her closets and storage facilities. She cared deeply for her career and her public image, and the objects in her collection reflect the thought and attention she devoted to her legacy.

Among her artifacts are magnificent gowns from films such as *Rosita* (1923), *Dorothy Vernon of Haddon Hall* (1924), and *Coquette* (1929). Pickford also donated precious items received while traveling the world with her husband, Douglas Fairbanks. The couple was greeted as royalty and given gifts of appreciation from the hosts of the nations they visited. The NHMLAC received three of these foreign treasures: a kimono from Japan, a matador's suit from Spain, and a headdress from Russia.

Nothing, however, evokes the image of Mary Pickford more than her donation of five coils of golden hair. Still glistening, the curls (each about eleven inches long) were shorn in June 1928. Today, these ringlets are among the top ten most requested items in the entire museum. Their impact is visceral, prompting a range of emotions from reverence to morbid curiosity. Children who have never heard of Pickford are instantly engaged: Can we clone her? Is that real hair? How does it stay curled?

The curiosity value of the curls, the exotic gifts, and the glorious costumes is a wonderful tool for opening the door to silent film history, grabbing visitors' attention and enticing them to stay, look, and learn about this movie pioneer. By donating these items and other memorabilia to the museum, Pickford provided the means to marvel at and better comprehend the twentieth century's definitive art form: the motion picture. ❧

Opposite, top: Tinted postcards from two of Pickford's earliest features: In the Bishop's Carriage *and* Caprice *(both 1913). No copies of the films are known to exist.*

Opposite, bottom left: Five of Pickford's famous golden curls.

Opposite, center right: One of two identical badges from the 1914 Motion Picture Exhibitors' Ball donated to the museum by Pickford. Her appearance at the event created a sensation among attendees.

Opposite, bottom right: Bejeweled headdress given to Pickford by the people of Russia during her 1926 visit to Moscow.

TEMPTATION.

MARY PICKFORD AS "MERCY" IN CAPRICE.

Paramount Pictures

MotionPicture EXHIBITORS' 2nd Annual Ball BOSTON 1914

Mary Pickford Chronology

Christel Schmidt

1892 — Mary Pickford is born Gladys Louise Smith on April 8 in Toronto, Ontario, Canada, to John Charles Smith and Charlotte Smith (née Hennessey).

1893–1898 — Charlotte gives birth to a daughter, Lottie, on June 9, 1893, and to a son, John (known as Jack), on August 18, 1896. John Charles and Charlotte separate in 1895. John Charles dies after a fall on February 11, 1898.

1900–1901 — Pickford, billed as Gladys Smith, makes her stage debut (along with sister, Lottie) in *The Silver King* at the Princess Theatre in Toronto on January 8, 1900. She continues to act in local productions for the next year and a half.

1901–1906 — In late 1901 Pickford begins touring the United States in third-rate melodramas. Eventually, acting becomes the entire family's trade, and they sometimes travel together in the same production. In August 1905 Pickford gets her first break when she is cast, along with the rest of her family, in *Edmund Burke* with Chauncey Olcott. The show tours until May 1906.

1907–1909 — After a brief return to melodrama, Pickford wins a small role in New York producer David Belasco's *The Warrens of Virginia*. Belasco gives her the stage name Mary Pickford, and she makes her Broadway debut on December 3, 1907. She continues acting in the play throughout its six-month New York run and then appears in the national tour, which ends in March 1909.

Pickford at age fourteen months.

Button of Pickford (then Gladys Smith) as a member of the Valentine Company in 1901.

1909– On April 19, 1909, Pickford audi-
1910   tions for director D. W. Griffith at
       the Biograph film studio in New
       York. She accepts Griffith's offer to
       join his stock company of actors,
       beginning her career in moving
       pictures. Pickford quickly moves
       into the front ranks of the com-
       pany's players and becomes a
       favorite with audiences. She writes
       scenarios for Biograph and the Selig
       Polyscope Company and shows an
       interest in all aspects of production.
       She also falls in love with fellow
       Biograph actor Owen Moore.
       In December 1910 she leaves
       Biograph for the Independent
       Motion Picture Company (IMP).

1911– Pickford marries Owen Moore on
1912   January 7, 1911. The couple works
       together at IMP, where they are
       often paired onscreen, through the
       summer. In the fall they join the
       Majestic Company. In January 1912
       Pickford returns (without Moore)
       to Griffith at Biograph. She resigns
       later that year after accepting a
       leading role in David Belasco's
       Broadway production *A Good
       Little Devil*.

Poster for My Baby *(1912).*

*A 1911 advertisement promoting Pickford and husband
Owen Moore in their first film for the Majestic Company.*

1913   On January 8, *A Good Little Devil* opens in New York. In May, while the play is still running, producer Adolph Zukor, founder of the feature-length movie company Famous Players in Famous Plays, films a movie version with the original stage cast. Soon after, Pickford leaves Broadway to join Zukor's company. Her first released feature, *In the Bishop's Carriage,* premieres on September 10, followed two months later by *Caprice.*

1914–
1915   Pickford makes fifteen movies in two years. *Hearts Adrift* opens in February 1914, with Pickford as a ragged castaway. It is so popular that Zukor puts the actress's name in lights at the cinemas that screen it. *Tess of the Storm Country,* which casts the star as a poor but feisty leader of a village of squatters, follows six weeks later, and Pickford attains unprecedented international fame. She closes out the year with *Behind the Scenes* (the tale of an ambitious actress) and *Cinderella.* Her 1915 films include *Mistress Nell* (about Nell Gwyn) and *Rags,* in which she plays another impoverished spitfire. Pickford's syndicated newspaper column, "Daily Talks," debuts on November 8, 1915, and thereafter appears six days a week across the nation.

Postcard for Tess of the Storm Country *(1914).*

Pickford and Russell Bassett in a scene from Behind the Scenes *(1914).*

Opposite: Poster for Cinderella *(1914).*

1916–1917 On March 10, 1916, Mary Pickford Rupp (who later changed her first name to Gwynne) is born to Pickford's sister, Lottie. After long negotiations, Pickford signs a groundbreaking contract on June 24, 1916, that gives the actress an impressive salary and a creative voice behind the scenes through her own production company. In August, Zukor and Walter E. Green form the Artcraft Pictures Corporation to distribute Pickford's movies outside the traditional block-booking system. Artcraft releases thirteen of her films, including two in 1917 in which she plays a child: *The Poor Little Rich Girl* and *Rebecca of Sunnybrook Farm*. Following America's entry into World War I on April 6, 1917, Pickford joins the effort to support soldiers, raise funds, and rally the home front. In July her patriotic movie *The Little American* casts her as a woman who is captured by the Germans and risks her life to help the Allies.

1918 In March the U.S. Treasury asks Pickford to join a national tour to sell war bonds, known as the Liberty Loan campaign. Meanwhile, she releases five films throughout the year, including the tragedy *Stella Maris* in which she plays two roles, one a homely, abused orphan. Her film contract ends in November. Pickford accepts an offer to make three movies with First National Pictures and obtains total creative control over her productions.

1919 Pickford's *Daddy-Long-Legs, The Heart O' the Hills*, and *The Hoodlum* are released. Meanwhile, on February 5, she joins Griffith and actors Charlie Chaplin and Douglas Fairbanks to cofound United Artists (UA), a corporation that distributes films produced by its founders. In the fall Pickford begins production on *Pollyanna*, her first movie for the new venture.

Pickford and her niece Gwynne on the set of Rebecca of Sunnybrook Farm *(1917).*

Pickford holds the American flag as she addresses troops stationed at Camp Kearny on November 16, 1918.

Christel Schmidt

1920   *Pollyanna* is released in January.
It is the actress's least favorite role,
but the film grosses over $1 million.
On March 2 Pickford divorces
Owen Moore. She marries
Douglas Fairbanks, with whom she
had been romantically involved for
several years, on March 28. The
pair go on a whirlwind European
honeymoon that makes headlines
around the world. In August they
return to Pickfair, their Beverly
Hills mansion, where they reign as
Hollywood's first power couple.
That summer, Pickford's mother,
Charlotte, adopts her granddaugh-
ter Mary Pickford Rupp (Gwynne).

1921–   Pickford releases three movies in
1922   1921, including the technically
innovative *Little Lord Fauntleroy*.
She decides to limit her future
output to one prestige picture a
year. In the fall she and Fairbanks
take a three-and-a-half-month trip
to Europe, one of many international tours they make throughout
the decade. Abroad, they are feted
by royalty, artists, and prominent
politicians; similarly, Pickfair
becomes a cultural mecca for the
powerful and well connected.
On January 21, 1922, Pickford and
Fairbanks jointly purchase a film
studio with a ten-acre lot in
West Hollywood for $150,000.
In November 1922 the actress
reprises her most famous role in
a lavish remake of her 1914 block-
buster *Tess of the Storm Country*.
As a follow-up, Pickford buys
the rights to the novel *Dorothy
Vernon of Haddon Hall* and hires
German filmmaker Ernst Lubitsch
to direct it.

Pickford and Fairbanks on the lawn of Pickfair in 1920.

Lobby card from Little Lord Fauntleroy *(1921).*

1923–1924 Pickford and Lubitsch clash over *Dorothy Vernon of Haddon Hall* in preproduction. Instead, they agree to make *Rosita,* a period drama about a provocative Spanish street singer to be filmed on a grand scale. Pickford hopes the story will present her in a new and sophisticated light. Although the film, released September 3, 1923, is commercially and critically successful, it alienates family viewers, who are a core fan base. Pickford films *Dorothy Vernon of Haddon Hall* with director Marshall Neilan. The film opens in March 1924, earning good reviews and a healthy box office. Nevertheless, it elicits the same response as *Rosita* among some moviegoers.

1925–1926 In early 1925 Pickford writes the scenario for *Little Annie Rooney* and starts production. To please fans who prefer her juvenile roles, she plays a rowdy tomboy. The film is released in the fall. Meanwhile, Pickford has already gone into production on *Sparrows* (1926). That film, a Dickensian tale about a band of abused orphans, is shot in the expressionist style popular in German cinema. In July 1926, on a six-month tour overseas, Pickford and Fairbanks visit Moscow. They enter the city in the former czar's railway car and are greeted by huge, ecstatic crowds; they are honored with gifts and celebrations that mirror the ovations they received on their honeymoon. They also meet Russian film director Sergei Eisenstein, and Pickford films a cameo appearance in *A Kiss from Mary Pickford* (1927).

1927–1928 Pickford joins thirty-six prominent members of the movie industry to cofound the Academy of Motion Picture Arts and Sciences in May 1927 (only three of the group are women). That month, she also starts production on *My Best Girl,* a romantic comedy featuring young actor Charles "Buddy" Rogers. The film opens to rave reviews in October. On March 21, 1928, Pickford's beloved mother and trusted adviser, Charlotte, dies of breast cancer. Three months later, Pickford makes front-page news when she cuts her world-famous curls into a stylish bob. At about this time, Pickford becomes the legal guardian of her niece Gwynne. In August she purchases the rights to *Coquette,* a successful Broadway play, to adapt into her first talking picture. Pickford is one of the first great stars to tackle the new medium.

1929 On April 12 *Coquette* is released to positive reviews. It is a box-office smash, making more money than any previous film that Pickford has produced. Next, she and Fairbanks agree to produce and star in *The Taming of the Shrew,* their first onscreen collaboration. Production, which begins in June and ends in early August, exacerbates strains in the marriage. The following month, the couple leaves on a four-month trip around the world, with stops in China, Egypt, Greece, India, and Singapore.

June 1924 cover of Motion Picture Magazine.

On January 2, 1930, Pickford and Fairbanks return from abroad. From late February to June, the actress tries to get her new production, *Forever Yours,* off the ground. After filming several reels, she shelves the project. On April 3 Pickford receives the Academy Award for Best Actress for her performance in *Coquette.* That summer, while Fairbanks travels alone in England, newspapers report rumors of trouble in their marriage. In the fall Pickford performs the starring role in *Kiki,* a film produced by Joseph Schenk. The French farce, released on March 14, 1931, is a financial disaster and the first Pickford movie ever to lose money. In November 1932 she begins production on *Secrets,* a retooling of the abandoned *Forever Yours,* opposite Leslie Howard. Her brother, Jack, dies in Paris on January 3, 1933, at age thirty-six. *Secrets,* released two and a half months later, is a box-office failure, and Pickford never appears in another movie. Cinema fans around the world are stunned when she files for divorce from Fairbanks on December 8.

Pickford and Mary Louise Miller on the set of Sparrows *(1926).*

Footage of Fairbanks and Pickford being feted in Moscow, from the Russian feature A Kiss from Mary Pickford *(1927). Pickford wears a headdress given to her by Russian fans, which she later donated to the National History Museum of Los Angeles County.*

Pickford hugs leading man Kenneth MacKenna in a scene from her unfinished 1930 production Forever Yours.

1934–1935   On October 3, 1934, Pickford debuts as the star of a six-month dramatic radio series sponsored by Standard Brands' Royal Gelatin on the NBC network. The following month, her inspirational book *Why Not Try God?* is published. The *Demi-Widow,* a novel, follows in August 1935. That summer, Pickford and Paramount Pictures cofounder Jesse L. Lasky form Pickford-Lasky Productions, agreeing to make several features and distribute them through United Artists. In October, Pickford begins a ten-month stint as president of UA, and her philosophical book, *My Rendezvous with Life,* is released.

1936–1939   On January 10, 1936, Pickford's divorce from Fairbanks is finalized. In February, Pickford launches *Parties at Pickfair,* a weekly radio program that airs nationwide. The show, which runs for five months, features celebrity guests who drop by for a mix of conversation and performances. In late June it is announced that Pickford-Lasky Productions will dissolve after their second movie, *The Gay Desperado* (1936), is completed. On December 9 Pickford's sister, Lottie, dies at age forty-three. Then, on June 27, 1937, after a long courtship, Pickford marries actor Buddy Rogers, her costar in *My Best Girl* (1927). In the fall she launches Mary Pickford Cosmetics, an enterprise that folds in the spring of 1939. More tragedy follows: her first husband, Owen Moore, dies on June 10, 1939. Just six months later, on December 12, Douglas Fairbanks dies of a heart attack in Santa Monica.

1940–1945   Pickford focuses her attention on her favorite charitable endeavors, including the Jewish Home for the Aged, the Motion Picture Relief Fund/Country House, the National Foundation for Infantile Paralysis, and the National Women's Party. In mid-1940, prior to America's entry into World War II, she participates in organizations that aid the Allies.

After America enters the war, Pickford sells war bonds and hosts weekly events for servicemen at Pickfair. Meanwhile, she fosters two children, Ronald and Roxanne, in 1942 and 1943, respectively, and later adopts them. In the summer of 1943 Pickford agrees to donate her personal film collection to the Library of Congress. She continues her involvement with war-related activities through 1945.

Pickford promotes her 1935 novel The Demi-Widow.

1946–1955 Pickford forms three small production companies in 1946; their releases include Douglas Sirk's *Sleep, My Love* (1947) and the Marx Brothers in *Love Happy* (1950). In the late 1940s director Billy Wilder asks Pickford to star in *Sunset Boulevard* (1950), but she declines. Producer Stanley Kramer offers her the lead role in the anticensorship movie *The Library* in the fall of 1951. Pickford flirts with the idea but turns it down. (The film is released in 1956 as *Storm Center*, starring Bette Davis.) On March 30, 1953, at the request of Mamie Eisenhower, Pickford begins a seven-week national tour promoting government savings bonds. *Sunshine and Shadow*, Pickford's autobiography (in progress for several years), is published in May 1955. That December, George Eastman House honors Pickford and eighteen other silent film figures for their work from 1915 to 1925. (Two years later, she receives another Eastman House award for her work from 1926 to 1930.)

1956–1965 In February 1956 Pickford (the last of United Artists' original founders) sells her company stock. That spring, she hosts a high-profile reunion party at Pickfair for 200 silent film industry veterans. In 1957 Pickford joins a committee to explore the possibility of creating a film museum in Los Angeles. Her involvement in the proposed Hollywood Museum continues for seven years. She attends the first White House Conference on Aging in January 1961 as a delegate from the state of California. In the fall of 1965 she is honored in Paris by the Cinémathèque Française with a monthlong retrospective of her work. Shortly afterward, Pickford retires from public life.

1976 On March 29 Pickford receives an honorary Oscar for her work in the film industry. The presentation is taped at Pickfair for the Academy Awards ceremony.

1979 On May 29 Pickford dies of a cerebral hemorrhage in Santa Monica. She is buried with her extended family in a private section of Forest Lawn Cemetery on May 31.

Pickford, host of the radio program Parties at Pickfair, *appears on the April 1936 cover of* Radio Mirror.

A 1947 family portrait shows Pickford with her third husband, Charles "Buddy" Rogers, and their adopted children Roxanne and Ronald.

Polaroid photo of Pickford, nearly seventy years old, standing next to a painting of her mother, Charlotte, in 1961. She would retire from public life just four years later.

LITTLE
MARY PICKFORD

Filmography

Christel Schmidt

Little Mary Pickford poster, 1915.

THIS FILMOGRAPHY was compiled from various sources, including the *American Film Institute Catalog of Motion Pictures Produced in the United States,* the International Federation of Film Archives database, *D. W. Griffith and the Biograph Company, Pickford: The Woman Who Made Hollywood,* and a list of credits collated by the late Robert Cushman. Extant titles were verified through screenings by the author. The films listed include those that Pickford acted in and, as indicated, those that she authored. The filmography is organized by production company and distributor (if applicable); titles are listed in order by release date; and key archival sources are noted.

ABBREVIATIONS

AMPAS. *Academy of Motion Picture Arts and Sciences*

BFI. *British Film Institute*

CF. *Cinémathèque Française*

CR. *Cinémathèque Royale*

GEH. *George Eastman House*

LC. *Library of Congress*

MoMA. *Museum of Modern Art*

NFA. *National Film Archive (Czech Republic)*

NFM. *Netherlands Film Museum*

RUR. *Gosfilmofond*

SFI. *Swedish Film Institute*

UCLA. *University of California– Los Angeles Film and Television Archive*

BIOGRAPH COMPANY

Two Memories. Released May 24, 1909. Material at LC and MoMA.

His Duty. Released May 31, 1909. Material at LC and MoMA.

The Violin Maker of Cremona. Released June 7, 1909. Material at LC and GEH.

The Lonely Villa. Released June 10, 1909. Material at LC, GEH, MoMA, and UCLA.

The Son's Return. Released June 14, 1909. Material at LC and UCLA.

The Faded Lilies. Released June 17, 1909. Material at LC and MoMA.

Her First Biscuits. Released June 17, 1909. Material at LC.

The Peachbasket Hat. Released June 24, 1909. Material at LC and MoMA.

The Way of Man. Released June 28, 1909. Material at LC and MoMA.

The Necklace. Released July 1, 1909. Material at LC and MoMA.

The Country Doctor. Released July 8, 1909. Material at LC, GEH, MoMA, and NFM.

The Cardinal's Conspiracy. Released July 12, 1909. Material at LC and MoMA.

The Renunciation. Released July 19, 1909. Material at LC and UCLA.

Tender Hearts. Released July 19, 1909. Material at MoMA.

Sweet and Twenty. Released July 22, 1909. Material at LC and MoMA.

The Slave. Released July 29, 1909. Material at LC and MoMA.

They Would Elope. Released August 9, 1909. Material at LC.

His Wife's Visitor. Released August 19, 1909. Material at LC.

The Indian Runner's Romance. Released August 23, 1909. Material at LC.

"Oh, Uncle." Released August 26, 1909. Material at LC and MoMA.

The Seventh Day. Released August 26, 1909. Material at LC and MoMA.

The Little Darling. Released September 2, 1909. Material at LC and MoMA.

The Sealed Room. Released September 2, 1909. Material at LC, MoMA, and UCLA.

"1776" or, The Hessian Renegades. Released September 6, 1909. Material at LC, BFI, GEH, and MoMA.

Getting Even (also author). Released September 13, 1909. Material at LC.

The Broken Locket. Released September 16, 1909. Material at LC.

In Old Kentucky. Released September 20, 1909. Material at LC.

The Awakening (also author). Released September 30, 1909. Material at LC.

The Little Teacher. Released October 11, 1909. Material at LC and BFI.

His Lost Love. Released October 18, 1909. Material at LC and MoMA.

In the Watches of the Night. Released October 25, 1909. Material at LC, GEH, and MoMA.

Lines of White in the Sullen Sea. Released October 28, 1909. Material at LC and MoMA.

The Gibson Goddess. Released November 1, 1909. Material at LC and MoMA.

What's Your Hurry? Released November 1, 1909. Material at LC and MoMA.

The Restoration. Released November 8, 1909. Material at LC, BFI, MoMA, and UCLA.

The Light that Came. Released November 11, 1909. Material at LC and GEH.

A Midnight Adventure. Released November 18, 1909. Material at LC.

The Mountaineer's Honor. Released November 25, 1909. Material at LC and MoMA.

The Trick that Failed. Released November 29, 1909. Material at LC.

Through the Breakers. Released December 6, 1909. Material at LC, BFI, GEH, and MoMA.

The Test. Released December 16, 1909. Material at LC and MoMA.

To Save Her Soul. Released December 27, 1909. Material at LC and MoMA.

The Day After (author only). Released December 30, 1909. Material at LC and MoMA.

The Heart of an Outlaw. Unreleased. 1909. Material at MoMA.

All on Account of the Milk. Released January 13, 1910. Material at LC and MoMA.

The Woman from Mellon's. Released February 3, 1910. Material at LC and UCLA.

The Englishman and the Girl. Released February 17, 1910. Material at LC.

The Newlyweds. Released March 3, 1910. Material at LC and MoMA.

The Thread of Destiny. Released March 7, 1910. Material at LC and MoMA.

The Twisted Trail. Released March 24, 1910. Material at LC.

The Smoker. Released March 31, 1910. Material at LC and UCLA.

As It Is in Life. Released April 6, 1910. Material at LC, BFI, GEH, and MoMA.

A Rich Revenge. Released April 7, 1910. Material at LC and MoMA.

A Romance of the Western Hills. Released April 11, 1910. Material at LC.

The Unchanging Sea. Released May 5, 1910. Material at LC, GEH, and MoMA.

Love among the Roses. Released May 9, 1910. Material at LC, BFI, and MoMA.

The Two Brothers. Released May 12, 1910. Material at LC, MoMA, and NFM.

Ramona. Released May 23, 1910. Material at LC, GEH, and MoMA.

In the Season of Buds. Released June 2, 1910. Material at LC and GEH.

Pickford objects to Billy Quirk's smelly cigar in The Smoker *(1910).*

A Victim of Jealousy. Released June 9, 1910. Material at LC and MoMA.

May and December (also author). Released June 20, 1910. Material at LC and MoMA.

Never Again. Released June 20, 1910. Material at LC, GEH, and UCLA.

A Child's Impulse. Released June 27, 1910. Material at LC and MoMA.

Muggsy's First Sweetheart. Released June 30, 1910. Material at LC and GEH.

What the Daisy Said. Released July 11, 1910. Material at LC and BFI.

The Call to Arms. Released July 25, 1910. Material at LC.

An Arcadian Maid. Released August 1, 1910. Material at LC, BFI, and UCLA.

When We Were in Our 'Teens. Released August 18, 1910. Material at LC.

The Sorrows of the Unfaithful. Released August 22, 1910. Material at LC.

Wilful Peggy. Released August 25, 1910. Material at LC and MoMA.

Muggsy Becomes a Hero. Released September 1, 1910. Material at LC and MoMA.

A Gold Necklace. Released October 6, 1910. Material at LC and MoMA.

A Lucky Toothache. Released October 13, 1910. Material at LC.

Waiter No. 5. Released November 3, 1910. Material at LC and MoMA.

Simple Charity. Released November 10, 1910. Material at LC, BFI, and MoMA.

The Song of the Wildwood Flute. Released November 21, 1910. Material at LC, BFI, and MoMA.

A Plain Song. Released November 28, 1910. Material at LC and BFI.

White Roses. Released December 22, 1910. Material at LC and BFI.

When a Man Loves. Released January 5, 1911. Material at LC and MoMA.

The Italian Barber. Released January 9, 1911. Material at LC and MoMA.

Three Sisters. Released February 2, 1911. Material at LC, BFI, and GEH.

A Decree of Destiny. Released March 6, 1911. Material at LC and GEH.

Madame Rex (author only). Released April 17, 1911. Material at MoMA.

The Mender of the Nets. Released February 15, 1912. Material at LC, BFI, GEH, and MoMA.

Iola's Promise. Released March 14, 1912. Material at LC, BFI, and UCLA.

Fate's Interception. Released April 8, 1912. Material at LC, BFI, GEH, MoMA, and UCLA.

The Female of the Species. Released April 15, 1912. Material at LC, BFI, GEH, MoMA, and UCLA.

Just Like a Woman. Released April 18, 1912. Material at LC and MoMA.

Won by a Fish. Released April 22, 1912. Material at LC and MoMA.

The Old Actor. Released May 6, 1912. Material at LC, BFI, GEH, and UCLA.

A Lodging for the Night. Released May 9, 1912. Material at LC.

A Beast at Bay. Released May 27, 1912. Material at LC, BFI, CF, GEH, and MoMA.

Home Folks. Released June 6, 1912. Material at LC, BFI, and MoMA.

Mischievous Peggy (Pickford) dons men's clothes and flirts with a barmaid in Wilful Peggy *(1910).*

Lena and the Geese (also author). Released June 17, 1912. Material at LC, AMPAS, MoMA, and UCLA.

The School Teacher and the Waif. Released June 27, 1912. Material at LC.

An Indian Summer. Released July 8, 1912. Material at LC and GEH.

The Narrow Road. Released August 1, 1912. Material at LC, GEH, and UCLA.

The Inner Circle. Released August 12, 1912. Material at LC and MoMA.

With the Enemy's Help. Released August 19, 1912. Material at LC and BFI.

A Pueblo Legend. Released August 29, 1912. Material at LC and GEH.

Friends. Released September 23, 1912. Material at LC, BFI, GEH, MoMA, and UCLA.

So Near, Yet so Far. Released September 30, 1912. Material at LC, BFI, GEH, and MoMA.

A Feud in the Kentucky Hills. Released October 3, 1912. Material at LC, BFI, GEH, and MoMA.

The One She Loved. Released October 21, 1912. Material at LC and GEH.

My Baby. Released November 14, 1912. Material at LC, GEH, and MoMA.

The Informer. Released November 21, 1912. Material at LC and GEH.

The New York Hat. Released December 5, 1912. Material at LC, BFI, GEH, MoMA, and UCLA.

The Unwelcome Guest. Released March 15, 1913. Material at LC, GEH, and UCLA.

Pickford makes a toast, puffs on a cigarette, and toys with another man as Owen Moore watches in The Dream *(1911).*

SELIG POLYSCOPE COMPANY[1]

Caught in the Act (author only).
Released March 9, 1911. No extant
material.

The Medallion (author only). Released
July 31, 1911. No extant material.

INDEPENDENT MOVING
PICTURE COMPANY

Their First Misunderstanding (also
author). Released January 9, 1911. No
extant material.[2]

The Dream (also author). Released
January 23, 1911. Material at LC.[3]

Maid or Man. Released January 30, 1911.
Material at MoMA.

The Mirror. Released February 9, 1911.
Material at GEH.

When the Cat's Away. Released
February 9, 1911. Material at LC, GEH,
and UCLA.

Her Darkest Hour. Released February 13,
1911. No extant material.

Artful Kate. Released February 23, 1911.
Material at LC, GEH, and UCLA.

A Manly Man. Released February 27,
1911. Material at LC and UCLA.

Pictureland. Released March 4, 1911. No
extant material.

The Message in the Bottle. Released
March 9, 1911. No extant material.

The Fisher-Maid. Released March 16,
1911. No extant material.

In Old Madrid. Released March 20, 1911.
Material at LC.

Sweet Memories. Released March 27,
1911. Material at LC.

The Stampede. Released April 17, 1911.
No extant material.

As a Boy Dreams. Released April 24,
1911. Material at AMPAS.[4]

Second Sight. Released May 1, 1911. No
extant material.

The Fair Dentist. Released May 8, 1911.
No extant material.

Pickford and King Baggot in the IMP short The Fair Dentist *(1911).*

For Her Brother's Sake. Released May 11, 1911. No extant material.

The Master and the Man. Released May 15, 1911. No extant material.

The Lighthouse Keeper. Released May 18, 1911. Material at LC.

Back to the Soil. Released June 8, 1911. No extant material.

In the Sultan's Garden. Released July 3, 1911. Material at LC.

For the Queen's Honor. Released July 6, 1911. No extant material.

A Gasoline Engagement. Released July 10, 1911. No extant material.

At a Quarter of Two. Released July 13, 1911. Fragment at LC.

Science. Released July 24, 1911. No extant material.

The Skating Bug. Released July 31, 1911. No extant material.

The Call of the Song. Released August 13, 1911. No extant material.

The Toss of a Coin. Released August 31, 1911. No extant material.

'Tween Two Loves. Released September 29, 1911. Material at LC and GEH.

The Rose's Story. Released October 2, 1911. No extant material.

The Sentinel Asleep. Released October 9, 1911. No extant material.

The Better Way. Released October 12, 1911. No extant material.

His Dress Shirt. Released October 30, 1911. No extant material.

A Timely Repentance. Released March 11, 1912. Fragment at LC.

MAJESTIC COMPANY

The Courting of Mary. Released November 26, 1911. No extant material.

Love Heeds Not the Showers. Released December 3, 1911. No extant material.

Little Red Riding Hood. Released December 17, 1911. Material at LC.

The Caddy's Dream. Released December 31, 1911. No extant material.

Honor Thy Father. Released February 9, 1912. No extant material.

KALEM COMPANY

When Fate Decrees (author only). June 4, 1913. No extant material.

FAMOUS PLAYERS FILM COMPANY (STATES RIGHTS)

In the Bishop's Carriage. Released September 10, 1913. No extant material.

Caprice. Released November 10, 1913. No extant material.

Hearts Adrift. Released February 10, 1914. No extant material.

A Good Little Devil. Released March 1, 1914. Incomplete copy at BFI.

Posters for Mistress Nell *(1915),* A Girl of Yesterday *(1915), and* Hulda from Holland *(1916).*

Tess of the Storm Country. Released March 20, 1914. Material at LC, CF, GEH, and UCLA.

FAMOUS PLAYERS FILM COMPANY (PARAMOUNT)

The Eagle's Mate. Released July 5, 1914. Material at BFI and GEH.

Such a Little Queen. Released September 21, 1914. No extant material.

Behind the Scenes. Released October 26, 1914. Material at GEH.

Cinderella. Released December 28, 1914. Material at LC and NFM.

Mistress Nell. Released February 1, 1915. Material at MoMA and NFA.

Fanchon the Cricket. Released May 10, 1915. Material at BFI, CF, and GEH.

The Dawn of a Tomorrow. Released June 6, 1915. Material at LC and SFI.

Little Pal. Released July 1, 1915. Material at CF.

Rags. Released August 2, 1915. Material at LC, CF, and GEH.

Esmeralda. Released September 6, 1915. No extant material.

A Girl of Yesterday (also author). Released October 7, 1915. No extant material.

Madame Butterfly. Released November 8, 1915. Material at LC, CF, and GEH.

The Foundling. Released January 3, 1916. Material at LC and GEH.

Poor Little Peppina. Released February 20, 1916. Material at LC and GEH.

The Eternal Grind. Released April 17, 1916. Material at CF.

Hulda from Holland. Released July 31, 1916. Material at NFA.

PICKFORD FILM CORPORATION
(ARTCRAFT PICTURES)

Less than the Dust. Released
November 6, 1916. Material at LC and
GEH.

The Pride of the Clan. Released
January 8, 1917. Material at LC and
GEH.

The Poor Little Rich Girl. Released
March 5, 1917. Material at LC,
AMPAS, GEH, and MoMA.

A Romance of the Redwoods. Released
May 14, 1917. Material at AMPAS and
GEH.

The Little American. Released July 2,
1917. Material at LC, GEH, and UCLA.

Rebecca of Sunnybrook Farm. Released
September 22, 1917. Material at LC,
AMPAS, CF, GEH, and UCLA.

A Little Princess. Released November 5,
1917. Material at LC, CF, GEH, and
NFM.

Stella Maris. Released January 21, 1918.
Material at LC, CF, GEH, and MoMA.

Amarilly of Clothes-Line Alley. Released
March 11, 1918. Material at LC, GEH,
and MoMA.

M'liss. Released April 18, 1918. Material
at LC, CF, and GEH.

How Could You, Jean? Released June 23,
1918. No extant material.

Johanna Enlists. Released September 29,
1918. Material at LC and GEH.

Poster for The Pride of the Clan *(1917).*

One Hundred Percent American. Released October 1918. Material at LC.[5]

Captain Kidd, Jr. Released April 6, 1919. No extant material.

MARY PICKFORD COMPANY (FIRST NATIONAL)

Daddy-Long-Legs. Released May 11, 1919. Material at LC, BFI, CF, GEH, NFA, NFM, and UCLA.

The Hoodlum. Released September 1, 1919. Material at AMPAS, CF, GEH, and RUR.

The Heart O' the Hills. Released November 17, 1919. Material at LC, CF, and GEH.

MARY PICKFORD COMPANY (UNITED ARTISTS)

Pollyanna. Released January 18, 1920. Material at LC, AMPAS, CF, CR, GEH, NFA, and RUR.

Suds. Released June 27, 1920. Material at LC, BFI, CF, GEH, NFA, and RUR.

The Love Light. Released January 9, 1921. Material at LC, CF, GEH, RUR, and UCLA.

Through the Back Door. Released May 17, 1921. Material at LC, CF, GEH, and RUR.

Little Lord Fauntleroy. Released September 11, 1921. Material at LC, CF, GEH, and RUR.

Tess of the Storm Country. Released November 12, 1922. Material at LC, GEH, and RUR.

Rosita. Released September 3, 1923. Material at CR, MoMA, NFA, and RUR.

Dorothy Vernon of Haddon Hall. Released March 15, 1924. Material at LC, CF, CR, GEH, and RUR.

Little Annie Rooney (also author). Released October 18, 1925. Material at LC, AMPAS, CF, and GEH.

Sparrows. Released September 19, 1926. Material at LC, AMPAS, CF, GEH, and UCLA.

My Best Girl. Released October 31, 1927. Material at LC, CF, CR, GEH, and UCLA.

Coquette (sound version). Released April 12, 1929. Material at LC, GEH, and AMPAS.

Coquette (silent version). Released April 12, 1929. Material at LC and CF.

The Taming of the Shrew (sound version). Released October 26, 1929. Material at LC, CF, and MoMA.

The Taming of the Shrew (silent version). Released October 26, 1929. Material at LC and GEH.

Forever Yours. Never completed, 1930. Fragment at LC.

ART CINEMA (UNITED ARTISTS)

Kiki. Released March 14, 1931. Material at LC and GEH.

PICKFORD CORPORATION (UNITED ARTISTS)

Secrets. Released March 15, 1933. Material at LC and UCLA.

Top: Poster for Captain Kidd, Jr. *(1919).*

Center: Pickford in the dream sequence from Suds *(1920).*

Bottom: Advertisement for Pickford's last film Secrets *(1933).*

Acknowledgments

Mary Pickford: Queen of the Movies is a collective work, and I am indebted to many publishing professionals, institutions, and writers for aiding its creation. In particular I am indebted to the Margaret Herrick Library at the Academy of Motion Picture Arts and Sciences for sharing the archive's remarkable Mary Pickford Collection. Indeed, it would have been impossible to fully honor Pickford's life and legacy without this material. I am also grateful to library director Linda Mehr, photo curator Matt Severson, and graphics librarian Anne Coco. I have benefited from the vast knowledge and infinite patience of Barbara Hall and Jenny Romero, as well as from the guidance of Joe Adamson, Val Almendarez, Mary Mallory, and Faye Thompson. And I cannot express how fortunate I was to have had the late Robert Cushman, former photo curator at the library, as a mentor. He blazed the trail of Pickford scholarship I walk on.

The Natural History Museum of Los Angeles County provided access to its incredible collection of Pickford artifacts. It is a privilege to showcase these pieces, especially the actress's costumes and curls. I am beholden to collections manager Beth Werling for her expertise and unstinting support and to photographer Candacy Taylor, who helped bring the collection to life. I also greatly appreciate the museum staff who went the extra mile to prepare these materials.

A number of archivists, curators, museum staff, and reference librarians offered vital assistance, including Nancy Kauffman (George Eastman House); Ron Magliozzi and Katie Trainor (Museum of Modern Art); Megan Forbes (Museum of the Moving Image); Holly Reed (National Archives), Kay Petersen (National Museum of American History); Karen Nickeson, Tom Lisanti, and Steve Massa (New York Public Library for the Performing Arts); Lizanne Reger (National Portrait Gallery); Susan Snyder (Bancroft Library); and Simon Elliot (UCLA Library).

Scans of original posters for *The Pride of the Clan* (1917) and *The Poor Little Rich Girl* (1917) were generously provided by Heritage Auctions (Noah Fleisher) and Matthew Wagenknecht, respectively. Permission to reprint the work of Edward Wagenknecht and James Card was granted by Walter Wagenknecht and George Eastman House (Amy Schelemanow).

Over the years, numerous colleagues and friends have aided and encouraged my work on Pickford, including Mark Betz, Kevin Brownlow, Siobhan Flynn, Jan-Christopher Horak, Eddie Richmond, Lynanne Rollins, Ed Stratmann, and Heather Ukryn. The indispensable Eileen Whitfield has generously shared information and offered wise counsel. I owe an important debt to the National Endowment for the Humanities for awarding me research fellowships in 2000 and 2004. The endowment provided essential assistance that made all my subsequent Pickford endeavors possible.

Without the support of the Library of Congress's Publishing Office, this book would not exist. Director Ralph Eubanks gave me a tremendous opportunity when he suggested I work on a Pickford book and remained a strong advocate for the project. I was especially privileged to have Margaret Wagner as an adviser, editor, and sounding board and to receive encouragement and guidance from Athena Angelos, John Cole, Amy Hess, Blaine Marshall, Elizabeth McDonald, Linda Osborne, Susan Reyburn, Evelyn Sinclair, and Tom Wiener. And I will always be thankful to brilliant photo editor Vincent Virga, who first recommended me to the publishing office.

For over a decade the Motion Picture, Broadcasting, and Recorded Sound Division at the Library of Congress has been my main resource for Pickford research. The dedicated and knowledgeable staff has kindly aided me at every turn. I am particularly grateful to reference librarians Rosemary Hanes, Zoran Sinobad, and Josie Walters-Johnston. I deeply appreciate the long-standing support of division chief Greg Lukow and Moving Image Section head Mike Mashon, as well as the assistance of Bryan Cornell, Karen Fishman, Brian Taves, and George Willeman. I am also indebted to Jan Grenci (Prints and Photographs Division) and Susan Claremont (Music Division), both of whom helped me navigate collections, and to Glen Krankowski and Domenic Sergi (Digital Scan Section) for technical advice and beautiful images. The ever-diligent Pat Padua (Music Division) offered his technical expertise, tireless support, and friendship.

It must have been Providence that brought gifted book designer Robert Wiser to this project. I thank him for his unerring taste and insight into Pickford. In addition, copy editor Linda Lotz's rigorous and meticulous work contributed immensely to the clarifying of the text.

Finally, I am grateful for the love and support of my family and friends, especially my mother Paula Schmidt, niece Hailee Wells, and best pal Hartley Napoleon Jones.

Pickford standing with her back to the camera in a 1920 promotional photograph.

Notes

INTRODUCTION
Molly Haskell

1   Quoted in Kevin Brownlow, *Mary Pickford Rediscovered: Rare Pictures of a Hollywood Legend* (New York: Harry N. Abrams, 1999), 13.
2   Ibid., 20.
3   Ibid., 34.
4   Ibid., 35.

THE NATURAL
Transitions in Mary Pickford's Acting from the Footlights to Her Greatest Role in Film
Eileen Whitfield

1   Eileen Whitfield, *Pickford: The Woman Who Made Hollywood* (Lexington: University Press of Kentucky, 1997), 127.
2   Pickford claimed she began acting at the age of five. In fact, she was seven years and eight months old.
3   Kim Marra, *Strange Duets: Impresarios and Actresses in the American Theatre, 1865–1914* (Iowa City: University of Iowa Press, 2006), 223.
4   Mary Pickford, interview by George Pratt, 1958, George Eastman House; Mary Pickford, *Sunshine and Shadow* (Garden City, NY: Doubleday, 1955), 59.
5   Barnett Braverman Collection, D. W. Griffith Papers, 1897–1954, Museum of Modern Art, New York.
6   Harry C. Carr, "How Griffith Picks His Leading Women," *Photoplay*, December 1918, 24.
7   Alison Smith, "Owen Talks about Mary," *Photoplay*, December 1919, 58.
8   Pickford, *Sunshine and Shadow*, 159.
9   Mary Pickford, interview with Tony Thomas, 1961, CBC Archives, Toronto.
10 Kemp Niver, *Mary Pickford, Comedienne* (Los Angeles: Ocare Research Group, 1969), 14.
11 Julian Johnson, "Mary Pickford: Herself and Her Career Part III," *Photoplay*, January 1916, 40.
12 Pickford, *Sunshine and Shadow*, 116. Pickford used a hand bite at least three times on film, in *A Beast at Bay* (1912), *Tess of the Storm Country* (1914), and *Kiki* (1931).
13 Robert Berkvist, "Stephen Sondheim Takes a Stab at Grand Guignol," *New York Times*, February 5, 1979, D1.
14 *Moving Picture World*, December 24, 1910, 1462.
15 Gish's image in talking films was much more steely; see especially *The Night of the Hunter* (1955).
16 Tom Gunning, *The Griffith Project*, vol. 4 (London: British Film Institute, 2000), 134.
17 In nickelodeons, Pickford played slaveys in *An Arcadian Maid* (1910), *Simple Charity* (1910), and *The Unwelcome Guest* (1913). In features, she played them in *The Foundling* (1916), *Stella Maris* (1918), *Johanna Enlists* (1918), and *Suds* (1920).
18 See, for instance, 1912's *The Female of the Species, The School Teacher and the Waif,* and *The New York Hat.*
19 Scrapbook 3 (ca. 1914–1933), FSA box A, number 19, Mary Pickford Collection, Margaret Herrick Library, Academy of Motion Picture Arts and Sciences.
20 Julian Johnson, "Mary Pickford: Herself and Her Career Conclusion," *Photoplay*, February 1916, 52. Johnson was describing Pickford's work in *The Dawn of a Tomorrow* (1915), but it captures the heart of her appeal.
21 Mary Pickford, interview by Arthur B. Friedman, May 1958, Columbia University Oral History Project.
22 Pickford, interview by Pratt.
23 See especially Pickford's versions of *M'liss* (1918) and *Heart O' the Hills* (1919).

Childhood Revisited
An Evaluation of Mary Pickford's Youngest Characters
Eileen Whitfield

1   Jerome L. Rodnitzky, *Feminist Phoenix: The Rise and Fall of a Feminist Counterculture* (West Port, CT: Praeger, 1999), 94; Marjorie Rosen, *Popcorn Venus* (New York: Coward, McCann and Geoghegan, 1973), 38.
2   In 1954 forty-year-old Mary Martin starred in the Broadway musical version of *Peter Pan*.
3   "'Good Little Devil' Gives Rare Delight," *New York Times*, January 9, 1913, 9; "At the Theatres ('A Good Little Devil')," *Washington Herald*, December 31, 1912, 4.
4   Wendell Phillips Dodge, "The Maude Adams of the 'Movies,'" *Theatre*, January 1913, 176.
5   "Grand Tripple [*sic*] Program Sunday (Mary Pickford in 'A Poor Little Rich Girl')," *Ogden Standard*, March 24, 1917, 6. Gwen's eleventh birthday is celebrated in the film.
6   Mary Pickford, "The Portrayal of Child Roles," *Vanity Fair*, December 1917, 75.
7   *Little Lord Fauntleroy* is the only feature in which Pickford plays a boy. She appears in the same film as Fauntleroy's mother.
8   John C. Tibbetts, "Mary Pickford and the American Growing Girl," *Journal of Popular Film and Television* 29, no. 2 (Summer 2001): 51.
9   Frances Marion, *Off with Their Heads: A Serio-Comic Tale of Hollywood* (New York: Macmillan, 1972), 73.
10 Beverly Lyon Clark, *Kiddie Lit: The Cultural Construction of Children's Literature in America* (Baltimore: Johns Hopkins University Press, 2003), 7.
11 Rosen, *Popcorn Venus*, 38, 44.
12 Pickford, "Portrayal of Child Roles," 75.
13 Such performances have also succeeded in the sound era. For instance, Julie Harris was twenty-six years old when she played a twelve-year-old in *The Member of the Wedding* (1952). Her performance was nominated for an Oscar.

The Smith family with Mabel Watson (left) and Edith Watson (right) in the late 1890s.

MARY PICKFORD
Passionate Producer
Kevin Brownlow

1. Samuel Goldwyn, *Behind the Screen* (New York: George H. Doran, 1923), 41–42.
2. Mary Pickford, interview by the author, 1965.
3. Ibid.
4. G. W. Bitzer, *Billy Bitzer: His Story* (New York: Farrar, Straus and Giroux, 1973), 73–74.
5. Mary Pickford, interview by George Pratt, 1958, George Eastman House.
6. Bitzer, *Billy Bitzer*, 74.
7. Campbell MacCullough, "What Makes Them Stars?" *Photoplay*, October 1928, 108.
8. Ibid.
9. Richard Schickel, *D. W. Griffith: An American Life* (New York: Simon and Schuster, 1984), 133–34.
10. Pickford, interview by author.
11. Schickel, *D. W. Griffith*, 157.
12. "When Mary Pickford Was the Girl with the Curls," *Literary Digest*, November 3, 1928, 60.
13. Adolph Zukor, with Dale Kramer, *The Public Is Never Wrong* (New York: Putnam, 1953), 110.
14. Frances Marion, *Off with Their Heads: A Serio-Comic Tale of Hollywood* (New York: Macmillan, 1972), 9–10.
15. Pickford, interview by author. Griffith frequently used the close-up; however, he did not invent it.
16. Zukor, *The Public Is Never Wrong*, 129.
17. Mary Pickford, interview by Arthur B. Friedman, May 1958, Columbia University Oral History Collection.
18. Pickford, interview by Pratt.
19. Pickford, interview by author.
20. Pickford, interview by Friedman.
21. Ibid.
22. Mary Pickford, *Sunshine and Shadow* (Garden City, NY: Doubleday, 1955), 180–81.
23. Ibid., 181.
24. Pickford, interview by Pratt.
25. Charles Higham, *Cecil B. DeMille* (New York: Scribner's, 1972), 66 (telegram dated February 19, 1917).

26. Pickford, interview by author.
27. Pickford (quoting Stephen Leacock), interview by Friedman.
28. Pickford, interview by Pratt.
29. Scott Eyman, *America's Sweetheart* (New York: D. I. Fine, 1990), 120.
30. Sidney Franklin, interview by the author, 1964.
31. Ibid.
32. Pickford, interview by author.
33. Adela Rogers St. Johns, *The Honeycomb* (Garden City, NY: Doubleday, 1969), 163.
34. "Making Film History," *Graphic*, February 11, 1928, n.p.
35. Adolphe Menjou, *It Took Nine Tailors* (New York: Whittlesey House, 1948), 82.
36. Pickford, interview by author.
37. Scott Eyman, *Ernst Lubitsch: Laughter in Paradise* (New York: Simon and Schuster, 1993), 95.
38. Pickford, interview by author.
39. Steven J. Ross, *Working Class Hollywood* (Princeton, NJ: Princeton University Press, 1998), 131.
40. Loyal Lucas, interview by the author, 1986.
41. Michael Ankerich, *Sound of Silence: Conversations with 16 Film and Stage Personalities Who Bridge the Gap between Silents and Talkies* (Jefferson, NC: McFarland, 1998), 6–7.
42. Charles Rosher, interview by the author, 1961.
43. Jack Spears, *Hollywood: The Golden Era* (South Brunswick, NJ: A. S. Barnes, 1971), 191.
44. Pickford, interview by author.
45. Louise Brooks, interview by the author, 1965.
46. Rosher, interview by author.
47. Richard Corliss, "Queen of the Movies," *Film Comment*, March–April 1998, 53–54.
48. Pickford, interview by Friedman.

FATHER OF THE FAMILY
Mary Pickford's Journey from
Breadwinner to Businesswoman
Christel Schmidt

1. Mary Pickford, *Sunshine and Shadow* (Garden City, NY: Doubleday, 1955), 31.

2. Ibid., 37.
3. Ibid., 42.
4. Ibid., 46, 28.
5. Elsie Janis, *So Far So Good!* (New York: E. P. Dutton, 1932), 26; Pickford, *Sunshine and Shadow*, 56.
6. Pickford, *Sunshine and Shadow*, 77.
7. Ibid., 85.
8. Ibid., 89–90.
9. "Edmund Burke at the Walnut," *Philadelphia Inquirer*, December 26, 1905, 4.
10. Pickford, *Sunshine and Shadow*, 85.
11. Mary Pickford, interview by Arthur B. Friedman, May 1958, Columbia University Oral History Project.
12. Pickford, *Sunshine and Shadow*, 95.
13. Ibid., 93.
14. Ibid., 100.
15. Ibid., 105.
16. Eileen Whitfield, *Pickford: The Woman Who Made Hollywood* (Lexington: University Press of Kentucky, 1997), 76.
17. Biograph refused to release the names of its actors until 1913.
18. Mary Pickford, interview by George Pratt, 1958, George Eastman House.
19. Karl K. Kitchen, "Mary Pickford: The Keenest Business Woman in the Film Game," *St. Louis Post*, May 11, 1919, C5.
20. Pickford, interview by Pratt.
21. Benjamin B. Hampton, *A History of the Movies* (New York: Covici, Friede, 1931), 148, 165.
22. Tom Field, "America's Sweetheart and the Flag's Best Press Agent Start Their Big Hurrah for Better Photoplay Art," *Photo-Play Journal*, April 1917, 21.
23. Hampton, *History of the Movies*, 174.
24. I. G. Edmonds and Reiko Mimura, *Paramount Pictures and the People Who Made Them* (San Diego, CA: A. S. Barnes; London: Tantivy Press, 1980), 88.
25. Pickford, interview by Friedman.
26. Whitfield, *Pickford*, 347.

254 *Notes to Pages 34–60*

27 Samuel Goldwyn, *Behind the Screen* (New York: George H. Doran, 1923), 42; Adolph Zukor, with Dale Kramer, *The Public Is Never Wrong* (New York: Putnam, 1953), 110; Frances Marion, *Off with Their Heads: A Serio-Comic Tale of Hollywood* (New York: Macmillan, 1972), 298; Kevin Brownlow, *Mary Pickford Rediscovered: Rare Pictures of a Hollywood Legend* (New York: Harry N. Abrams, 1999), 42.

28 Charles Chaplin, *My Autobiography* (New York: Simon and Schuster, 1964), 223. An article in the *St. Louis Post-Dispatch* on March 23, 1920, quotes Chaplin as saying, "The rarest thing in the world is a woman who is both beautiful and intelligent at the same time. When I meet that combination I am going to marry it."

29 Chaplin, *Autobiography*, 223.

30 Quoted in Gladys Hall, "Discoveries about Myself," *Motion Picture Magazine*, May 1930, 98.

31 Julia Shawell, "Mary Pickford's Empty Arms," *Pictorial Review*, January 1934, 18.

32 Irene Kuhn, "Mary Pickford's Choice," *New Movie Magazine*, November 1934, 66.

33 Janet Mercer, "The Fairbanks Social War Is On!" *Photoplay*, August 1936, 96.

34 Ibid.

35 "Mary Pickford Quits Dolls at Five; 17 Years an Actress; Makes $100,000 Year at 22," *Washington Post*, April 2, 1916, ES12.

36 "Leaders Honored by 12,000 Women," *New York Times*, March 19, 1926, 21.

37 "Mary Pickford Purchases Seals," *Equal Rights*, December 1, 1938, 375.

38 Pickford, interview by Friedman.

Pickford and Fairbanks
A MODERN MARRIAGE
Christel Schmidt

1 There was even parity in the naming of their home, Pickfair—a combination of each of their last names.

2 Rebecca Davis, "Not Marriage at All, but Simple Harlotry: The Companionate Marriage Controversy," *Journal of American History*, March 2008, 1140.

3 Adela Rogers St. Johns, "The Married Life of Doug and Mary," *Photoplay*, February 1927, 134.

4 Benjamin McArthur, *Actors and American Culture, 1880–1920* (Iowa City: University of Iowa Press, 2000), 68.

5 Carol Van Wyck, "Friendly Advice on Girls' Problems: Should a Wife Work?" *Photoplay*, March 1927, 88.

6 Adela Rogers St. Johns, "Why Does the World Love Mary?" *Photoplay*, December 1921, 110.

7 Pickford's third marriage, to Charles "Buddy" Rogers, was particularly troubled, as evidenced by a private investigator's report (July 9, 1958) regarding Rogers's liaisons and legal separation papers (dated March 1960) that were never filed. Both are located in the Pickford Collection at the Academy of Motion Picture Arts and Sciences.

8 Colleen Moore, *Silent Star* (Garden City, NY: Doubleday, 1968), 169.

"LITTLE MARY"
FORMIDABLE PHILANTHROPIST
Alison Trope

1 Randolph Bartlett, "Mary, the Well Beloved," *Photoplay*, April 1920, 28–29, 116–17.

2 Benjamin McArthur, *Actors and American Culture, 1880–1920* (Iowa City: University of Iowa Press, 2000), 85–98.

3 Kenneth L. Kusmer, "The Functions of Organized Charity in the Progressive Era: Chicago as Case Study," *Journal of American History* 60, no. 3 (December 1973): 657–78.

4 Tom Field, "America's Sweetheart and the Flag's Best Press Agent Start Their Big Hurrah for Better Photoplay Art," *Photo-Play Journal*, April 1917, 20–21. The two interests are also captured in various issues of the syndicated newspaper column "Daily Talks."

5 Quoted in Bernard Rosenberg and Harry Silverstein, *The Real Tinsel* (New York: Macmillan, 1970), 176.

6 *St. Louis Globe*, April 22, 1918, file 224, scrapbook 6, 1918, Mary Pickford Collection, Margaret Herrick Library, Academy of Motion Picture Arts and Sciences (AMPAS).

7 File 224, scrapbook 6, 1918, Pickford Collection, Herrick Library, AMPAS; Leslie Midkiff DeBauche, *Reel Patriotism: The Movies and World War I* (Madison: University of Wisconsin Press, 1997), 71.

8 Billy Bates, "The Pickford-Fairbanks Wooing," *Photoplay*, June 1920, 70, 73.

9 "Record Made by Popular Movie Star in Bond Sales," *Pittsburgh Dispatch*, April 20, 1918, 1; "Pittsburgh Pours Millions into Nation's War Treasury in Response to Appeal by Film Star," *Pittsburgh Post*, April 20, 1918, 1.

10 "Hearing before the Committee on Ways and Means, House of Representatives with Reference to the New Revenue Bill" (Washington, DC: Government Printing Office, June 24, 1918), 1247–61; "Film Folk to Launch Great Service Plan," *Los Angeles Times*, May 25, 1918, 113.

11 "Film Folk to Launch Great Service Plan."

12 "Plan Home for Film Players," *Los Angeles Times*, August 8, 1918, 118.

13 *The Passing Parade*, January 1, 1939, LWO 5320, reel 5, A8–11.

14 Ibid.

15 In addition to the museum venture and payroll program, Pickford and other stars devised other money-making plans to subsidize the fund, including the Screen Star's Shop, which sold items donated by stars such as Pickford. "Filmdom Goes into Business," *Los Angeles Times*, June 24, 1930, A10.

16 *The Passing Parade*, January 1, 1939.

17 In January 2009 the fund disclosed plans to shut down the hospital and nursing home by the end of the year. According to the *Los Angeles Times*, the hospital admitted more than 500

patients in 2008, in addition to the 100 long-term residents. The article framed the facilities as a $10 million annual drain on the fund's budget since 2004, despite fund-raisers that generated $12 million to $15 million a year. Lisa Girion and Richard Verrier, "Actors' Hospital to Close; the Motion Picture and Television Fund Says Financial Problems Will Force It to Shut Two Facilities by Year's End," *Los Angeles Times,* January 15, 2009, A1.

18 25th Anniversary Motion Picture Country House and Hospital, pamphlet 137, file 1525, Pickford Collection, Herrick Library, AMPAS.

19 Eileen Whitfield, *Pickford: The Woman Who Made Hollywood* (Lexington: University Press of Kentucky, 1997), 208, 210–11.

20 "Verbatim Transcript of Organization Banquet of AMPAS," May 11, 1927, Special Collections, Herrick Library, AMPAS.

21 File 1530, Museum of Modern Art, Pickford Collection, Herrick Library, AMPAS.

22 Aline Mosby, "Mary Pickford to Disinherit Hollywood—Lack of Museum Irks Star," *Los Angeles Herald Express,* March 20, 1956, sec. C.

23 This sentiment proved to be a common refrain in Pickford's comments to the press. In her correspondence files, she also makes marginal notes that the museum "must be here in Hollywood." Given the failure to erect a museum in Los Angeles, Pickford's will left her film collection to the Library of Congress.

24 "Hollywood Museum Groundbreaking," file 1460, Hollywood Museum, Special Collections, Herrick Library, AMPAS.

25 Mary Pickford, interview by Arthur B. Friedman, May 1958, Columbia University Oral History Project.

26 Ed Edstrom, "Be Active, Grow Old Gracefully," *Los Angeles Examiner,* November 16, 1960, sec. 2, p. 3, file 1601, Pickford Collection, Herrick Library, AMPAS.

27 Whitfield, *Pickford*, 318.

28 Ibid., 227–28, 332, 366.

29 Pickford, interview by Friedman.

30 This trust was a spin-off of another trust formed after her mother's death in 1928, likely with the strategic goal of avoiding taxes on her mother's estate. Pickford's assets were largely in her mother's name. File 2259, box 236, Pickford Collection, Herrick Library, AMPAS.

AMERICA'S SWEETHEART
Edward Wagenknecht
(Notes by Christel Schmidt)

1 D. J. "Pop" Grauman was a motion picture exhibitor in San Francisco during the 1910s. His son, Sid Grauman, co-owned a number of historic movie theaters in Hollywood, including Grauman's Chinese Theater and Grauman's Egyptian Theater.

2 Wagenknecht's original German text has been translated here. Friedrich Schiller, *Maiden of Orleans, a Romantic Tragedy,* trans. John T. Krumpelmann (Chapel Hill: University of North Carolina Press, 1959), 118.

3 Gerald R. McDonald, review of *Sunshine and Shadow, Films in Review* 6 (June–July 1955): 295–97.

4 See Card's "The Films of Mary Pickford" in this volume.

5 Charles Edward Russell, *Julia Marlowe: Her Life and Art* (New York: D. Appleton, 1926), 366.

6 "A Romance of the Redwoods," *Moving Picture World,* May 26, 1917, 1300.

7 James Card, "The Films of Mary Pickford," *Image* 8, no. 4 (1959): 184.

8 In 1997 the Giornate del Cinema Muto began a yearly retrospective of D. W. Griffith's work in cinema. The films were shown in chronological order and included Pickford's Biograph films from 1909 to 1912.

DRESSING THE PART
Mary Pickford's Use of Costume
Beth Werling

1 Mary Pickford, "Daily Talks: The Magic Clothes Brush," *Dallas Morning News,* November 19, 1915, 8.

2 See Christel Schmidt's "Father of the Family" in this volume.

3 Mary Pickford, "Daily Talks: The Question of Clothes," *Dallas Morning News,* November 11, 1915, 8.

4 "Clothes Seen on the Stage," *Theatre Magazine,* June 1916, 376.

5 Madge Bellamy, *Darling of the Twenties* (Vestal, NY: Vestal Press, 1989), 5.

6 Quoted in Katherine Synon, "The Unspoiled Mary Pickford," *Photoplay,* September, 1914, 36.

7 Harriette Underhill, "Among Us Mortals' at the Equity Ball and Elsewhere: Mary Pickford, Douglas Fairbanks, Laurette Taylor, Alexander Clark Jr. and Connie Talmadge Are among Those Present," *New York Tribune,* November 26, 1922, 2; Alexander Walker, *Sex and the Movies: The Celluloid Sacrifice* (Baltimore: Penguin, 1968), 60.

8 "'Dorothy Vernon' Picture Rights Go to Pickford," *Morning Oregonian,* September 17, 1922, 3.

9 Press book for *Dorothy Vernon of Haddon Hall,* 38, LP20113, Copyright Collection, Motion Picture Reading Room, Library of Congress.

10 Press book for *Little Annie Rooney,* n.p., LP21807, Copyright Collection, Motion Picture Reading Room, Library of Congress.

11 Ibid.

AMERICAN IDOL
Mary Pickford,
World War I, and the Making
of a National Icon
Christel Schmidt

1 "13 Subscribers Add Nearly $5,000,000 to Liberty Total," *Philadelphia Inquirer,* April 10, 1918, 4.

2   In her memoir *Sunshine and Shadow* (Garden City, NY: Doubleday, 1955), Pickford claims that D. J. Grauman was the first to call her America's Sweetheart. See also "Comment and Criticism," *Fort Worth Star Telegram*, July 12, 1914, 12, and Warren Nolan, "The Nicknames Our Heroes Wear: Whether 'Fighting Marine,' 'Lone Eagle,' or 'Oil King,' the Great in All Walks of Life Get Tags Reflecting Their Dominant Traits," *New York Times*, February 10, 1929.

3   Pickford's "Daily Talks" column was published nationally by the McClure Newspaper Syndicate from November 1915 through August 1917. It was believed to be ghostwritten by Frances Marion and Izola L. Forrester.

4   Mary Pickford, "Daily Talks: From across the Seas," *Duluth News-Tribune*, March 13, 1916, 6.

5   Mary Pickford, "Daily Talks: Gifts and Letters I Receive," *Dallas Morning News*, December 15, 1915, 11.

6   "Refuse 40,000 Place in Citizens' Parade," *New York Times*, May 5, 1916, 6.

7   Mary Pickford, "Daily Talks: The Preparedness Parade," *Dallas Morning News*, June 17, 1916, 11.

8   Letter from Jesse L. Lasky to Cecil B. DeMille, March 5, 1917, reel 157, Cecil B. DeMille Collection, Motion Picture, Broadcasting, and Recorded Sound Division, Library of Congress.

9   "Mary Likes 'Rebecca,'" *Oregonian*, September 17, 1917, 7.

10 Kevin Brownlow, *Mary Pickford Rediscovered: Rare Pictures of a Hollywood Legend* (New York: Harry N. Abrams, 1999), 133.

11 The alternative ending can be found in outtakes for *The Little American* at the George Eastman House.

12 Brownlow, *Mary Pickford Rediscovered*, 251, n. 131.

13 "Mary Pickford Puts Her Money in Bonds," *San Jose Mercury Herald*, June 2, 1917, 12.

14 Sales for the first Liberty Loan drive may have been sluggish. One day before Pickford spoke in San Francisco, in an interview with the *San Jose Evening News*, she expressed dismay that "people are so backward in buying the Liberty bonds."

15 "Mary Pickford Dances to Aid Liberty Bonds," *San Francisco Chronicle*, June 14, 1917, 11.

16 R. E. Austin, "The Little American, Modern Movie Factor," *Duluth News-Tribune*, June 24, 1917, 1.

17 Robert S. Birchard, *Cecil B. DeMille's Hollywood* (Lexington: University Press of Kentucky, 2004), 108.

18 Producer Jesse L. Lasky acknowledged the difficulties some war films faced in 1917, writing, "Where some months ago they [audiences] would not attend subjects with war and battlefield backgrounds, they now seem eager for war pictures." Letter from Jesse L. Lasky to Cecil B. DeMille, March 26, 1918, reel 157, Cecil B. DeMille Collection, Motion Picture, Broadcasting, and Recorded Sound Division, Library of Congress.

19 In 1919 the short was released in Canada as *One Hundred Percent Canadian*. During World War II, Canada's National War Finance Committee reissued the film with a prologue and an epilogue (shot in the fall of 1943) featuring Pickford.

20 The incredible rise and influence of cinema celebrities in the 1910s—especially Pickford, Chaplin, and Fairbanks—made actors important cultural figures and opened the door to an elite world that was previously closed to them.

21 "Surge to Buy Bonds," *Washington Post*, April 7, 1918, 8.

22 "Film Trio Starts on Liberty Loan Drive: Fairbanks, Chaplin, and Mary Pickford Separate at Washington," *Los Angeles Times*, April 7, 1918, 13.

23 Apparently, during her one-week hiatus, Pickford canceled only one Liberty Loan appearance (in Boston on April 17, 1918).

24 Austin, "The Little American," 1; Grace Kingsley, "Mary Pickford Does Her Bit: Famous Actress to Help Liberty Loan," *Los Angeles Times*, March 16, 1918, 13; "More than Otherwise," *Macon Weekly Telegraph*, April 17, 1918, 6.

25 "Mr. Shaw and Movie Folks," *Biloxi (MS) Daily Herald*, April 25, 1918, 2.

26 In the summer of 1918, at a hearing before the House Ways and Means Committee, Congressman Charles H. Sloan connected the large salaries of actors, including Pickford, to "conditions created by the war." Newspaper columnist Mae Tinee wrote a defense of movie stars who had been accused of joining the third Liberty Loan tour for publicity: "All for Their Country," *Chicago Daily Tribune*, April 14, 1918.

27 "Love Mesh Mocks Screen," *Kansas City Star*, July 2, 1919, 11.

28 "Mary and Doug in France Made a Hit in Person," *Los Angeles Times*, August 1, 1920, 16.

29 *Montgomery Advertiser*, July 6, 1920, 4.

30 Jacob Mogelever (chief, Promotion Section, Treasury Department) to Mary Pickford, January 22, 1953, box 106.f 1272, Mary Pickford Collection, Margaret Herrick Library, Academy of Motion Picture Arts and Sciences.

31 "Mary Pickford Sixty Years Old," *New York Times*, April 10, 1953.

Laws of Attraction
MARY PICKFORD, MOVIES, AND THE EVOLUTION OF FAME
Eileen Whitfield

1   *Letchworth Citizen* (England), June 25, 1910, quoted in Anthony Slide, *The Griffith Actresses* (South Brunswick, NJ: A. S. Barnes, 1973), 67.

2   Review of *Tess of the Storm Country*, *Variety*, April 13, 1914.

3   Julian Johnson, "Mary Pickford: Herself and Her Career," *Photoplay*, February 1916, 50.

4   Arlene Croce, "Golden Girl," *New Yorker*, September 22, 1997, 132.

5   Alistair Cooke, *Douglas Fairbanks: The Making of a Screen Character* (New York: Museum of Modern Art, 1940), 21.

6   Mary Pickford, *Sunshine and Shadow* (Garden City, NY: Doubleday, 1955), 208.

7   Alexander Woollcott, "Strenuous Honeymoon," *Everybody's Magazine,* November 1920, 37.

8   Ibid.

9   *Times* (London), January 24, 1920, Pickford scrapbooks, Mary Pickford Collection, Margaret Herrick Library, Academy of Motion Picture Arts and Sciences (AMPAS).

10   *Pall Mall Gazette,* June 24, 1920, Pickford scrapbooks, Pickford Collection, Herrick Library, AMPAS.

11   *Aberdeen Press,* June 25, 1920, Pickford scrapbooks, Pickford Collection, Herrick Library, AMPAS.

12   Mary Pickford, "Ambassadors," *Saturday Evening Post,* August 23, 1930, 7.

13   Ibid.

CROWN OF GLORY
THE RISE AND FALL OF THE MARY PICKFORD CURLS
Christel Schmidt

1   Mary Pickford, "Please May I Bob My Hair," *Liberty Magazine,* June 30, 1928, 30.

2   "Mary Pickford Wins Honors in Good Role," *Fort Worth Star-Telegram,* March 4, 1915, 7.

3   Adolph Zukor, with Dale Kramer, *The Public Is Never Wrong* (New York: Putnam, 1953), 173.

4   "They Are All Trying to Be Mary Pickfords," *Los Angeles Times,* May 11, 1915, III1.

5   Zukor, *The Public Is Never Wrong,* 173.

6   Louis Reeves Harrison, "Two Unlovely Black Eyes," *Moving Picture World,* August 25, 1917, 1190.

7   Louis Reeves Harrison, "The Exhibitor's Mirror," *Moving Picture World,* September 8, 1917, 1508.

8   Alla Nazimova starred in *The Brat* (1919), and Norma Talmadge played Tessibel Skinner in *The Secret of the Storm Country* (1917), a sequel to Pickford's 1914 *Tess of the Storm Country.* A number of other actresses appeared in child roles during this period, including Bessie Love, Marie Doro, and Marguerite Clark.

9   Mary Pickford, "Daily Talks: To Be or Not to Be a Vampire," *Duluth News Tribune,* May 9, 1916, 8.

10   Marguerite Mooers Marshall, "How the Movies Are Molding Us Over," *St. Louis Post-Dispatch,* September 6, 1919, 13.

11   "'Are All Men Alike' Title of Big Film," *Montgomery Adviser,* November 14, 1920, 6.

12   Anna Rittenhouse, "School Girls Set Fashions—Their Elders Follow," *Lexington Herald,* March 7, 1920, 1.

13   "Bans Bobbed Hair," *Los Angeles Times,* March 28, 1921, II9.

14   Harry Carr, "Wright Book Coming Soon," *Los Angeles Times,* August 15, 1921, I14.

15   "To Bob or Not to Bob" was the title of numerous magazine and newspaper articles that discussed women's dilemma over cutting their hair in the 1920s.

16   "Girls Bewail Loss of Locks as Bobbed Hair Style Passes," *Fort Wayne New Sentinel,* June 30, 1921, 2.

17   "The 'Old-Fashioned Girls' Triumph," *Montgomery Adviser,* March 5, 1922, 31; "'Bobs' and 'Longs' to Play Baseball Today," *Albuquerque Morning Journal,* July 9, 1922, 1.

18   "Doug Likes Her in a Long Skirt," *Chicago Daily Tribune,* June 1, 1920, 5. Pickford later denied this was true and claimed that "she was the boss in the Fairbanks household and wore her skirts just as short or long as she wanted to." "Doug and Mary to Make Extended Tour," *Salt Lake Telegram,* September 25, 1922, 8.

19   "Mary Pickford Talks of Various Subjects," *Baltimore American,* August 14, 1921, 5.

20   "Mary Selects Six Parisien [*sic*] Gowns for Return Home," *Salt Lake Telegram,* October 12, 1921, 1; "Pickford Talks of Various Subjects," 5; "Modern Styles Kill Romance, America's Sweetheart States," *Duluth News Tribune,* March 27, 1921, 5.

21   "Long Skirts and Business," *Miami Herald,* October 17, 1921, 4.

22   Grace Wilcox, "How Gloria Swanson Spent $10,000 in Paris," *Los Angeles Times,* August 27, 1922, III13.

23   Mrs. Lydig Hoyt, "What Is Good Taste," *Los Angeles Times,* June 15, 1924, I19.

24   James R. Quirk, "The Public Just Won't Let Mary Pickford Grow Up," *Photoplay,* September 1925, 36.

25   "Lois Moran Renounces Demureness," *Los Angeles Times,* November 6, 1927, C13.

26   Mary Pickford, "To Bob or Not to Bob: Why I Have Not Bobbed Mine," *Pictorial Review,* April 1927, 9.

27   "Gossiping with Mary Pickford," *Chicago Daily News,* January 22, 1928, F6.

28   Pickford, "Please May I Bob My Hair," 28.

29   Ibid.

30   "Mary Bids Good-bye to Curlhood," *Motion Picture Magazine,* October 1928, 59.

31   Mary Pickford, *Sunshine and Shadow* (Garden City, NY: Doubleday, 1955), 294–95.

BLOOD AND SYMPATHY
RACE AND THE FILMS OF MARY PICKFORD
Elizabeth Binggeli

1   Clark appeared in blackface in the 1918 feature *Uncle Tom's Cabin* in which she played Little Eva, a white child, and Topsy, a slave girl.

2   Iris Barry, *Let's Go to the Movies* (New York: Arno Press, 1972), 58.

3   Richard Dyer, *White* (London: Routledge, 1997), 10.

4   Ibid., 24–25.

5   Ibid., 16–17.

6 Linda Arvidson Griffith, *When the Movies Were Young* (New York: E. P. Dutton, 1925), 168.

7 Conversation with Christel Schmidt, 2009. The photo of Morton appeared on the front page of the *Pittsburgh Courier* on August 11, 1923. The photo of Pickford was published in the *Chicago Daily Tribune* on November 25, 1923.

8 Pickford's Nina in the now-lost 1914 film *Hearts Adrift* was not explicitly racialized; rather, she was a character who had "gone savage" during her long stay on a desert island.

9 "Mary Pickford Talks of Her Life as a Japanese," *Columbus (GA) Enquirer-Sun*, December 15, 1915.

10 Christel Schmidt identified this IMP short at UCLA. My analysis of the film relies on her description.

11 Review of *Madame Butterfly, Variety,* November 12, 1915.

12 Adolph Zukor, with Dale Kramer, *The Public Is Never Wrong* (New York: Putnam, 1953), 173.

13 Jeremiah 13.23.

14 Pickford's 1922 *Tess of the Storm Country* was a remake of her successful 1914 film of the same name. My comments refer to the later version.

15 In *Hoodlum* (1919), for example, Pickford plays a spoiled society girl whose goodness is revealed only after she learns to appreciate life in the slums.

16 The Valentine Company production of *Uncle Tom's Cabin* ran at the Princess Theatre for one week from April 8 to 13, 1901.

17 Mary Pickford, "Daily Talks: Pickaninnies," *Anaconda Standard* 27, no. 197 (March 20, 1916): 6. "Daily Talks" was a nationally syndicated newspaper column purportedly authored by Pickford. Although it may have been ghostwritten, the content was most likely endorsed by Pickford, and in any case, the column worked to build Pickford's star persona in the eyes of her audience.

18 Matthew 6:26, 10:29–31; Harriet Beecher Stowe, *Uncle Tom's Cabin: Life among the Lowly* (Boston: J. P. Jewett, 1852), 128.

19 Stowe, *Uncle Tom's Cabin,* 363.

THE FILMS OF MARY PICKFORD
James Card
(Notes by Christel Schmidt)

1 Iris Barry, *Let's Go to the Movies* (New York: Arno Press, 1972), 103, 200.

2 Richard Griffith, *The Movies* (New York: Simon and Schuster, 1981), 57. There are still few works that offer a serious discussion and analysis of Pickford's movies. However, there have been a number of excellent publications on the actress since Card wrote his essay in 1959, including Richard Corliss's *Queen of the Movies,* Jeanine Basinger's *Silent Stars,* Kevin Brownlow's *Mary Pickford Rediscovered,* and Eileen Whitfield's *Pickford.* Pickford has also been discussed in several film history books, including William K. Everson's *American Silent Film* (New York: Oxford University Press, 1978), and Richard Koszarski's *An Evening's Entertainment* (New York: Scribner, 1990).

3 Paul Rotha, *Film Till Now* (London: Vision-Mayflower, 1960), 176.

4 Vachel Lindsay, *The Art of the Moving Picture* (New York: Macmillan, 1922), 27–28.

5 Quoted in "Cinema: Shrewd," *Time,* May 11, 1931, 46. There is no evidence that Pickford ever purchased any movies in order to destroy them. She owned the rights to and held film materials representing the majority of her work. In the early 1920s she purchased more than seventy of her Biograph movies from film producer Nathan Hirsh. A 1925 inventory of the Pickford holdings revealed that she had already accumulated most of the material she would later donate to the Library of Congress.

6 See "The Mary Pickford Film Collection at the Library of Congress" in this volume.

7 Mary Pickford, *Sunshine and Shadow* (Garden City, NY: Doubleday, 1955), 227.

8 Pickford was actually seventeen when she began working at Biograph.

9 Shot in 1913, *A Good Little Devil* was the first feature Pickford made, but it was the fourth to be released, after *In the Bishop's Carriage* (1913), *Caprice* (1913), and *Hearts Adrift* (1914).

10 Today the George Eastman House has film material on thirty-five Pickford features and thirty-five shorts, the majority of which can be screened. See the filmography for details.

Mary Pickford and the Archival Film Movement
Christel Schmidt

The epigraph is from "Mary Pickford Seen at Screening of *The Eagles Mate,*" Mary Pickford scrapbook 4 (ca. 1914–1933), PSA box A, number 19, Museum of Modern Art

1 Quoted in Brader Matthews, "The Statue of Snow," *Munsey's Magazine,* October 1906.

2 Her anxieties were justified. A March 28, 1922, *New York Times* review of Harry Carey in *Man to Man* noted that a Pickford one-reeler, screened as a prologue to the feature, was "so awful that they have turned it into a burlesque" and remarked, "it's fun to ... laugh at what was once taken so seriously."

3 In the early 1920s Hirsh reissued the one-reelers with an excess of new intertitles that not only expanded them to two reels but also altered the stories. Pickford was displeased that these Biograph reissues were being screened in direct competition with her new releases.

4 "Cinema: Shrewd," *Time,* May 11, 1931, 46.

5 Matthews, "Statue of Snow."

6   See Alison Trope's "'Little Mary': Formidable Philanthropist" in this volume.

7   "The Post Impressionist: 'Her Picture as She Was,'" *Washington Post,* November 21, 1935, 8.

8   Pickford's anxieties about exhibition continued. On February 5, 1936, a *New York Times* article noted that audiences were laughing at silent film screenings at MoMA. Alison Trope's dissertation, "Mysteries of the Celluloid Museum: Showcasing the Art and Artifacts of Cinema" (University of Southern California, 1999), also documents the "resistance from some … audiences" to silent movies at MoMA's 1936 film screenings. Trope quotes a January 1937 MoMA bulletin that acknowledged it was "not easy for all students to approach the film seriously" (57).

9   "Mary Pickford Talks of Letter While Clerks Here Talk of Her: 'America's Sweetheart,' Greatly Concerned about U.S. Preservation of Films for Posterity, Disrupts Archives Office Force, House Cafe," *Washington Post,* May 8, 1938, R15.

10   See Christel Schmidt's "The Mary Pickford Film Collection at the Library of Congress" and James Card's "The Films of Mary Pickford," both in this volume.

11   Pickford's frustration over the lack of a film archive or museum in Los Angeles can be found in various newspaper reports, including "Failure of Film Museum Idea Stirs Ire of Mary Pickford," *Bethlehem Globe,* March 21, 1956, and "Mary Pickford to Disinherit Hollywood: Lack of Museum Irks Star," *Los Angeles Evening Herald,* March 20, 1956. The following month, Pickford was contacted by Richard F. Brown, the chief curator of art at the Los Angeles County Museum (and later by John Anson Ford, a supervisor with the Third District County of Los Angeles Board of Supervisors), to discuss plans to develop a film museum near the Hollywood Bowl. In 1957 she accepted an invitation to join the Los Angeles County Motion Picture Committee, which was established to research the viability of a film museum in Los Angeles. For more information, see the Hollywood Museum paper files in the Pickford Collection at the Academy of Motion Picture Arts and Sciences.

12   She may have been inspired by the George Eastman House, which is located in the former home of the Eastman Kodak founder.

13   The event marked the seventieth anniversary of the first copyrighted film, *Fred Ott's Sneeze* (1894).

14   The history of the 1960s Hollywood Museum can be found in Alison Trope, *Stardust Monuments: The Selling and Saving of Hollywood* (Hanover, NH: Dartmouth College Press, 2011). There is no connection between the 1960s Hollywood Museum and other organizations with the same name.

15   According to Anthony Slide's *Nitrate Won't Wait* (Jefferson, NC: McFarland, 1992), the university's film archive began, "at least on paper," in 1965.

THE MARY PICKFORD FILM COLLECTION AT THE LIBRARY OF CONGRESS
Christel Schmidt

1   Pickford did not donate her entire film collection to the Library in 1946. The actress chose to withhold several titles, most of which she did not appear in. However, five of her movies—the Biograph shorts *His Wife's Visitor* (1909), *A Plain Song* (1910), and *When a Man Loves* (1911) and the features *Rosita* (1923) and *Secrets* (1933)—were among those held back. *His Wife's Visitor* and *Rosita* later decomposed before they could be preserved, but the other titles were given to the Library in subsequent donations.

THE MARY PICKFORD COSTUME AND EPHEMERA COLLECTION AT THE NATURAL HISTORY MUSEUM OF LOS ANGELES COUNTY
Beth Werling

1   The museum was originally called the Los Angeles County Museum of History, Art and Science when it opened in 1913. In 1965 the institution split into two entities—the Natural History Museum of Los Angeles County and the Los Angeles County Museum of Art.

FILMOGRAPHY
Christel Schmidt

Pickford also made an appearance in the following films: *All-Star Production of Patriotic Episodes for the Second Liberty Loan* (1917), *A Kiss from Mary Pickford* (1926), and *The Gaucho* (1927).

1   Pickford credits herself as author of the two titles released by Selig in "Unspoiled by Fame Is Mary Pickford," *New York Dramatic Mirror,* March 19, 1913, 28.

2   Pickford credits herself as author in ibid.

3   Pickford credits herself as author in ibid.

4   This title had been missing from all previously published Pickford filmographies. Film enthusiast Scott Taylor rediscovered it on a Grapevine Video. In addition, an image of Pickford from the film appeared in an ad in the *Washington Herald* on August 20, 1911.

5   A reissued version found at UCLA, titled *One Hundred Percent Canadian,* was released in Canada with an added prologue during World War II.

Pickford with an unidentified child while filming Fanchon the Cricket *(1915).*

Bibliography

Arvidson, Linda. *When the Movies Were Young*. New York: Dover, 1969.

Balio, Tino. *United Artists: The Company Built by the Stars*. Madison: University of Wisconsin Press, 1976.

Barry, Iris. *Let's Go to the Movies*. New York: Arno Press, 1972.

Basinger, Jeanine. *Silent Stars*. New York: Knopf, 1999.

Bellamy, Madge. *Darling of the Twenties*. Vestal, NY: Vestal Press, 1989.

Birchard, Robert S. *Cecil B. DeMille's Hollywood*. Lexington: University Press of Kentucky, 2004.

Bitzer, G. W. *Billy Bitzer: His Story*. New York: Farrar, Straus and Giroux. 1973.

Brownlow, Kevin. *Mary Pickford Rediscovered: Rare Pictures of a Hollywood Legend*. Introduction and photograph selection by Robert Cushman. New York: Harry N. Abrams, 1999.

————. *Parade's Gone By*. New York: Knopf, 1968.

————. *War, the West, and the Wilderness*. New York: Knopf, 1979.

Brownmiller, Susan. *Femininity*. New York: Linden Press/Simon and Schuster, 1984.

Campbell, Craig W. *Reel America and World War I: A Comprehensive Filmography and History of Motion Pictures in the United States, 1914–1920*. Jefferson, NC: McFarland, 1985.

Chaplin, Charles. *My Autobiography*. New York: Simon and Schuster, 1964.

Chierichetti, David. *Hollywood Director: The Career of Mitchell Leisen*. New York: Curtis Books, 1973.

Collins, Suzanne. "Calling All Stars: Emerging Political Authority and Cultural Policy in the Propaganda Campaign of World War I." PhD diss., New York University, 2008.

Cooke, Alistair. *Douglas Fairbanks: The Making of a Screen Character*. New York: Museum of Modern Art, 1940.

Corson, Richard. *Fashions in Hair: The First Five Thousand Years*. New York: Hastings House, 1965.

Cushman, Robert B. *A Tribute to Mary Pickford*. Washington, DC: American Film Institute, 1970.

DeBauche, Leslie Midkiff. *Reel Patriotism: The Movies and World War I*. Madison: University of Wisconsin Press, 1997.

DeCordova, Richard. *Picture Personalities: The Emergence of the Star System in America*. Urbana: University of Illinois Press, 1990.

Dibbets, Karel, and Bert Hogenkamp. *Film and the First World War*. Amsterdam: Amsterdam University Press, 1995.

Duff Gordon, Lucy, Lady. *Discretions and Indiscretions*. New York: Frederick A. Stokes, 1932.

Dyer, Richard. *White*. London: Routledge, 1997.

Edmonds, I. G., and Reiko Mimura. *Paramount Pictures and the People Who Made Them*. San Diego, CA: A. S. Barnes; London: Tantivy Press, 1980.

Eyman, Scott. *America's Sweetheart*. New York: D. I. Fine, 1990.

————. *Ernst Lubitsch: Laughter in Paradise*. New York: Simon and Schuster, 1993.

Fairbanks, Douglas, Jr. *The Salad Days*. New York: Doubleday, 1988.

Finnegan, John Patrick. *Against the Specter of a Dragon: The Campaign for American Military Preparedness, 1914–1917*. Westport, CT: Greenwood Press, 1974.

Goldwyn, Samuel. *Behind the Screen*. New York: George H. Doran, 1923.

Graham, Cooper, Steven Higgins, Elaine Mancini, and Laoa Louiz Vieira. *D. W. Griffith and the Biograph Company*. Metuchen, NJ: n.p., 1985.

Gunning, Tom. *D. W. Griffith and the Origins of American Narrative Film: The Early Years at Biograph*. Urbana: University of Illinois Press, 1991.

Hampton, Benjamin B. *A History of the Movies*. New York: Covici, Friede, 1931.

Hancock, Ralph, and Letitia Fairbanks. *Douglas Fairbanks: The Fourth Musketeer*. New York: Henry Holt, 1953.

Janis, Elsie. *So Far, So Good!* New York: E. P. Dutton, 1932.

Keil, Charlie, and Ben Singer. *American Cinema of the 1910s: Themes and Variations*. New Brunswick, NJ: Rutgers University Press, 2009.

Lane, Christina Merrel. "Hollywood Star Couples: Classical Era Romance and Marriage." PhD diss., University of Texas in Austin, 1999.

Lewis, Philip C. *Trouping; How the Show Came to Town*. New York: Harper and Row, 1973.

Lindsay, Vachel. *The Art of the Moving Picture*. New York: Macmillan, 1915.

Louvish, Simon. *Cecil B. DeMille: A Life in Art*. New York: Thomas Dunne Books/St. Martin's Press, 2008.

Lowrey, Carolyn. *First One Hundred Noted Men and Women of the Screen*. New York: Moffat, Yard, 1920.

Marion, Frances. *Off with Their Heads: A Serio-comic Tale of Hollywood*. New York: Macmillan, 1972.

Marra, Kim. *Strange Duets: Impresarios and Actresses in the American Theatre, 1865–1914*. Iowa City: University of Iowa Press, 2006.

May, Elaine Tyler. *Great Expectations: Marriage and Divorce in Post-Victorian America*. Chicago: University of Chicago Press, 1980.

May, Lary. *Screening out the Past: The Birth of Mass Culture and the Motion Picture Industry*. New York: Oxford University Press, 1980.

McArthur, Benjamin. *Actors and American Culture, 1880–1920*. Iowa City: University of Iowa Press, 2000.

Menjou, Adolphe. *It Took Nine Taylors*. New York: Whittlesey House, 1948.

Moore, Colleen. *Silent Star*. Garden City, NY: Doubleday, 1968.

Niver, Kemp. *Mary Pickford, Comedienne*. Los Angeles: Ocare Research Group, 1969.

Pickford, Mary. *Sunshine and Shadow*. Garden City, NY: Doubleday, 1955.

Rogers St. Johns, Adela. *The Honeycomb*. Garden City, NY: Doubleday, 1969.

Rosenberg, Bernard, and Harry Silverstein. *The Real Tinsel*. New York: Macmillan, 1970.

Ross, Steven J. *Working Class Hollywood*. Princeton, NJ: Princeton University Press, 1998.

Schickel, Richard. *D. W. Griffith: An American Life*. New York: Simon and Schuster, 1984.

———. *His Picture in the Papers: A Speculation on Celebrity in America Based on the Life of Douglas Fairbanks, Sr.* New York: Charterhouse, 1973.

Schneider, Dorothy, and Carl J. Schneider. *American Women in the Progressive Era, 1900–1920*. New York: Facts on File, 1993.

Spears, Jack. *Hollywood: The Golden Era*. South Brunswick, NJ: A. S. Barnes, 1971.

Stowe, Harriet Beecher. *Uncle Tom's Cabin: Life among the Lowly*. Boston: J. P. Jewett, 1852.

Wagenknecht, Edward. *The Movies in the Age of Innocence*. Norman: University of Oklahoma Press, 1962.

Walker, Alexander. *Sex in the Movies: The Celluloid Sacrifice*. Baltimore: Penguin, 1968.

Whitfield, Eileen. *Pickford: The Woman Who Made Hollywood*. Lexington: University Press of Kentucky, 1997.

Yurka, Blanche. *Bohemian Girl: Blanche Yurka's Theatrical Life*. Athens: Ohio University Press, 1970.

Zukor, Adolph, with Dale Kramer. *The Public Is Never Wrong*. New York: Putnam, 1953

Contributors

ELIZABETH BINGGELI received her PhD in English from the University of Southern California and teaches at Immaculate Heart High School in Los Angeles. Her work has appeared in *Cinema Journal, African American Review,* and *Arizona Quarterly.* She is the coproducer of the documentary film *Palace of Silents,* a history of the Silent Movie Theater of Los Angeles.

KEVIN BROWNLOW is a film historian, author, and filmmaker. He has written several books on the silent era, including *Behind the Mask of Innocence, Mary Pickford Rediscovered,* and *The Parade's Gone By.* He restored the feature films *Napoleon* (1927) and *The Four Horsemen of the Apocalypse* (1921). These and other achievements led to his honorary Oscar in 2010, which recognized his preeminence in the field. He is now working on a documentary on star-producer Douglas Fairbanks.

JAMES CARD (1915–2000) was the founder and first curator of the Motion Picture Department at the George Eastman House in Rochester, New York. He was an avid collector and promoter of silent movies. In 1994 he published the book *Seductive Cinema: The Art of Silent Film.*

ROBERT CUSHMAN (1946–2009) was the photograph curator for the Margaret Herrick Library from 1972 until his death in July 2009. During his tenure, he developed and expanded the institution's photographic collection to over 10 million items, acquiring major studio collections as well as those from individuals such as Cecil B. DeMille, Douglas Fairbanks, and Katharine Hepburn. He coauthored two books on Hollywood's Chinese Theatre and was the photo editor of *Mary Pickford Rediscovered* and *Douglas Fairbanks.*

MOLLY HASKELL is a film critic and author whose books include *From Reverence to Rape: The Treatment of Women in the Movies; Love and Other Infectious Diseases: A Memoir;* and, most recently, *Frankly, My Dear: Gone with the Wind Revisited.* She has taught at Columbia, Barnard, and Sarah Lawrence; served as a film critic for *New York* magazine and *Vogue;* and has written for many other publications, including the *New York Times, New York Review of Books, Town & Country,* the *Guardian,* and the *Nation.* Her work was featured in the Library of America's 2006 *American Movie Critics,* edited by Philip Lopate, and she won a Guggenheim Fellowship in 2010.

CHRISTEL SCHMIDT is a film historian, writer, and editor. She was awarded two fellowships from the National Endowment for the Humanities for her work on Mary Pickford. She also coedited *Silent Movies: The Birth of Film and the Triumph of Movie Culture.* She is currently researching and writing about the careers of stage actresses during the Progressive Era.

ALISON TROPE, PHD, is a clinical associate professor of communication in the Annenberg School for Communication and Journalism at the University of Southern California in Los Angeles. She is the author of *Stardust Monuments: The Saving and Selling of Hollywood* and is currently researching and writing about the history of Hollywood philanthropy and activism.

EDWARD WAGENKNECHT (1900–2004) was a professor of English at Boston University and a prolific writer. He published biographies on several major figures from the nineteenth and early twentieth centuries, including Charles Dickens, singer Jenny Lind, and Mark Twain. His book *Movies in the Age of Innocence* recounts his memories of watching silent movies.

BETH WERLING is a collections manager in the History Department of the Natural History Museum of Los Angeles County, where she is responsible for overseeing the institution's cinema collections. Her essay on the museum's collection of motion picture costumes was published in *Style and Seduction: The Art of Hollywood Costume Design.*

EILEEN WHITFIELD began her career as an actor, appearing on the stage in New York and Canada, on the CBC, and in commercials. She became a journalist in 1982, editing and writing for *Saturday Night* and *Toronto Life* magazines and contributing to Canada's national newspapers, the *Globe and Mail* and the *National Post.* She is an independent scholar of silent film and wrote the biography *Pickford: The Woman Who Made Hollywood.*

Pickford and Fairbanks begin their honeymoon on the S.S. Lapland in June 1920.

Photo Credits and Permissions

Joan Crawford and Douglas Fairbanks Jr.
with Pickford, circa 1929.

Index